VANGUARD

The Advanced Detachment of the African Revolution

The Political Report to the Seventh Congress of the African People's Socialist Party

By Chairman Omali Yeshitela

Foreword by Luwezi Kinshasa

Portions previously published in *The Burning Spear* newspaper and on the TheBurningSpear.com

Cover design by David Lance

ISBN-13: 978-1-891624-15-5

Printed in the U.S.
First Edition 2019

African People's Socialist Party USA
1245 18th Avenue South
St. Petersburg, FL 33705
727-827-6620
info@apspuhuru.org

Published by Burning Spear Publications
1245 18th Avenue South
St. Petersburg, FL 33705
burningspearmarketplace.com

Dedication

To members of the
African People's Socialist Party,
the steadfast Vanguard
for whom this report was written.

To all members and sectors of the
Uhuru Movement who have placed
your faith in the Party.

To the African working class,
whose victory will liberate and unite
Africa and Africans forcibly dispersed
throughout the world, and deliver the
critical blow in the destruction of colonial
capitalism, the advent of world socialism,
the precursor to communism and the end of
all national oppression and class exploitation.

Contents

Part III: Solidarity Statements

Part IV: Photos

Foreword

This book, like its title, is the vanguard of all books. It is more than a publication for intellectual stimulation - it is literally a tool to advance humanity's struggle against capitalism through revolution.

It is the cutting edge of all political books. It is the only coherent voice putting forth revolution as the only solution, to end white power imperialism and elevate the African working class to power.

This latest work by Chairman Omali Yeshitela, like his previous works, is about leading the Revolution. The difference this time is that the crisis of a desperate imperialism is in uncharted territory, characterized by its continuous decline and permanent wars of aggression; a decline spearheaded by the ongoing victories and constant struggles of the oppressed nations and colonized peoples the world over.

Crises abound! A few examples are: the indecisiveness and chaotic exit of Britain from the European Union (Brexit), yellow vests in France, the military defeat of U.S proxies in Syria, the existence of Chinese, French, Japanese and U.S. military bases occupying the same land mass in Djibouti in Africa, so on and so forth.

Chairman Omali's pronouncement of a new era of revolutionary struggle brings hope and optimism to the oppressed African nation, as well as all colonized and freedom-loving peoples on the planet. It informs us that we must strike a thousand blows against this dying capitalist system.

We are not seeking a multipolar or tripolar capitalist world. African Internationalism tells us that a free and unified African nation cannot coexist with parasitic capitalism.

This book leads in every aspect, from economic work, to genuine liberation of women to white solidarity with black power.

True to being the spearhead of the African Revolution, this is the leading call to establish a united and liberated African state, as the home of black power for the forcibly dispersed African nation.

For Europeans all over the word—in Europe, North America, Australia, New Zealand, South Africa, South America and elsewhere—the road to genuine solidarity begins with black power.

It is true that with African Internationalism the dispersed and dispossessed African working class is reclaiming its place at the forefront of both the African Revolution and the worldwide revolution.

The seeds of African Internationalism's work on the Continent are taking root. It is only a matter of time before we see the explosion of the contest between neocolonialism, also known as white power in black face, and African Internationalist revolutionaries.

The ever-developing philosophy of African Internationalism is bursting with innovative political analysis and groundbreaking economic projects. It is spreading to all four corners of the world. Honest forces and people of integrity, tired of reactionary parasites that occupy the political scene in their respective countries, seek new leadership to steer the world in a direction that leads to total liberation from imperialism.

Yeshitelism, aka African Internationalism, is that new direction, to rescue humanity from the brutal domination and exploitation of oppressed nations by oppressor nations, from the barbarity of often U.S.-led undeclared, unending wars of aggression in Africa, the Middle East and Afghanistan. The monstrous greed of imperialist white power always wants more and gives nothing to the oppressed.

Traditional Marxists in Europe are fundamentally concerned with the struggles to overthrow the rule of the aristocracy and of the bourgeoisie. They are not concerned about the enslavement of Africans and other colonized peoples. Chairman Omali explains that real change begins by snatching imperialism at its pedestal of colonial slavery.

African Internationalism is producing a blueprint for a revolutionary process that points the way forward for everybody who is irreversibly opposed to any kind of imperialist opportunism. It offers everyone integrity and a real future for humanity, through joining the struggle to free Africa and the African nation, which is essential to free the world.

Younger activists who are preoccupied with the world's uncertain future, or who despise the recklessness and selfishness of the white ruling class, will find redemption in African Internationalism.

African Internationalism is struggling to uproot parasitic capitalism, which began some 600 years ago. It has no stake whatsoever in maintaining or in compromising with parasitic capitalism. It is the scientific worldview of the colonized African working class.

This worldview is quite different from the so-called Marxists whose struggles were born of the need to organize and free white workers from the white nobility and bourgeoisie.

We are the ones who are forwarding the legacy of the great Marcus Garvey. We are taking his fight for African Fundamentalism to its logical conclusion.

We are the African nation, led by the African working class, laying out our own path to full international freedom, sovereignty and power.

African Internationalism gives the African working class confidence to speak to the world based on its own scientific investigations of imperialist society.

If we genuinely want to make revolution, if we genuinely want to mobilize the starving, emaciated African workers in Africa and around the world, a new revolutionary consciousness is necessary.

Only African Internationalism will move the African working class from a constant state of rebellion to a revolutionary process.

The African working class has been waiting five decades for a new theory to move us forward, to complete the Black Revolution of the Sixties, to bring an end to 600 years of white imperialism in Africa and the rest of the world.

Learn and evangelize African Internationalism

The African population is the most youthful in the world. We are connecting current generations of young people to revolutionary life. The youth that want to have a future must learn and apply African Internationalism.

We have inherited two harmful things from colonialism: the African petty bourgeoisie and the neocolonial state.

Our goal is to create a new world, a new Africa and a new world order.

Chairman Omali is giving revolutionary knowledge to a new generation of African workers and peasants.

African Internationalism teaches us how Western parasitism was born and how to forward revolution against parasitic capitalism. It offers a new proletarian culture in opposition to the decadent culture of the bourgeoisie. It introduces new standards for what it means to be a communist. It serves as a point of re-entry to revolution for African youth. It is also the basis of the upcoming communist international movement.

In this new outstanding publication, Chairman Omali defines the African working class as the pedestal upon which real socialism is being built.

African Internationalism is the gigantic social hurricane that will bring imperialism to its knees and make way for a new humanity to emerge, of workers, for workers.

Chairman Omali has spent his over 50 years in political life solving unanswered questions left by giants such as Malcolm X, Kwame Nkrumah, Patrice Lumumba and Huey P. Newton, after the military defeat of the Black Revolution of the Sixties.

This book reaffirms the legacy of Omali Yeshitela as simply the finest theoretician of his time; as the scientist who solved the theoretical questions of the African Revolution.

Vanguard expresses his undying faith that the masses of African workers everywhere will adopt, endorse and own African Internationalism.

Our Movement, the longest-standing national liberation movement against white imperialism, is equipped with the most mature and advanced revolutionary theory. It stands at a historical juncture that will determine the world's destiny.

Chairman Omali's vision is guiding the greatest storm threatening to engulf and destroy white imperialism. There is no chance for the imperialist parasites to survive.

African Internationalism not only explains the defeat of the Black Revolution of the Sixties, it explains how to reorganize the African Revolution.

Chairman Omali has lived through assassinations of our revolutionary leaders, through demoralization in the wake of the defeat of the Black Revolution of the Sixties and he is now experiencing the excitement of certain victory in the struggle for African liberation.

Black people, science, future, optimism, power, working class, revolution, Africa and black power—spoken in the same breath! You will certainly not see that in the bourgeois press. This is African liberation in the era of the final offensive against imperialism.

We are confident and we are clear after being on the longest road to freedom. Our journey through oppression is coming to a close. The African working class is bringing white power to its timely death.

The African Internationalist voice will be the center of revolutionary philosophy. This is the growing trend in the world.

All Africans dissatisfied with flag independence and civil rights, indirect rule and all other reforms won against European imperialist oppressors, can look no further than Chairman Omali's theory and work.

The ideological vacuum left by the assassinations and overthrow of Nkrumah, Lumumba, Garvey, Malcolm X and other key leaders has been filled with revolutionary theory advanced to its highest form.

The African proletariat has the eradication of parasitic capitalism as its main strategic goal.

As colonized people, we are not just fighting to recapture our land and resources. With African Internationalism, we are recapturing our minds.

The struggle for world socialism, far from being outdated, is indeed the struggle for the future of humanity, whose gates can only be genuinely unlocked by the most wretched African workers.

The African People's Socialist Party is the focal point of the world's revolutionary thought that aims to overthrow flag independence—U.S-led imperialism and black puppets.

No other force except for the African working class, through its Advanced Detachment, the African People's Socialist Party, has given itself the objectives of defeating the U.S. white ruling class and white power, and winning white solidarity with black power.

Chairman Omali has worked overtime to win African people and the best of humanity to African Internationalism as the road that leads to genuine world revolution and socialism!

This book is the best introduction on how to become an active, living part of the final offensive against 600 years of foreign European domination over our Continent and people.

Vanguard Up!

Forward to the Victorious African Nation!

Luwezi Kinshasa, Secretary General
African Socialist International

Preface

The Seventh Congress of the African People's Socialist Party makes history!

Through the tireless efforts of Chairman Omali Yeshitela completing and turning over the historical Seventh Congress Political Report and leading an entire committee to build this monumental occurrence, the Seventh Congress of the African People's Socialist Party (APSP) transformed the Black Power Movement, declaring that the "Black Revolution is Alive!" and that the Party is the Vanguard—the Advanced Detachment of the African Revolution.

The African People's Socialist Party convened its first day of the historic Seventh Congress on October 6, 2018 in St. Louis, Missouri—ground zero for African resistance.

African people and comrades from throughout the U.S. and the world, and our long-time allies from Unión del Barrio, traveled long distances to be part of this event laying out the future for a liberated, socialist Africa.

The Congress opened with chants such as "Vanguard, Vanguard we must lead; African people must be free!" and "Fly it high, Red, Black and Green; forward to our victory!"

National Central Committee commences the Congress

The highest body of the African People's Socialist Party, the National Central Committee, moved everyone to their feet with a powerful processional. Carrying decorated spears and the most revolutionary African garb, they took the stage in spear formation.

First up was Southern Regional Representative Kobina Bantushango and Northern Regional Representative Nana Yaw Grant.

Then came Director of the All African People's Development and Empowerment Project (AAPDEP) Dr. Aisha Fields, President of the African National Women's Organization (ANWO) Yejide Orunmila and President of the International People's Democratic Uhuru Movement (InPDUM) Kalambayi Andenet.

Marching toward the front of the stage came the Director of Agitation and Propaganda (Agit-Prop) Akilé Anai, the Deputy Chairwoman Ona Zené Yeshitela and the Secretary General of the African Socialist International (ASI) Luwezi Kinshasa.

Finally Chairman Omali Yeshitela, leader of the African nation, took the stage wielding the most elaborate spear. Resounding applause filled the auditorium as Chairman Omali took center stage, raised his spear and declared "Izwe Lethu i Afrika!" (Africa is our land!) The audience gave a thunderous response, "i Afrika, Izwe Lethu!"

Drumming group Ngoma in Motion further set the tone of this historic moment with lively rhythms that gave this introduction a dynamic African character. Then the Party's own Freedom Mass Choir & Band performed its first song of the event, "African People Must Be Free!"

Secretary General Luwezi Kinshasa then officially convened the Congress, assuring the African nation of its victory in the struggle for total liberation and the destruction of parasitic capitalism and colonialism.

Unión del Barrio's Under-Secretary Benjamín Prado gave a tribute to their 35-year principled relationship with the Party and acknowledged the late Pablo Aceves—long-time member of Unión del Barrio and close Compañero.

There were video messages of solidarity from around the world in unity with the Party and our resolve to be a liberated African nation, including Ramiro Sebastián Fúnez and his new organization, ANTICONQUISTA, APSP Kenya Chairwoman M. Kask, APSP Occupied Azania (South Africa) Secretary General Asa Anpu and a letter from Lisa Davis, Vice Chair of the Black is Back Coalition for Social Justice, Peace and Reparations (BIBC).

Chairman Omali delivers the Political Report

Chairman Omali Yeshitela re-took the stage and presented the powerful Seventh Congress Political Report to the world.

In the morning he completed Chapter I, moving to Chapter IV after lunch to highlight some of the most important details to be internalized by our Movement—not before recognizing some important figures in the historical development of the Party, including Vincent Lawrence, early member of the Party, and Unión del Barrio.

The Chairman commended Secretary General Luwezi Kinshasa and his selfless leadership in organizing the comrades on the Continent and recognized the brilliant work of Deputy Chair Ona Zené Yeshitela who has taken the Party's work to an entirely new level.

Annual appeal exceeds goal

Later in the afternoon, the Office of the Deputy Chair presented an exciting video review of the work of the Black Power Blueprint, the African People's Education and Defense Fund (APEDF) and Black Star Industries (BSI).

They recognized some of the top donors to the Party's economic development initiatives and presented gifts to New York state assemblyman Charles Barron and Unión del Barrio.

Movement veterans Omowale Kefing, Gaida Kambon, Chimurenga Selembao and again Vincent Lawrence were also recognized for their critical contributions to the establishment and development of the Party.

Some of the victories to occur during the first two days were the Party's ability to exceed its $75,000 pledge goal for 2019 by at least $10,000, and the 11 new members who committed to join the Party to carry out the work to its successful conclusion.

The Black Power Masquerade and Awards Ball

The evening of October 6 was spent at the beautiful Black Power Masquerade and Awards Ball, where St. Louis community activists and Party members received community awards.

Comrade Tafarie Mugeri, Chair of APSP Occupied Azania, was awarded Comrade of the Quarter.

There were vibrant cultural performances like African drumming by the Ngoma brothers, along with stilt walkers, a best-dressed contest and a delicious dinner. The downstairs floor was dedicated to dancing, a silent auction and photos.

Day two of the Congress

Day two began with a special tribute by ANWO President Yejide Orunmila to the courageous African women throughout history who fought against colonialism wherever they were located.

October 7 was New York state assemblyman Charles Barron's birthday and he opened his presentation with an expression of respect for the Party and the Chairman, saying that participation in this Congress was how he wanted to spend his 68th birthday.

Assemblyman Barron has held office in New York as a city councilman and now state assemblyman. The former Black Panther discussed his approach and strategy for using electoral politics to serve the African community.

The Party is building the political economy of the African nation

The second half of day two was dedicated to presenting the Party's approach to the economic question.

Chairman Omali introduced the Party's strategy for the development of dual and contending power in preparation for self-government with a presentation on "The Political Economy of the African Nation."

This brilliant presentation laid the foundation for the report delivered by the Office of Deputy Chair called "The Political and Economic are One: Dual and Contending State Power."

This workshop showcased members of this office from the different regions of the U.S. who discussed the Party's successful and long-standing institutions as well as our prospective projects including the St. Louis Uhuru Jiko community kitchen, the One Africa! One Nation! Marketplace and the Gary Brooks Community Garden.

Congress moves to the Party's own center

Day three through seven moved from the Better Family Life community center to our very own Uhuru House on West Florissant Avenue.

Each day began with the raising of the Red, Black and Green African flag on a 50-foot flagpole. This flag was voted on by the African nation at the Universal Negro Improvement Association and African Communities League (UNIA-ACL) convention nearly a century ago, where Africans determined to reconsolidate our own national identity.

The Party's honor guard marched militantly to raise and lower the flag in a traditional, ceremonial manner every morning and evening of the Congress.

The African community in St. Louis—from the elders to the children applauding and saluting from school buses—

was inspired to see true examples of black power in their community.

Some people went so far as to stop traffic, get out of their cars and participate in the ceremony!

Attendees hear reports on the Party's work

To open day four, a tribute to African martyrs was given by InPDUM President Kalambayi Andenet.

Her presentation expanded the definition of the martyr beyond what is typically known as someone killed by the state or "vertical violence." She recognized that all violence stems from Africans being colonized and having no power over our own lives.

The week advanced with dynamic reports and briefings from the Party's various departments and constituent organizations.

Reports were given on the work of the Office of the Chairman by Chief of Staff Ekenge Mayele.

The Department of Agitation and Propaganda's workshop was led by its Director Akilé Anai who is also Editor-In-Chief of *The Burning Spear* newspaper.

Chimurenga Selembao of the Office of National Security led a workshop on security protocols for the Party. Northern Regional and Southern Regional Representatives Nana Yaw Grant and Kobina Bantushango reported on the work and future plans for their respective regions.

AAPDEP Director Dr. Aisha Fields presented on the current health, infrastructure and environmental situation of Africans on the Continent and throughout the world, and on AAPDEP's economic institution Zenzele Consignment in Hunstville, Alabama.

Reports were delivered by InPDUM President Kalambayi Andenet, ANWO President Yejide Orunmila, African People's

Solidarity Committee (APSC) Chairwoman Penny Hess and Uhuru Solidarity Movement (USM) Chair Jesse Nevel.

Comrades Tafarie Mugeri and M. Kask—the Chairs of APSP Occupied Azania and APSP Kenya respectively—reported on the work being done on the ground in their regions, advancing many constituent organizations such as the African Internationalist Student Organization (AISO) and ANWO.

The reports from each department and constituent organization focused on the victories of these areas as well as the contradictions that prohibited them from carrying out the work called for by the Chairman in its fullest capacity.

These dynamic presentations rekindled the determination of all participants to get involved and take the Party to new levels.

Building revolutionary spirit and culture

In the whirlwind of dynamic reports, presentations and festivities was the celebration of the revolutionary birthdays of Chairman Omali Yeshitela and Deputy Chair Ona Zené Yeshitela, who share the same birthday, October 9.

The Party surprised them with a delicious cake, music and heartfelt statements that brought people to tears or caused uncontrollable laughter.

There were three ceremonies of rebirth that served to strip comrades of their colonial names and to give them names that the African nation deemed appropriate to their revolutionary qualities. These comrades were Christine Wilson and Brandee Ebert who took on the names Shupavu Kirima and Kundai Bajikikayi, respectively.

Overflowing at this Seventh Congress was the culture of African people—from spoken word to the amazing Freedom Mass Choir & Band directed by Comrade Elikya Bwanya

Ngoma. Performing original, revolutionary compositions, this choir set the standard for culture in the Revolution.

A culmination of talent and genius of the African working class was seen at the Congress Culture Night, where comrades performed poetry and stand-up comedy, sang songs, rapped, danced and concluded the evening with the "African Nation Fight Song."

Voting on Party matters at the Congress

Another important aspect of the Congress was the voting process. Several things were voted on at the Congress, including the adoption of the Chairman's Political Report, the Constitution, applications for reinstatement of two expelled Party members and elections of the National Central Committee. Each vote was handled with much seriousness, employing committees and commissions to make sure no details were overlooked.

The slate of the National Central Committee was voted up, presenting the NCC with Chairman Omali Yeshitela, ASI Secretary General Luwezi Kinshasa, Deputy Chair Ona Zené Yeshitela, Agit-Prop Director Akilé Anai, Southern Regional Representative Kobina Bantushango, Northern Regional Representative Nana Yaw Grant and the NCC's newest member, Midwest Regional Representative Shupavu Kirima.

Also sitting on the NCC are the Chairman-appointed positions of InPDUM's International President Kalambayi Andenet, ANWO's International President Yejide Orunmila and AAPDEP's International Director Aisha Fields.

The highest body of the Party—the Congress—being able to vote, on who can be reinstated to the Party, as well as on various resolutions that carry Party work forward, the Political Report and the Constitution, is the greatest example of the African working class seizing power.

No Party or organization in the world today exhibits such profound leadership of the African poor and working class.

For many Party members, this was their first Congress, but it transformed old and new forces alike.

Chairman Omali Yeshitela announced that the first Congress of the African Socialist International would be held in Occupied Azania in 2023!

This is a call to all Party members to take the work seriously and advance the interests of the poor and working class in leading a successful Revolution.

We are winning!

Part I

Political Report to the Seventh Congress of the African People's Socialist Party

I. The Vanguard, the Advanced Detachment

Uhuru! Comrades, delegates, observers and supporters of the Seventh Congress of the African People's Socialist Party!

During the five years since our Sixth Congress there have been many changes in the world and within our Party. All of them have served to reinforce the significance of the African People's Socialist Party which for more than 46 years has provided leadership for the African nation and the oppressed and exploited workers of the world.

Comrades! This Seventh Party Congress constitutes a firm salute to the indefatigable work of the African People's Socialist Party to forward the struggle for the liberation and unification of Africa and African people under the leadership of the African working class.

The continued, unrelenting dedication of our Party to complete the Black Revolution of the Sixties is alive in the theme of this Congress: "The African People's Socialist Party, Vanguard! Advanced Detachment of the African Revolution."

Although our assertion that we are the Vanguard and Advanced Detachment sets us apart from other organizations, it is not something said in contention with others. This is a declaration to you, the members of our Party, calling on you to recognize the magnitude of your Party membership and the role you have volunteered to carry out in the struggle for the liberation and unification of Africa and African people worldwide.

An example of an advanced detachment is a unit or group of soldiers that goes out first to lead and pave the way for the army in battle.

For our Party the Advanced Detachment or Vanguard means that we have freely and enthusiastically stepped forward to lead the struggle for the total liberation and unification of Africa and our entire dispersed African nation wherever we are located.

Unlike any other African organization on the planet, our Party is very serious about seizing African state power on our African continent. Our goal is to wrest back our land, our stolen resources and the value of our stolen labor, under the leadership of the African working class in a liberated, socialist Africa.

We understand that no oppressed people has ever become free without the intervention of an organization of trained, disciplined cadres who are committed to winning liberation by overcoming every obstacle, including our own limitations.

We are a Party of professional revolutionaries. Our members have a variety of occupations. We are school teachers, barbers, construction workers, taxi drivers and the like. We are also students, prisoners, office workers and welders. We are cooks and even lawyers. But whatever our occupation, our *profession* is revolution.

We are not dilettantes, simply committed to faddish political work in our spare time. In fact, our profession as revolutionaries guarantees that there is no time when we are not advancing the struggle for the liberation of our people. This is what it means to be the Vanguard, the Advanced Detachment.

The African People's Socialist Party was created to complete our Revolution that had been crushed by a vicious U.S.-led counterinsurgency that defeated the Black Revolution of the Sixties as it expressed itself globally.

There was no other organization in the African world that both survived the counterinsurgency and took up the task to go beyond survival and mere adaption to our inherited conditions of defeat. Our Party was bent on advancing the Revolution, the struggle for the total liberation and unification of Africa and the forcibly dispersed African nation everywhere.

We have done much advanced work to resolve the many theoretical issues that otherwise would have been left unresolved by the ruthless colonial-capitalist defeat of our Movement just as the most important questions were surfacing in our struggle.

We are practical revolutionaries. We are not an organization of consumers and dispensers of information. We have chosen to lead in every way. We have chosen to be the Advanced Detachment of the African working class. We have chosen to be the Vanguard.

Our Party understands that in order to change the world, to end our oppression we must have the organizational vehicle to do so and willing and trained cadres to carry out the task. This is why we are able to say African People's Socialist Party and Vanguard in the same breath.

The African People's Socialist Party is boldly declaring our intent to forge the revolutionary process to defeat imperialism. We are not just talking; we are preparing to govern. We know parasitic capitalism was created and is maintained through its cruel, rapacious attachment to Our Africa and our people. Our intention is to overturn it and replace it through a worldwide socialist revolution based in the forcibly dispersed international African nation wherever we are located.

The success of our Party is the critical factor in the liberation and unification of Africa and the entire suffering African nation. It is not a little thing. It is for this reason we were able to report to our Party's Plenary in February 2012 that building the Party is not only a crucial task of the African People's Socialist Party and our members, "it is also the fundamental task of the African Revolution at this critical juncture."

The African People's Socialist Party: the revolutionary vehicle

Years ago, in 1986, we summed up the qualities of our Party that made it necessary to characterize the African People's Socialist Party as the Vanguard in the pamphlet, "Build and Consolidate the African People's Socialist Party."[1]

We paraphrased a statement by former Black Panther leader Huey P. Newton when he was a revolutionary during the Black Revolution of the Sixties, which stated, "The party must be the ox upon whose back the masses ride."

We pointed out that two 19th century European revolutionaries, Karl Marx and Friedrich Engels, authored a similar statement:

> *The Communists, therefore, are on the one hand, practically, the most advanced and resolute section of the working-class parties of every country, that section which pushes forward all others; on the other hand, theoretically, they have over the great mass of the proletariat the advantage of clearly understanding the line of march, the conditions, and the ultimate general results of the proletarian movement.*[2]

We noted that it was left to V.I. Lenin, the 20th century Russian revolutionary, however, to successfully build and lead the revolutionary organization spoken of by Marx, Engels and later Newton.

We quoted Lenin as saying, "Give us an organization of revolutionaries, and we will overturn Russia,"[3] and explained

---

1 Yeshitela, Omali. "Build and Consolidate the African People's Socialist Party," Marcus Garvey Club, 1986.

2 Marx, Karl, and Friedrich Engels. *Selected Works*, p. 46, International Publishers, 1986.

3 Lenin, V.I. *Collected Works*, Vol. 5, p. 467, Foreign Language Publishing House, Moscow, 1961.

that Lenin set upon the task to build the revolutionary organization that indeed overturned Russia and became the prototype for revolutionary organizations of the oppressed and exploited peoples throughout the world.

Such a party is the Vanguard, the Advanced Detachment of the working class. It is a party of communists, a party of a new type. Such a party is the African People's Socialist Party.

Our task then as now is to unite our people under the leadership of the black working class in the struggle for political independence, African liberation and socialism.

This Political Report must win the unity of our Party members and the participants in our Seventh Congress to the recognition of the gravity of your role as cadres, the Advanced Detachment of the African Revolution. This Political Report will demonstrate the material basis, to be found in the history and accomplishments of the Party and our understanding of the acute crisis of the parasitic capitalist system, for having the confidence and courage to take up your proper role as leaders of the African Revolution.

Our Political Report to the 2017 Party Plenary was titled "Putting Revolution Back on the Agenda!" In this report we began to show how the Party is the Advanced Detachment:

> *First of all, the imperialist crisis, the uneasy equilibrium with which we have been contending, is manifesting itself with ever-greater clarity in the political arena, especially as seen in the 2016 U.S. presidential campaign and election.*
>
> *Secondly, the neocolonial African assimilationist tendency of our community, while opposed to the election of Trump, is making every effort to support the colonial-capitalist system. The assimilationists are doing everything possible to keep Africans loyal to the system and the electoral process—primarily*

to the ruling Democratic party from whence flows their economic security, semblance of power and influence.

The African People's Socialist Party is the revolutionary vehicle of the advanced detachment through which the conscious and organized African working class continues to wage the struggle for the socialist liberation and unification of our dispersed African nation.

Instead of spontaneity, which allows the issue of the moment to determine our trajectory, our work is based on a plan stemming from a scientific theory. We continue to check up on our work, to measure our successes and correct our errors, to make certain that our practice reflects and validates our theory.

The Party Congress and our plenaries allow us to bring the membership of the Party into this democratic process of charting our course. They grant the Party leadership the authority to require centralized discipline from all our members and constituent organizations....

The Sixth Party Congress participants adopted the Political Report after serious discussions that began more than three months prior to the convening of the Congress. The Political Report was truly a document of our whole Party and the tasks, the five-year plan laid out in the Political Report, constitutes the Party's direction that was voted for by the whole Party.

Our Plenary process is the method the Party has adopted to continue summing up our work of making our plan reality and guaranteeing that we do not veer off on some opportunistic gambit based on the whims of any Party organization, committee, member or leader.[4]

The resolutions and mandates adopted at our congresses safeguard our Party against spontaneity and opportunism, factors that distinguish our Party and contribute to its continuity, which is key to our strategic approach.

Our congresses and plenaries are critical because since the defeat of the Black Revolution of the Sixties more than two generations ago, the African People's Socialist Party is the organization that assumed custody of the revolutionary struggle of the African working class and peasantry, indeed of the entire African nation.

We are the Party that constitutes a historical continuum from the previous era of the Black Revolution of the Sixties to its incipient resurgence today.

Our mission has never been determined by the events of the moment. Events come and go, elections are held, coups overturn governments, police violence escalates from time to time, our struggle faces setbacks, but the social system that has arisen from slavery and colonialism remains the same. This is the essential ingredient that must inform our analysis during each period.

Our congresses and plenaries contribute to our ability to hold the line to protect, defend and solve the problems of the Revolution. This is what revolutionaries do. This is what a revolutionary party does.

It is also true that the system of oppression under which the entire world and we live and struggle, is a parasitic capitalist system that owes its existence to and is nourished by slavery and colonialism. The legitimacy of any movement of the oppressed must ultimately be judged by its opposition

---

4 Yeshitela, Omali. *Putting Revolution Back on the Agenda: Political Report to the 2017 Plenary of the African People's Socialist Party*, apspuhuru.org/2017-plenary-political-report/

to slavery, colonialism and the capitalist system birthed by slavery and colonialism.

Africans and the peoples of the world suffer from a dictatorship of a white nationalist imperialist bourgeoisie currently headquartered in the U.S.

Our Party is the custodian of the African Revolution

While the selection of Barack Hussein Obama as the first African U.S. president and the August 9, 2014 police murder of 18-year-old Mike Brown in Ferguson, Missouri may have affected how we carried out our strategy and tactics, the reality of the parasitic capitalist colonial domination of Africa and the world remained the same. This reality shapes our worldview. It makes us African Internationalists.

We addressed the critical role of our Party in the continuing process of solving the problems of the Revolution in the Political Report to the 2016 Plenary:

> *Since our inception in 1972, our Party has functioned as the primary custodian of the African liberation struggle. We have summed up all the lessons and contradictions of our revolutionary Movement to reunite the African nation and liberate and unite Africa and African people worldwide under the leadership of the African working class.*
>
> *The African Liberation Movement suffered major setbacks since the defeat of the Black Revolution of the 1960s. Not only were giants like Patrice Lumumba of Congo and Kwame Nkrumah of Ghana brutally murdered and overthrown by repulsive, shameless, European-created neocolonial stooges, but our Movement was never able to resolve many of the key ideological and political questions facing our people. This demoralized our people whose dreams*

and aspirations were spoiled by the disillusionment that followed our Movement's defeat and demise.

Inside the U.S. it was left to our Party to sum up the significance of the life and death of Malcolm X and Dr. Martin Luther King and the destruction of the Black Panther Party along with the accompanying assassinations and imprisonments.

It was the African People's Socialist Party that forced the world to recognize that the African Liberation Movement is one struggle being waged across the globe on different fronts by a forcibly dispersed African nation held in colonial slavery in Africa and elsewhere over the last several hundred years.

It was our philosophy, African Internationalism, that brought this understanding to the forefront. Without African Internationalism it would be impossible to understand why Africans, sometimes called by an assortment of different names, suffer impoverishment, brutality and imposed ignorance all over the world.[5]

As we state in the Political Report to our Party's 2010 Fifth Congress, published as *One People! One Party! One Destiny!*:

Would capitalism and the resultant European wealth and African impoverishment have occurred without the European attack on Africa, its division, African slavery and dispersal, colonialism and neocolonialism?

5 Yeshitela, Omali. *Organize to Win! Organize to Govern! Political Report to the 2016 Plenary of the African People's Socialist Party,* apspuhuru.org/2016-plenary-political-report/

> *The answer is No! No! No! and a thousand times, No!*[6]

In the Political Report to the Party's 2016 Plenary we clarified:

> *It was African Internationalism that helped to locate the millions of Africans that otherwise would be missing from history by false national identities that facilitate our colonization everywhere and deny Africans the confidence and resources that come from recognition that as a nation Africans are more than a billion and a half strong...*
>
> *Our Party, through practice and theory, continues up to now to help people understand that despite the ongoing efforts by the U.S. to demonstrate otherwise, the Black Revolution of the Sixties did not simply go away because our militants tired of struggle or came to enjoy our oppressed status in the U.S. Our Revolution was militarily defeated through assassinations, mass jailings, slander and unrelenting harassment. In a word, it was a war without terms that silenced our struggle.*
>
> *This is the understanding that allowed the African People's Socialist Party to recognize that the African charlatans, including Barack Hussein Obama, were elevated to high places as neocolonial substitutes for genuine revolutionary African leaders of the past.*
>
> *Indeed, these charlatans, every one of them, are a result of the defeat of the Revolution, not of its success.*

---

6 Yeshitela, Omali. *One People! One Party! One Destiny! The Political Report to the Fifth Congress of the African People's Socialist Party-USA*, p. 42, Burning Spear Uhuru Publications, St. Petersburg, FL, 2010.

We have led and participated in campaigns throughout the U.S. and all over the world informed by this understanding and steeled by practice that involved virtually every form of struggle.

This is why we can confidently say we are best prepared to lead our people to the reunification of the African nation and the liberation and unification of our African Motherland.

Unlike most who see the growing unrest roiling the world—the unremitting wars and the threats to U.S. hegemony in Africa, Asia, Latin America, the Middle East and increasingly the African domestic colony of the U.S.—with alarm, we of the African People's Socialist Party recognize this as an era of general imperialist crisis.[7]

Certainly this is why the Political Report to the Party's Sixth Congress was titled *An Uneasy Equilibrium: The African Revolution versus Parasitic Capitalism*, where we summed up:

The science of African Internationalism enabled our Party to avoid the ideological pitfalls that validate the assumption of the superiority of white people. Thus, we have never been diverted from our mission of capturing power and uniting Africa and our nation under the leadership of the African working class.

Our Party brought science to our defeated African Liberation Movement at a time when it was generally bogged down in racial and cultural nationalism that indulged in candlelit ceremonies, religious obscurantism and nostalgia for an often imaginary African past. Through African

7 Yeshitela, *Organize to Win! Organize to Govern!*

> *Internationalism we were able to discover the material basis for the exploitation and oppression of Africans and others in this world.*
>
> *With African Internationalism we can understand the material forces at work in the movement of history. We can clearly see the current shift in the balance of power between the oppressor and the oppressed, between Europe and the rest of us, between the "white man" and the "black man."*[8]

We recognize the reality that there is a great contest between an imperialist past that has defined the world for the last five hundred years and a liberated future of a totally free and reunited African nation and the emancipation of the colonized peoples worldwide.

Our Party fights for the interests of the African working class

All societies contain an advanced sector. These are people who, for whatever reason, stand out because of their willingness to step forward to address the pressing problems found in society at any given time. It is they who generally attempt to sum up the areas of social concern and to put forward solutions. The individuals who take on this important social task are those who comprise the advanced sector.

Political parties are parties that are comprised of these individuals. But political parties are also parties of particular classes. In the development of capitalism, political parties have historically been representatives of the colonial-capitalist class. They represent the selfish interests of that class even though the colonial-capitalist class, because it is a minority,

8 Yeshitela, Omali. *An Uneasy Equilibrium: The African Revolution versus Parasitic Capitalism. The Political Report to the Sixth Congress of the African People's Socialist Party*, p. 59. Burning Spear Publications, 2014.

exploiting class, must usually disguise its class rule as the popular will of the oppressed and exploited masses.

Today, the African working class has our own organization that fights for the selfish interests of our class. Up to now most of our political activism has taken place inside the ranks of the parties of our oppressors, the colonial-capitalist rulers of society. They have been able to continue their rule because we have not had our own working class parties to advance our own selfish class interests that are diametrically opposed to the interests of our oppressors.

As colonial subjects of imperialist white power, Africans have only had access to the electoral process since the 1960s. Before that time our political interests were usually determined by the white colonial rulers or by the African petty bourgeoisie and organizations they established.

In the U.S. some of these petty bourgeois-led organizations won popular acclaim because of their successful mobilization of the oppressed African masses to become directly involved in the movement for basic democratic rights under colonialism.

Similarly, on the continent of Africa it was the African petty bourgeoisie that rose to prominence in the quest for political independence within the capitalist system presided over by imperialist white power. While some of the demands of the pro-independence African petty bourgeoisie appeared to be radical, they were generally incapable of challenging the capitalist system that has its origin in our colonial domination. This meant that the outcome was a capitalist outcome that now had African management.

A meaningful, notable exception to this was the Universal Negro Improvement Association (UNIA) that was organized by Marcus Garvey to pursue the liberation of Africa and Africans globally and the achievement of our independent capacity for self-government.

The UNIA organized branches throughout the world with a membership of 6 to 11 million Africans. It created groundbreaking economic institutions that included a steamship line, factories, recording companies and a host of other economic projects intended to initiate a threatening, independent, anti-colonial international economy for African people.

The Garvey Movement was incessantly attacked by international imperialist white power, especially the U.S. government that falsely charged and imprisoned Garvey before deporting him to Jamaica, his place of birth.

While the UNIA never touted its working class constitution, it was the working class character of the Garvey Movement that won Garvey the enmity of the African petty bourgeoisie of the era in the first quarter of the 20th century.

Many of them, especially the distinguished W.E.B. Du Bois, cooperated with the U.S. government and others to destroy the Garvey Movement in part because of its black working class composition.

We are the Garveyites of the 21st century. Like Garvey, we do speak to the interests of the African nation as expressed through the interests and worldview of the independently organized African working class. The philosophy of the UNIA was African Fundamentalism, not Pan-Africanism.[9] The

9 The Pan-Africanist Movement recognized a relationship among Africans worldwide, but was incapable of seeing Africans as part of the same dispersed nation that had to be physically liberated and united. Anyone could call him/herself Pan-Africanist regardless of whether he/she was revolutionary or reactionary. As a political movement we can trace the history of Pan-Africanism to the late 1800s. However, the first recorded or recognized Pan-Africanist Conference occurred in England in 1900. The movement took on political significance in 1919 when W.E.B. Du Bois who was editor of the NAACP magazine *The Crisis*, organized a conference in Paris, France. Under the influence of the assimilationist Du Bois, Pan-Africanism became a primary adversary of the millions-strong movement led by Marcus Garvey. African Internationalism is a theory that requires practice and which stands unabashedly for the total unification and liberation of Africa and African people everywhere under one socialist government led by the African working class.

worldview of our Party, 21st century Garveyites, is African Internationalism. Again, not Pan-Africanism.

As the party of the African working class we are always consciously contending with the parties and interests of the oppressor nation and the exploiting capitalist class.

The African People's Socialist Party is not *the* African working class; we are its Advanced Detachment, its general staff, its Vanguard which, like the class parties of the oppressors, looks out for the interests of the whole class whether the whole class is at any given moment capable of recognizing what its class interests are.

The African working class is always in a posture of resistance. This is most obvious in the behavior of young working class Africans who consciously defy convention that usually defines how "reasonable," "civilized" behavior should look. They are constantly breaking out of the social boundaries imposed on our community by colonialism and in many cases, they set new social and cultural trends which, after initial strong ruling class and African petty bourgeois denunciation, are co-opted by proper colonial society.

The resistance of the African working class can be seen in the spontaneous rebellions and threats of rebellion that require an oppressive presence of the domestic colonial military police waging barely disguised war in every African community within the U.S. and the entire world.

When the African working class does not have access to its own African People's Socialist Party, their defiance is most often not politically motivated and directed. When it is occasionally politically directed, it comes under the influence of the white rulers, sometimes transmitted by radical sectors of the African petty bourgeoisie. We have seen this recently in the aftermath of the 2014 uprising in St. Louis-Ferguson following the colonial police murder of Mike Brown.

We have also seen the result of this indirect ruling class influence over the masses of African workers in Occupied Azania (South Africa) with the rise of the African National Congress, Nelson Mandela and a host of other radical sectors of the African petty bourgeoisie.

Similarly, African working class protests are roiling the African continent, including the Democratic Republic of Congo. The weakness of the African Revolution is again exposed by the fact that the majority of the African working class and poor peasantry do not have the advantage of the African People's Socialist Party, its own party fighting for the selfish interests of the colonized African working class.

The African People's Socialist Party has been the instrument of the African working class that continues to rally the class to its own interests, to its own side, so to speak.

Our Party leads the entire African nation

However, our Party is not only the Advanced Detachment of the African working class, but, as we have said before, we are the Vanguard of the entire African National Revolution. We have accepted the responsibility of liberating Africa and the entire forcibly dispersed African nation that suffers under the cruel weight of colonialism everywhere.

The African People's Socialist Party is the leadership of the African working class, the most consistently revolutionary component of the African nation, but because the African working class is the main social force of a colonized African *nation*, our responsibility is greater than simply leadership of the working class.

The leadership of the Advanced Detachment of the African working class is an absolute necessity for the liberation of the entire colonized African population, including the African petty bourgeoisie that has an entirely different definition of what liberation means.

The African petty bourgeoisie wants equality with the colonizer, preferably with the colonial ruling class. One sector of the African petty bourgeoisie wants to get rid of the colonizer and its domination of the African nation. It is a patriotic sector of the African petty bourgeoisie because of its opposition to white colonial domination. However, this sector is not interested in overturning the system of capitalism that was created through colonial slavery.

In the Political Report to the Party's Third Congress, held in St. Petersburg, Florida in September 1990 we defined the difference between petty bourgeois national liberation and the national liberation of the African working class. Although this passage speaks specifically to the situation of the U.S. domestic colonialism of our people, the principle is universal:

> *The "national liberation" of the aspiring black petty bourgeoisie is a "liberation" from the limitations of its development into a full-blown bourgeoisie, [limitations] which are imposed on it by domestic colonialism, the imperialist rule by foreign gangsters. Within this concept of "national liberation" is the germ of a future, continuing exploitation of the African working class by a black bourgeoisie that has been liberated from the "national" oppression which prevented the emergence of a free, independent black boss. Such a "national liberation" is not in the interests of the colonized African working class.*
>
> *The national liberation of the working class is a liberation which will sweep away all forms of oppression and exploitation. The national liberation of the domestically colonized African working class is not only interested in removing the oppression of foreign rule, it is also interested in destroying the*

> *class rule which exploits the workers and toiling masses of all countries where the capitalist system prevails. The national liberation of the working class is explicitly anti-capitalist and consciously a part of the worldwide socialist movement.*[10]

In many writings we have often quoted V.I. Lenin, the Russian revolutionary who designed the vanguard party that has influenced the definition of revolutionary parties since that time. The African People's Socialist Party is a Leninist-type Party, based on democratic centralism.

Lenin stated: "We are the Party of a class, and therefore *almost* the entire class should act under the leadership of our Party."[11]

In the pamphlet "Build and Consolidate the African People's Socialist Party," we explained, following the quote from Lenin:

> *However, within the domestically colonized population of the U.S. the two main contending social forces are the black working class comprising 88 to 94 percent of the population, and the primitive black petty bourgeoisie which, generally speaking has an inordinate amount of influence presently due to the military defeat of the Black Revolution of the Sixties. Its influence is also tied to one or another sector of the colonial white ruling class or the capitalist/colonialist State itself.*
>
> *In the past when the political activity and ideology of the black petty bourgeoisie was generalized as an anti-colonial struggle for democratic rights, the*

10 Yeshitela, Omali. *Izwe Lethu i Afrika*, p. 72. Burning Spear Publications, 1991.

11 Lenin, V.I. *Collected Works*, Vol. 7, p. 260. Foreign Language Publishing House, Moscow, 1961.

> *black petty bourgeoisie constituted a progressive influence within our movement.*
>
> *However, with the victory of the struggle for democratic rights which came as a concession to the black petty bourgeoisie and at the expense of the Black Revolution of the Sixties, the black petty bourgeoisie realized its fundamental political aim and lost any historically-derived progressive character it once had.*
>
> *Thus the mantle of leadership—both for the struggle for national liberation and socialism—has fallen upon the shoulders of the most despised and feared black working class.*
>
> *Therefore, as the advanced detachment of the black working class, the African People's Socialist Party assumes the leadership not only for "almost the entire class," but also for almost the entire people.*[12]

This is why we say we are the Advanced Detachment or Vanguard of the *African* Revolution. The fact is that we are involved in a struggle for national liberation within which there is also a raging class struggle that grows sharper with the crisis of imperialism.

The revolutionary aspirations of our people for happiness, the return of hundreds of years of stolen resources and the construction of a socialist system wherein material want can be conquered will be determined by the African working class having its own independent political vehicle, its Advanced Detachment, leading the struggle.

We are that Vanguard. It is the profound duty of the leaders and members of our Party to eagerly, enthusiastically,

12 Yeshitela, "Build and Consolidate," p. 25.

accept this responsibility at this Congress to take our Party and people to the future that Africans desire and deserve.

Our Party was born in an era of defeat

The U.S. government is currently the wounded, reactionary chief imperialist regime of the world that led the counterrevolutionary response of international imperialism to crush the liberation struggles of the peoples during the period of the 1960s when revolution was the main trend of the entire world.

At our 1972 inception, the African People's Socialist Party inherited a political terrain characterized by the fact that the masses had been shot and jailed out of political life. Revolution is characterized by the mass, unbridled participation of the oppressed people in political life and it was the defeat of the Black Revolution of the Sixties that ended this mass participation.

Our Party has been busy organizing with the intent of reintroducing the people to political life. We have created various organizations to win the active participation of African people to the task of overturning the colonial government's violent program to prevent us from rising up again. An example of such an organization is the International People's Democratic Uhuru Movement (InPDUM).

Programs to prevent or crush anti-colonial resistance are called counterinsurgency programs. Counterinsurgency employs every form of warfare: psychological, economic, political, etc. However, all counterinsurgency relies on military force in the final analysis.

Central to most counterinsurgency programs is what the colonial power calls population and resource control. This is why the prisons are filled with Africans who might be otherwise available for revolutionary organization. This is also why there is an unrelenting murderous presence of colonial occupying military police in every African community in the U.S. and most places in the world.

Like the U.S. colonial government, however, our Party has always understood that it is only a matter of time before the African working class reclaims our station at the forefront of the Revolution. This is why we never forsook revolution for some opportunist substitute.

When Mike Brown was murdered by a white nationalist citizen in police uniform, it proved to be the straw that broke the proverbial camel's back. It ignited a fierce resistance among the young African working class in St. Louis-Ferguson that mobilized Africans throughout the U.S.

Our history and the Sixth Congress of our Party prepared us for this moment of imperialist crisis and rising consciousness among many sectors within the colonized African nation.

Since our Sixth Congress five years ago, our Party has intensified our work on every front.

We are winning!

Comrades! Delegates, Brothers and Sisters! We salute the history of unending resistance of our people and the great advancement of the people's struggle under the unrelenting leadership of its Advanced Detachment, the African People's Socialist Party!

Izwe Lethu i Afrika!

II. Our Party solved the problems of the Revolution

The African People's Socialist Party was born in the heat of struggle, at a time when the U.S. government was bent on destroying the Black Revolution of the Sixties. Together with the heroic revolution of the people of Viet Nam against U.S. colonial occupation, the Black Revolution constituted an existential threat to imperialist white power.

The freedom movement of African people within current U.S. borders had broken from the absolute leadership of the liberal sector of the African petty bourgeoisie and was fighting to become one with the anti-colonial movements sweeping the planet. All the peoples of all countries wanted freedom from the capitalist parasite that had come into existence through colonial slavery and dominated the world.

The Chinese, Korean and Cuban revolutions had ignited the imaginations of oppressed peoples everywhere. Capitalism had been born as global white power and defined itself as such. The world capitalists had previously predicted their own invincibility as custodians of the planet. Many of the oppressed had also been convinced of this until the revolutions of oppressed peoples achieved universality and shook the imperialist world at its foundation.

Africans within the U.S. were affected by the escalating scope of anti-colonial revolutions. Many were forced to reevaluate the definition of our struggle in the U.S. as simply one for civil rights within the existing social system. We began to recognize the struggle for civil rights as being rooted in philosophical idealism and patriotism to the very system and people responsible for our oppression.

My own personal political history began to solidify during this period of anti-colonial upheaval. I was fortunate to have been born during the era when anti-colonial struggle was the main trend in the world. These revolutions resulted in political independence for India, followed quickly by the success of the Chinese Revolution of 1949, an era that was reshaping the economic, political and ideological contours of the world. I was thereby able to envision a future shorn of white colonial domination.

My personal political development initially moved me to join the U.S. military in an ill-informed youthful attempt to extricate myself and my future from the prevailing blatant white domination in the southern U.S. city of my birth.

I found that the U.S. army was a reflection and guardian of the injustices I attempted to evade through my enlistment. As a consequence of my struggles in the military, I was grudgingly granted a discharge. Shortly thereafter I found my footing in the organized resistance by joining the Student Nonviolent Coordinating Committee (SNCC), a youthful and dynamic front of the Civil Rights Movement that was responsible for raising the slogan-demand for black power in 1966.

The black power demand put SNCC on a collision course with the U.S. government and the liberal leaders of the Civil Rights Movement, leaders who owed their success to their relationship with sectors of the white ruling class. SNCC became a target of the colonial state, but events were moving too fast to immediately contain the growing anti-colonial radicalization of the African population within current U.S. borders.

In Florida, I was jailed for my political activities in St. Petersburg and Gainesville and sentenced to a five-year prison term at the end of 1966. At the same time in Oakland, California, the Black Panther Party, influenced by SNCC work in Lowndes County, Alabama, exploded on the scene in dramatic fashion.

The terror of the counterinsurgency unleashed by the U.S. colonial state within U.S. borders was laying waste to much of the anti-colonial resistance. The Black Panther Party was a primary target because of its explosive growth and influence among the most oppressed sectors of the colonized African population. I was also constantly in and out of prison because of similar work, primarily in Florida and Kentucky at the time.

It was during one of my frequent prison stints that it became clear to me that the era of "protest politics" was over, that our people had to really fight for power. We had to have a political party, the most effective vehicle for capturing and wielding power. Black power had to be translated as our own black "state power."

By 1972 when our Party was formed, the Black Revolution of the Sixties was on its last leg as a generalized expression of organized mass struggle. The Black Panther Party, which had borne the brunt of the domestic assault by the U.S. colonial state, had lost most semblances of a revolutionary organization. Many of its leaders had been jailed, exiled and killed, and others, after years of assault and eventual political isolation, were driven to paranoid political immobilization. By this time the Black Panther Party had little semblance of its former self.

Party's Oakland years revive the African Revolution

The African People's Socialist Party took up the gauntlet. In 1986, three years before his death, Huey P. Newton, the founder of the Black Panther Party who once achieved international stature as a prominent revolutionary leader, stated at our Uhuru House in Oakland, California at one of his last public political speeches:

> *You might not have the Black Panther Party but you have the Uhuru House; you might not*

> *have* The Black Panther *newspaper but you have* The Burning Spear. *So they really haven't done anything by crushing one organization.*[1]

Indeed, the existence of the Uhuru House in Oakland, California, which at the time was the international headquarters of our Party, was part of our work to resuscitate the African Revolution.

Newton was only able to have a venue and an audience for his statement because of our Party and the Movement we had created in Oakland where the U.S. was already performing dirges marking the demise of the U.S.-based African Liberation Movement.

Our Party was organizing resistance to the criminal charges being pressed against Newton by the colonial state at the time. His presence at the Uhuru House was due to our insistence that he fight back. We assured him that we could bring the people to his defense from ridiculous allegations associated with a school the Panthers once owned that had been destroyed by fire, likely ignited by the U.S. government.

The African People's Socialist Party led the campaign to bring Huey P. Newton back into political life in Oakland. When he was assassinated in 1989, it was we who organized the mass resistance against attempts by bourgeois colonial media to slander his name into political revulsion and irrelevance.

It was our Party that supported Newton's widow after his assassination and we who obtained the mortician that presided over his funeral. It was the African People's Socialist Party that organized the honor guard of uniformed members of our Party at the public viewing of Newton's body attended by more than 10,000 people. We printed the program for his funeral.

1 Newton, Huey P. "The Last Speeches of Huey P. Newton," p. 1. Burning Spear Publications, 1990.

While the official funeral happened in a major church in Oakland, it was our Party that held the mass People's Funeral outside the church, conducted by Oakland Party leader Comrade Biko Lumumba from atop a Party van surrounded by thousands of working class Africans who could not get in the church. We also led the spontaneous funeral march of thousands that accompanied Newton's hearse at the conclusion of the official ceremony.

The participation of the African People's Socialist Party in the funeral of Huey P. Newton was a continuation of our work in Oakland and was a concrete transition in a historical moment. The African People's Socialist Party was the rising revolutionary force, the current Advanced Detachment of the African Revolution providing an honorable, if belated, departure for the leadership of the past.

The presence of the African People's Socialist Party in Oakland influenced the consciousness of our people and our movement for liberation. Our decision to reclaim the definition of Newton and the Black Panther Party transformed the colonial narrative and changed the course of history.

We defeated the efforts of the colonial ruling class media to characterize Newton by the last difficult years of his life when he had succumbed to the decades of jailings and repression that successfully isolated and demoralized him, reducing him to the stature and habits of too many of our colonized brothers and sisters during the height of the counterinsurgency in the U.S.

On the morning after the announcement of his death, bourgeois colonial newspapers described Newton as a "bum" and criminal, his epitaph as written by our hated class enemies and national oppressor. On the same morning, our Party held rallies at the site of his assassination and showed videos of the heroic days of the Black Panther Party when it had been the revolutionary center of our movement.

It was our Party that held the march that led hundreds of Africans through the streets of Oakland, deserted of all domestic occupation military forces, chanting, "Who killed Huey? Don't tell no lie! The government, the government, the FBI!"

Without the intervention of the Party, the state and its media would have succeeded in the attempt to demean the movement for African liberation by discrediting Newton and the Black Panther Party.

Left to their own devices, the hated imperialist rulers would have created the myth that they detested Newton because he was a "bum" and a criminal and not because he led an incredible liberation movement that raised many working class African people from the depths of the social, spiritual and political morass created for us by U.S. colonial capitalism.

Although the attempt continues to be made to define Newton outside of his role as a leader of our struggle against colonial-capitalist domination, our Party rescued the definition of our anti-colonial struggle from the poisoned sewer of white nationalist contempt that rose up with Newton's assassination.

It is only because the African working class and our colonized nation had an Advanced Detachment, a revolutionary Party that functions as the general staff of our struggle for national liberation, unification and socialism, that the colonial rulers were unable to rewrite our history of revolutionary resistance.

The Revolution continued to exist after the demise of Newton and the Black Panther Party. The Revolution continued to exist in the form of the African People's Socialist Party.

Party has always functioned as the Advanced Detachment

It is a law of dialectics that the old must give way for the new. This applies to the dynamics within our anti-colonial movement as well as the dynamic between our liberation struggle and the parasitic capitalist system. This is why we are not intimidated by what appears to be the strength of our colonial-capitalist oppressors at the moment. All evidence exposes the reality that U.S. bluster today is the anxious braggadocio of symptomatic impotence, the bluster of an imperialism in decline on its deathbed.

We never tailed the masses as did so many others. We exposed the bourgeois selections of Nelson Mandela and Barack Hussein Obama as the imposition of neocolonialism, even when the masses wanted them to represent a victory for the African people. The African People's Socialist Party always led, even through periods when our positions were temporarily unpopular, until the truth of the Party's analysis revealed itself to the masses.

We have always fought to defend the anti-colonial revolution of the African nation. We have always functioned as the Advanced Detachment of our nation and class, dragging our struggle to new heights from the depths of defeat.

There were others who organized different events around any number of issues during this period. Some were repudiating past commitments to revolution and, for some, "coalition-building" became the buzzword for the way forward.

The African People's Socialist Party, our organization, was determined to solve the problems of the Revolution.

Our people and our movement needed a revolutionary party of steeled cadres guided by revolutionary principles and advanced revolutionary theory. We had to fiercely fight to build the party of the African working class, the only social force capable of leading the struggle of African national liberation, unification and socialism to its successful conclusion.

The African working class, under the leadership of its own revolutionary party, conscious of its own selfish interests and guided by the revolutionary theory of African Internationalism, had to lead our struggle for victory over colonial capitalism and usher in a new world free of class exploitation and human oppression.

Comrades! The Advanced Detachment understands that revolution is not an event; it is a process. Revolution is a science and an art that requires for its leadership advanced revolutionary theory and a disciplined organization of professional revolutionaries.

My Political Report to our Sixth Congress, *An Uneasy Equilibrium*, spoke to the Party's work to maintain the life and direction of the Black Revolution of the Sixties:

> *Since the defeat of the Black Revolution of the Sixties the masses of the people have been sidelined, pushed out of political life. What passes for struggle is relegated most often to single-issue activism that is nothing but an appendage to social media militancy or liberal and other bourgeois schemes.*
>
> *The significance of our Party lies in the fact that we have never surrendered or deviated from the path of the same African Revolution that motivated the imperialist white power attacks in the 20th century. We continue to lead despite the general setbacks suffered by our movement as a whole.*
>
> *We are the only organization that correctly analyzed the fact that the Black Revolution of the '60s was defeated by imperialist counterinsurgency—a*

> *military attack intended to keep our people and our movement from ever rising up again.*[2]

Comrades! Brothers and Sisters! Delegates to the Seventh Congress of our Party:

When our Party came to Oakland, it was not in anticipation that we would be there to fight for a dignified departure of Comrade Huey P. Newton.

We did not go to Oakland to preside over the passage of an era of black revolutionary struggle.

Our presence in Oakland was a natural consequence of the Party's growth and our determination to complete the Black Revolution of the Sixties.

Our political trek began with the founding of the African People's Socialist Party, an act which in and of itself raised our struggle to a higher level even as the U.S. government was confident of its success in destroying it.

In 1972 in Florida when the Black Rights Fighters of Fort Myers and the Gainesville Black Study Group joined with the Junta of Militant Organizations (JOMO) to form the African People's Socialist Party, we were working to build the inaugural African Liberation Day mobilization scheduled for May 27 in Washington, DC.

Our participation in the subsequent African Liberation Day mobilizations from that point on has been to continue the revolutionary trajectory of our movement that was being effectively crushed by U.S. imperialism within its borders.

Solving the problems of the Revolution

The task of solving the problems of the Revolution meant that we had to resolve the host of organizational, political and theoretical contradictions blocking the progress of revolutionary development.

---

2 Yeshitela, Omali. *An Uneasy Equilibrium,* pp. 25-26. Burning Spear Publications, 2014.

Our organizational response was the creation of the African People's Socialist Party, an organization of professional revolutionaries, as the necessary vehicle for advancing the interests of our nation under the revolutionary leadership of the African working class.

With the development of the Party we opened up new fronts of struggle throughout the African world.

Theoretically, our Party opened up a major offensive against outdated, failed philosophical worldviews and vigorously advanced struggles against the hostile ideology of the colonial oppressor class and its devotees within our colonized community.

We made determined struggles against philosophical idealism. This included incessant ideological war against the definition of our struggle as being against "racism," which can only be an effort to perfect the system of oppression by changing the minds or "feelings" of white colonial oppressors.

This has included an ideological offensive against religious obscurantism and various expressions of mysticism and the notion that our liberation will result from speeches by some individual genius or the discovery of secret documents that, once received, would automatically confer freedom upon our people.

The theory of African Internationalism, necessary for the success of our Revolution, was developed to provide an ongoing guide for our struggle in the wake of the demonstrated inadequacies of organized, practiced, idealist and metaphysically-influenced Marxism that did not recognize the centrality of parasitism and the colonial question.

As the Advanced Detachment, only we have been able to spread our theory and grow our political influence through the publication of our 50-year-old political journal, *The Burning Spear* newspaper, read by thousands of Africans in colonies throughout the world and within the brutal colonial prison concentration camps.

Our internet radio station, Uhuru Radio and the two FM radio stations, Black Power 96.3 and 100.1, owned by constituent organizations of our Movement enhanced this work of anti-colonial socialist Party propaganda.

Solved the problem of African unification

Another problem that had gone unaddressed since the U.S. government's effective destruction of the Garvey Movement in the early part of the last century was the question of African unification and liberation.

Africans *can* be united globally once again under a single leadership with a single center. Like Garvey, we know that a liberated and united Africa can only occur under a single revolutionary organizational leadership.

We passed the resolution calling for the establishment of the African Socialist International (ASI) at our First Congress in 1981, but our work to build the unity of the international African Liberation Movement preceded this Congress by many years. We organized the first U.S.-based support committee for the Zimbabwe African National Union (ZANU) that at the time in the early 1970s was engaged in armed struggle against the white settler regime of Rhodesia.

We also led much of the work of the Pan Africanist Congress of Azania (PAC) during its early stages in the U.S., placing staff in its New York United Nations office and sponsoring and escorting PAC leaders to events in the U.S., many of which were organized by our Party.

We spoke at the United Nations and participated in several demonstrations there in support of the PAC. We reprinted many of their publications for their use in propaganda work.

Our efforts to win ZANU and PAC leadership to formal participation in the African Socialist International were unsuccessful. Our Party pursued the efforts up to the points when negotiated settlements resulted in transfer of direct political power from the white settler-colonialists to African neocolonial custody in the form of ZANU in Zimbabwe and to the African National Congress in Occupied Azania.

The transfer of direct political power to the African petty bourgeoisie revealed the ideological weaknesses of ZANU and PAC, leading them to abandon their efforts for revolutionary seizure of real African worker-peasant power, instead functioning within the neocolonial state structures previously utilized by the white settler-colonialists of Rhodesia and South Africa.

Party brought political and economic together as one

From its inception our Party united the struggle for political independence with concrete work to build African economic self-reliance through programs of dual and contending African working class power. We have always known that the political and economic are one.

Who created the decades-old economic institutions to teach African anti-colonial self-reliance? It was we who organized Ujamaa Restaurant in Florida in 1972 and African Connections bookstore in Louisville, Kentucky in 1979. We opened the first African-owned commercial newspaper, and later a bookstore and record shop in Gainesville, Florida, even as we built Spear Graphics and then Uhuru Bakery Cafe in Oakland in the 1980s.

Throughout the years we have never been without our own independent economic infrastructure, committed to ensuring that our Party would never be economically beholden to anyone or anything that would demand political adherence to another worldview.

Uhuru Foods & Pies was born in Oakland in 1980 and is still growing today. The dynamic Uhuru Furniture stores in

Philadelphia and Oakland continue to thrive after nearly 30 years of operation.

The Party established a nonprofit entity, the African People's Education and Defense Fund (APEDF) to host community programs in defense of the human and civil rights of the African community.

APEDF today encompasses Uhuru Furniture & Collectibles, the African Independence Workforce Program and other economic programs of the Party created over the past three or more decades.

We have built dynamic Uhuru Houses with their Akwaaba Halls in St. Petersburg, Florida; Oakland, California and now in St. Louis, Missouri.

We created Black Star Industries that includes Uhuru Foods & Pies, Planet Uhuru Apparel, One Africa! One Nation! Marketplaces, Burning Spear Publications and other institutions that comprise the foundation of a liberated African working class economy, an expression of dual and contending power.

In the early 2000s, the Party formed the All African People's Development and Empowerment Project (AAPDEP) to bring African skilled scientists, engineers and doctors into organization under the leadership of the African working class.

AAPDEP opened Zenzele Consignment in Huntsville, Alabama, a consignment shop that functions as an ongoing resource-generating institution for the organization.

Zenzele will function as the headquarters of AAPDEP where the community can shop and volunteer and where the organization's national and international projects can be showcased.

For the past eight years, Deputy Chair Ona Zené Yeshitela has headed up the Party's economic front catapulting our existing institutions into a new level of success with a growing list of economic entities.

The Black Power Blueprint is our latest economic front

Our Seventh Congress taking place in part at our latest Uhuru House in St. Louis, Missouri is simply a continuation of our history of leading by example, as the Advanced Detachment. We are practical revolutionaries. This is why we initiated the Black Power Blueprint, a major project that is helping to transform the entire African colony of St. Louis.

We have renovated the 9,000 square foot building that was a community eyesore just a few months ago on a major thoroughfare. It was a property, like so many in St. Louis, waiting to be added to the list of gentrified booty for the array of realtors and "investors" that perennially lurk in the shadows, working with financial institutions, government officials and neocolonial sycophants to undermine our communities to a status of inhabitability as a prelude for moving us out.

Instead, with the determined direct leadership of the Office of Deputy Chair Ona Zené Yeshitela, we are advancing dynamic economic initiatives. When we say that politics is concentrated economics and that the political and economic are one, we mean exactly what is being demonstrated in St. Louis.

The pending St. Louis Uhuru Bakery and Cafe is part of the Black Power Blueprint plan along with the intended workforce development program to train Africans who have been given felony convictions by the colonial state and prison system that are used to lock Africans out of employment possibilities.

The amazing array of economic institutions developed and/ or led by Deputy Chair Ona Zené Yeshitela are consistent with the Party's drive to pursue by example our ongoing, 600-year-old struggle against foreign and alien colonial domination of African people.

Party made reparations a mass demand

Another problem solved by our Party was to give reality to the demand for reparations that had been talked about within the national liberation movement for generations. It was we who took the reparations demand out of the straitjacket of purely legal and legislative approaches.

We are the organization that gave the reparations demand a mass and concrete character. We deepened the theoretical and political basis for the demand and began the practical process of acquiring reparations that made it a reality and not just wishful thinking.

When our Party began this work, the so-called reparations movement was only considering compensation for African colonial-slavery. It was we who recognized that the rate of exploitation of Africa and African people has grown greater since the formal end of our legal enslavement.

The existing reparations movement of today bears the imprint of the work of the Advanced Detachment of the African working class and forcibly dispersed nation. It bears the imprint of the African People's Socialist Party.

It was we who made the reparations demand a mass demand of our people. In 1982, we formed the African National Reparations Organization (ANRO). ANRO held reparations tribunals throughout the United States for 12 years.

In fact most of the noted reparations activists of today gained their reparations involvement through a direct or indirect relationship to the work of our Party.

Only the Advanced Detachment would be able to use the political device of international law and the Universal Declaration of Human Rights, giving the right of oppressed peoples to bring their case before the bourgeois world court. Only African Internationalism could inform us of the necessary conclusion that reparations are owed because of parasitic capitalism and our stolen labor, land and resources.

Our understanding that the reparations demand is a function of the Revolution allowed the Party to open a serious front among the colonizer population. Through the reparations demand, we are able to win thousands of "whites" to conscious participation in the assault on white nationalist colonialism. For some, their introduction to active political life was and is in the reparations work created and led by our Party.

Our Party solved the problem of white people

It is our Party that took the mystery out of the question of "white" people. We brought the definition of white people down to Earth, destroying the myths of biological and religious determinism. We advanced the often unpopular declaration that white people are people whose behavior can be explained by a scientific historical materialist analysis.

We resolved the outstanding question of white people in a practical way with the formation of the African People's Solidarity Committee (APSC) in 1976, the organization of whites working under our leadership with the strategic assignment of collecting reparations from North Americans to forward our struggle for African national liberation.

Party built revolutionary mass organizations

The African People's Socialist Party created mass organizations that made it unnecessary for us to abandon our revolutionary trajectory in order to win non-revolutionary masses to the revolutionary politics, programs and leadership of the Party.

Politically we initiated various campaigns and relationships to defeat the U.S. counterinsurgency and protect and advance the interests of the African working class that had suffered the brunt of the defeat of our revolutionary movement.

The African People's Socialist Party led major campaigns to recognize and free many of the political prisoners who fell during the counterinsurgency when imperialism was most determined to destroy any semblance of resistance.

Pitts and Lee, Al Courtney, Connie Tucker, Dessie Woods, Angela Davis, Huey P. Newton, Fleeta Drumgo, George Jackson, Sundiata Acoli, Assata Shakur, the San Quentin Six, Republic of New Afrika 11, Freddie Lee Roberts, Mafundi Lake and myself are some of the people we defended and sometimes freed when their arrests and imprisonment were being used to crush the Revolution and the spirit of the people.

At a time when there was no other organized African response, we formed the African National Prison Organization (ANPO) in 1979 which we created as millions of Africans were being caught up in the net of colonial mass incarceration.

In 1991 the International People's Democratic Uhuru Movement (InPDUM) was formed in Chicago to fight the counterinsurgency and defend the democratic rights of the African community. InPDUM waged countless campaigns to defend and free African political prisoners and prisoners of war, as well as thousands of victims of colonial police violence and murder.

We formed the African National Women's Organization (ANWO) in response to the oppression of African women and as a vehicle of the Party to bring masses of African women into political life, the Party and the Revolution.

An excerpt from the Political Report to the Fifth Congress stated quite simply:

> *...ANWO could become the powerful home to African women who are constantly under some form of assault by a myriad of contradictions*

> *peculiar to African women. ANWO would provide a mass organization for women who need to confront their oppression and exploitation. It would allow the Party to develop a reserve for the Revolution through helping women to recognize the universal contradictions confronting our people and class that are located in the specific contradictions they are confronting as women.*[3]

Party's legacy of internationalist solidarity

As the Vanguard Party, representing our class and nation, we have stood unconditionally with the struggles of colonized peoples around the world.

We have always demonstrated practical unity with the people of Occupied Palestine in their righteous struggle to liberate their land and people from the illegitimate white settler-colony of Israel that functions as a forward military base of U.S. imperialism.

Even before the success of Iranian national liberation from U.S. neocolonialism in 1979, our Party had occupied picket lines and hosted forums and events designed to expose and fight against the U.S.-backed regime of Shah Reza Pahlavi. We encountered violent mass white colonial opposition in the U.S. to our organized support of the Iranian people following the seizure of the U.S. embassy in Tehran by Iranian militants.

July 1979 was also the time of the defeat of the U.S.-supported Somoza regime in Nicaragua by the Sandinista National Liberation Front (FSLN). Without waiting for an invitation, the African People's Socialist Party organized many public political forums in the Northern California Bay Area in support of the Sandinista-led revolution. Even before the flight and temporary escape by Somoza from his bunker in

3 Yeshitela, Omali. *One People! One Party! One Destiny!*, pp. 117-118. Burning Spear Publications, 2010.

Nicaragua's capital, Managua, our Party functioned as part of the U.S. Front of the Sandinista Movement.

In the 1970s the African People's Socialist Party entered into a brief relationship with the Puerto Rican Socialist Party (PRSP). We participated with the PRSP in a thousands-strong mass anti-colonial mobilization in Philadelphia in 1976.

Shortly after the Party organized the first World Tribunal on Reparations for Black People in the U.S. in Brooklyn, New York, we were in Belfast, Ireland where we developed unity from the Irish Republican Socialist Party (IRSP) with our struggle for national liberation from U.S. colonialism.

The Irish Republican Socialist Party organized a joint press conference with our Party to publicly announce its support for our demand for reparations to African people. This allowed our Party to denounce British colonial occupation of Northern Ireland and express our support for Irish resistance and the revolutionary liberation of Northern Ireland.

In 1985 the Party entered into an enduring fraternal relationship, an alliance with Unión del Barrio, a most influential component of the Mexican national liberation movement.

Some of these relationships were formed during a time of extreme backward race nationalism within sectors of the African national liberation movement. It was a time when there was a common refrain that the international relations we were establishing were "white too." Some insisted that our Movement could not establish alliances and relations with others until "we get ourselves together," whatever that meant beyond a demand that the African working class remain isolated.

We are African Internationalists. We have always recognized the importance of uniting with *all* the peoples of the world in the fight to overturn the parasitic system of colonial capitalism that has the world in its death grip. We have always been committed to international solidarity. We refused to accept the isolation demanded by the African petty bourgeoisie. We have always taken the strategic approach that anti-colonial struggle anywhere in the world is part of our struggle to defeat U.S. imperialism and parasitic capitalism.

III. How the Party survived the counterinsurgency

Comrades! Since its inception in 1972, our Party has been the only force that through theory and practice exposed the historical basis both for the rise of the Black Power Movement of the 1960s and its demise.

We are the singular voice that waged tireless political struggle and fierce on-the-ground campaigns showing that the demise of our courageous movement of the 60s was brought about by a violent and devastating U.S. government counteroffensive, known in military terms as *counterinsurgency.*

The will to struggle and the heady confidence of the African working class feeling the power of its own leadership did not go out of style or lose favor among the masses, as fabricated in the U.S. government's narrative of our defeat.

By the mid- to late-'70s, almost all those so-called revolutionary African leaders and organizations inside the U.S. and around the world that had actually survived the U.S. government's murderous assault were now compliant with imperialism's myths about what happened to us and our historic liberation struggle.

Contrary to the ruling class lies, the African working class did not suddenly develop a preference for heroin and crack cocaine, poverty, homelessness, police murder and years in prison over self-determination and political power. We did not abandon our children or willingly turn them over to their kidnappers in the U.S. foster care and prison systems. We did not gladly give up our power and leadership to the African petty bourgeoisie, the neocolonial class.

As we have said many times, the African working class inside this country, which had been for centuries the revolutionary moral compass for oppressed peoples around the world, was now criminal, hated and detested in the U.S. government's carefully crafted counterinsurgent plan.

After more than a decade of concerted struggle, hard-fought-for rights were rapidly taken away and the conditions of the African working class were soon worse than they had been before we rose up.

Counterinsurgency is what the U.S. and imperialist powers of parasitic capitalism do to colonized peoples when we fight for our freedom and independence through revolution. The heroic peoples of Viet Nam, Chile and Nicaragua, and African people in Congo, Kenya and South Africa were among many others who bore the brunt of imperialist counterinsurgency.

A counterinsurgency is a war without terms. When white people fight each other, they have the Geneva Convention, defined as "rules that apply in times of armed conflict and seek to protect people who are not or are no longer taking part in hostilities; these include the sick and wounded of armed forces on the field, wounded, sick, and shipwrecked members of armed forces at sea, prisoners of war, and civilians."[1]

When they fight *us*, however, the Geneva Convention does not apply and they do anything they want, including to civilians, the wounded, the sick and prisoners of war.

Almost 30 years ago, we summed up in my 1991 book, *Black Power Since the '60s: The struggle against opportunism within the U.S. front of the Black Liberation Movement:*

> *While ever-present since our forced sojourn within this U.S. North American hell, this counterinsurgency has achieved a different character since its effective use during the Black Revolution of the Sixties to destroy our movement for happiness and repossession of our stolen resources.*

1 "Geneva Conventions," *Wikipedia.org.*

Essentially this counterinsurgency changed character from one which, while it attacked the whole African people, had its primary emphasis on the destruction of specific individuals and organizations, to one which has as its primary target the entire African people especially the revolutionary African working class.

There are various components to the counterinsurgency; it employs each branch of the government and a host of state-connected institutions as well as the bourgeois media and other instruments of mass culture controlled by the U.S. colonialist state and ruling class.

Of particular significance to this discussion is the use of drugs and neocolonialism as components of the counterinsurgency. The impact of drugs in the African community is well known if not even exaggerated.

For several years the white ruling class media have quite selectively overwhelmed our consciousness with images of drugged-out African mothers, African children who are born addicted, African illnesses and wretchedness which are due to drug use, and of course the violent African youths who are victims of and, responsible for the torrent of violence and homicide that characterizes so much of our existence.

Indeed, the media have consciously worked to criminalize the African community and people mostly through manipulation of the drug issue.

The selective usage of the media has defined the African in the popular consciousness (this includes too much of the African consciousness as well) as a criminal entity suffering from self-inflicted "ills that beset us," or as a community on the road to "self-destruction."

It is no longer the vicious colonial repression—as exemplified by the fact that more than a quarter of our male youth are tied to the prison system, or that the infant mortality rate within our colonized community is at least twice that for white people or the vicious police and white citizen violence constantly directed at African people—that defines our existence.

It is no longer the economic exploitation that denies us work within the legal capitalist economy while at the same time charging us more for shoddier goods from housing and transportation to food and healthcare, that defines our reality.

It is no longer the African oppressed by colonial white power who we are aware of, but the thankless, criminally-violent, drug-addicted African who has tried the patience of civilized white society for the last time.

And indeed drugs, violence and crime do haunt our community. But they do so as a part of a vicious U.S. government-imposed counterinsurgency that is designed to crush any attempts by our desperate people to realize national liberation.[2]

Revolution was the main trend in the world

Only our Party has provided a historic and class analysis of the development of the Black Revolution of the Sixties that must be understood by militants and activists attempting to interpret the state of our struggle today.

---

2 Yeshitela, Omali. *Black Power Since the '60s: The struggle against opportunism within the U.S. front of the Black Liberation Movement*, p. 2. Burning Spear Publications, 1991.

One critical point is the profound correlation between the historical events occurring in Africa and other places throughout the colonial world and the freedom movement of Africans inside the U.S.

As I wrote in 1997 in the pamphlet, "Why I became a revolutionary,"

> *I am fortunate to have been born in an era of great transformation in the world. It was a time when the basic social contradictions of this country became obvious for all to see, especially those contradictions which revolve around the 'race' question.*
>
> *The 1940s was also the era in which great movements against direct white rule, or colonialism, were occurring worldwide. In 1947 India achieved formal independence from England and the great Chinese revolution occurred in 1949. Other revolutionary anti-colonial movements were sweeping Africa, Asia and Latin America.*[3]

It was this period that most determined how we understand the nature and character of our struggle today.

The image and bold initiatives of Kwame Nkrumah, first president of independent Ghana and the implacable stance of Patrice Lumumba are etched in the consciousness of all who look back at that era of universal struggle of African people.

We were made confident of our road to liberation by the incorruptible visage of Malcolm X and the massive mobilizations for democratic rights organized by Dr. Martin Luther King Jr.

---

3 Yeshitela, Omali. "Social Justice and Economic Development for the African Community: Why I Became a Revolutionary," p. 2. Burning Spear Uhuru Publications, 1997.

The scenes of courageous young Africans from the Student Nonviolent Coordinating Committee, the Junta of Militant Organizations and the Black Panther Party, to name just a few examples of the high resistance of the time, leave many Africans at a loss. Why the current lack of direction for the mass movement today? Why the absence of universal opposition to our colonial domination as a people?

Only the African People's Socialist Party has answered these questions. The answers lay in the counterinsurgency.

Bourgeois thinkers in this country have come up with a shallow explanation for the rise of anti-colonial liberation struggles during or following both the First and Second Imperialist Wars to redivide the world. The massive phenomenon known as the Marcus Garvey Movement followed on the heels of the First Imperialist World War while the historic Civil Rights Movement rose up in the years following the Second Imperialist War.

They tell us that African soldiers and other colonial subjects who participated in those wars in defense of our colonial oppressors were inspired by our first glimpse of freedom when we visited other lands as soldiers for the empire.

There may be some truth to the fact that many of the colonized were able to leave our neighborhoods and villages and experience the larger world for the first time since white power took over our lives.

Nevertheless, an understanding of the explosive and generalized growth of the struggles for national liberation in the U.S. and around the world must be sought beyond the self-laudatory explanations of the international colonial bourgeoisie.

Historically, the colonial rulers have always employed their subjects to fight their predatory wars, whether between themselves or against other colonial subjects. The British used Africans from other African colonies in their attacks against the courageous Kenya Land and Freedom Army, or Mau Mau. The Mau Mau successfully stood up to the British empire for many years before the brutal, terroristic British counterinsurgency campaign was able to crush the heroic struggle in the 1960s.

The French deployed troops from their various colonies in their vain efforts to defeat the magnificent, life- and freedom-affirming Vietnamese Revolution liberating Viet Nam from French colonialism. Seventy-one percent of French troops fighting France's colonial war against the Vietnamese were actually subjects from Algeria, Senegal, Ivory Coast and other French colonies.

When the U.S. entered that war on the side of French imperialism in an attempt to maintain the colonial slavery of the Vietnamese people, it is said that 50 to 65 percent of the troops on the front lines were domestically colonized Africans, not to mention Mexicans, Filipinos and Puerto Ricans, other forces also colonized inside the U.S.

It is true that the participation of Africans and other colonial subjects in these imperialist wars did introduce thousands of us to contemporary military training and the invaluable experience of fighting under enemy fire without panic. This aided the anti-colonial armed struggles being waged in our own interests against our colonial oppressors.

Participation in the U.S. wars also served to destroy the colonial myth of the courage and indestructibility of the "white man" and even provided legal opportunities for actually killing him. White men could die at the hand of a lowly "nigger." They could scream in pain, just like an African being burned to death by a white lynch mob in the U.S. This was instructive.

The greatest value of the Second Imperialist World War for the struggle against colonialism, however, is the fact that the imperialist bandits who were in fierce struggle against each other to redivide the world (the "world" meaning us and our lands) were unable to give our oppression their usual ruthless attention. The war had left many of the colonial powers exhausted and preoccupied.

In some cases the imperialists actually required the colonized to take on some of the colonial responsibilities previously in the sole control of the colonizer. All of this provided us political space that we, the colonized everywhere, used to organize against our oppressors.

Inside the U.S. thousands of African people risked their lives and limbs fighting in the First Imperialist War for the interests and freedom of white people only to be targeted upon return to the U.S. with lynchings, Jim Crow, unspeakable violence and assault by those same white people after the war. African and colonized peoples worldwide faced a similar situation.

As the fever for independence swept the colonial world, hungry for our own freedom and independence following the war, more than 11 million African people here and around the world flocked to the African national liberation movement led by Marcus Garvey.

British colonial subjects inside England created real class struggle

With the end of the Second Imperialist War the world economy changed hands from the British, who, up to that time controlled 25 percent of the world's population and territory, to those of the U.S. The myth of British tea-sipping white civility as the imperialist-in-chief was destroyed by the German bombing of London and other cities in England and by rising struggles for national liberation inside British colonies.

Out of desperation following the war, the British made a call to their colonial subjects from throughout the world to "come home" to rebuild England, thereby growing a domestic or internal colony similar to that in the U.S.

Soon thousands of colonial workers were recruited to relocate to England to be exploited in the process of reconstructing the former colonial power that now lay in ruins. This influx of Africans and South Asians into the imperialist center initiated real class struggle that ruptured the facade of class peace. Previously, the unity of British workers with their ruling class had made it unnecessary to arm the English police.

The internal class struggle in England had been smothered by the abundance of colonial booty that filled markets, dinner tables, urban department stores and provided holidays and home ownership for workers and the bourgeoisie alike. Class struggle was also muted by the transfer of excess white population to the resource-generating far reaches of the empire—Southern Africa, Kenya, India, Australia, Canada.

Today, the British do not boast so loudly of a pacifist police department. Increasingly, the armed British police force inside England is no different from the arm of the state called the "army" when it is deployed in Kenya, Nigeria, Rhodesia (now Zimbabwe), South Africa, India and Ireland. The "United Kingdom" is a lot less united today as a consequence of the importation of labor and class struggle from the British colonies.

While many colonies were able to win nominal independence through people's struggle in the years following the Second Imperialist War, imperialist powers retained economic and political domination over African people. The imperialist strategy of neocolonialism, or white power in black face, carried out by the African and colonized petty bourgeoisie, proved to be an essential tool of counterinsurgency.

Class forces at work in the rise of the Civil Rights Movement

The U.S. did not suffer the consequences of war being fought within its domestic borders and became the center of the capitalist world economy. This is reflected in what is known as the Bretton Woods Conference—the 1944 United Nations Monetary and Financial Conference which established the World Bank and International Monetary Fund that relocated the center of the world capitalist financial system to the U.S.

The European imperialist powers were now forced to share with the U.S. their previously dominated markets and resources from their colonial bounty. Raw materials from the colonies that were opened up to U.S. exploitation began to generate a critical need for U.S. workers to transform them into finished products. Workers from Eastern Europe, having become a part of the Soviet Bloc after the war, were no longer available to the U.S. as in the past.

The bourgeois solution for the U.S. worker shortage was located in the southern states among the domestically colonized African working class. The problem was that the relations of production in the South required Africans to be tied to the intense, backbreaking toil associated with the labor-intensive capitalism in jobs such as sharecropping, mining and agricultural work.

The southern based, labor-intensive, colonial-capitalist system was opposed to any kind of change that might challenge its profit and domination and the existing relations of production that protected it. These relations of production were justified by the ideology of white nationalism, which had used terrorist violence for its perpetuation since the earliest days of our enslavement on southern plantations.

It was for these reasons that African laborers were denied the right to the minimum education that would be necessary for workers in the capital-intensive production in northern factories. This is why the liberal U.S. bourgeoisie supported the nonviolent effort to legalize education and basic civil rights for the oppressed African workers in the South.

The apartheid regime of South Africa was influenced by and built on the same relations of production that existed within the U.S. where Africans were totally disenfranchised and defined as subhuman. There was such a thing as "nigger work" that placed restrictions on where Africans could work and what we were permitted to do within those work spaces.

Separate toilets, drinking fountains and neighborhoods were also used to define Africans as less human than the North Americans or whites who set the standard for human identity. The colonial state which included the white population in the South also initiated deadly prohibitions on all social interactions, especially sexual, between the colonizer and colonized, essentially between African men and North American women.

These deadly prohibitions involved massive government-sanctioned lynchings, human burnings, torture, white mob attacks destroying whole African towns, rape and general degradation of African people for which, as of the 1950s, no white perpetrator was ever prosecuted.

A crude but generally accepted ideologically backward definition of African humanity was a logical expression of the economic base of a slavery-generated social system. It is a definition that prevails up to this day, not only for Africans within the U.S., but for Africans in general, all of whom were brought into a relationship with Europe through the global, colonial-slavery related economy.

Nor is this backward ideological assumption restricted to what are generally regarded as reactionary, Klan, Boers or fascist types of Europeans or whites. We are talking here about the ideological foundation of capitalism that permeates all of Europe, other capitalist-dominated societies and essentially the entire world. Happy Christian families, liberals and cookie-baking grandmothers all embraced this ideology and carried out this violence.

African workers attempting to leave the U.S. South for the capital-intensive production of the North often had to do so under extremely dangerous circumstances. In many instances, Africans risked their lives to acquire the education necessary for laborers in capital-intensive production.

These contradictions led to the alliance between members of the liberal sector of the colonial bourgeoisie, as represented by U.S. senator and vice president Hubert Horatio Humphrey and former U.S. presidents John Fitzgerald Kennedy and Lyndon Baines Johnson, and the liberal colonized African petty bourgeoisie. Both needed change and access to African workers, but for entirely different reasons. Both needed a "revolution from above" that would not overturn the entire colonial capitalist system.

The African working class, perennial victims of this terror and the arbitrary extra-legal and often very subjective, personalized violence, desperately needed relief from this situation. We wanted to be able to see a future where our children would not be locked into indeterminate, relentless brutality with poverty and backbreaking "nigger work."

The colonized, liberal African petty bourgeoisie also needed democratic changes for its own protection from this arbitrary extrajudicial treatment. Even petty bourgeois, educated and otherwise assimilated Africans were subjected to the vicious whims of uncultured, uneducated, reactionary whites who functioned as extensions of the white colonial state in their treatment of Africans.

Additionally, the selfish interests of the African petty bourgeoisie required mass access to the electoral process as a means of acquiring an ability to integrate into the capitalist economic system, which is the definition of "equality" for the African petty bourgeoisie.

They needed the African masses to have the ability to vote so they, the African petty bourgeoisie, could be elected to office and positions of power to integrate into the capitalist system as co-predators. These petty bourgeois forces became the burgeoning neocolonialists. Many had no neocolonialist aspirations; often they merely wanted to be part of the existing setup. Some, suffering severe self-alienation, just wanted to be with white people.

The "revolution from above" that we have come to know as the Civil Rights Movement was funded by the liberal white colonial rulers. This explains why the movement had to be based on philosophical nonviolence. The white rulers were not about to fund a movement that would engage in armed resistance to white terror that might destroy our colonial domination.

As we analyzed in the book *Izwe Lethu i Afrika,* the Political Report to our Third Congress back in 1990:

> *The alliance between the liberal oppressor and the liberal oppressed was an alliance which required a limited or partial "revolution". This partial revolution would result in the oppressed African working masses being able to sell their exploited labor to the liberal bourgeoisie and would give access to electorally gained white power to the African primitive petty bourgeoisie.*
>
> *Along with the natural aspirations of the oppressed domestically colonized African people for national liberation, this was the real political and economic basis for the Civil Rights Movement that mobilized and gave consciousness to millions of African people throughout the U.S. and the world.*

This was the real political and economic basis for the heroic resistance of the wretched toiling African masses of the South.

Both the white liberal oppressors and the oppressed liberal African petty bourgeoisie were determined to obscure the actual material basis of the struggle known as the Civil Rights Movement and the real stakes that were involved. Both were determined to keep the masses of African people convinced that we were struggling to change the feelings of white people toward Africans or that we were fighting for the right to live with the white oppressor-nation U.S. North American population.

Thus a purely idealistic ideological cover was given to our struggle by the liberal African primitive petty bourgeoisie. We were not told that we must be committed to philosophical nonviolence because we were involved in a limited revolution designed to serve the interests of the liberal sector of our colonial oppressors who would never support a genuine revolution of our oppressed people. Instead we were told that such a philosophical commitment to nonviolence was morally cleansing and empowering.

However, there was always an undercurrent of resistance to the philosophical idealism, tactics, strategies and political objectives of the liberal African primitive petty bourgeoisie from the broad perimeter of the Black Liberation Movement. Much of this resistance came from the masses of oppressed African working people who sometimes participated in the movement despite these differences....[4]

---

4 Yeshitela, Omali. *Izwe Lethu i Afrika (Africa is Our Land): Political Report to the 3rd Party Congress of the African People's Socialist Party*, pp. 5-6. Burning Spear Publications, 1991.

The problem for the white rulers and their compliant African minions was the fact that the fodder for this movement, the impoverished and brutalized Africans of the southern U.S., would discover our own interests in the struggle for the democracy being sought by the liberals, colonizer and colonized alike. In the struggle to change the world these African toilers would ourselves be changed.

We summed up in the article, "Advanced Detachment," written for *The Burning Spear* in 1985 and which appears in the book, *Omali Yeshitela Speaks:*

> *During the 1950s the alliance between our movement and the liberal bourgeoisie consolidated itself in mass struggle. In the process our movement began to achieve a revolutionary character. This movement activated the African victims of U.S. colonialism as conscious participants, and impacted on the consciousness and practical life of all the people inside the U.S. This powerful movement overthrew the immediate form of capitalist rule of the Southern white ruling class and achieved legal democratic rights for African people.*[5]

The rise of the conscious African working class

The need for change was aptly summed up by the Student Nonviolent Coordinating Committee in its slogan-demand for black power, coming in 1966 *after* the petty bourgeois-led Civil Rights Movement had realized its aims with the enactment of the Civil Rights Bill in 1964 and the Voting Rights Act of 1965.

The outcome of the alliance "was something that neither the liberal bourgeoisie nor the black petty bourgeoisie could predict, namely the emergence of an African proletariat rising

5 Yeshitela, Omali. "Advanced Detachment," *Omali Yeshitela Speaks*, p. 287. Burning Spear Uhuru Publications, 2005.

up from the bowels of America itself,"[6] as we observed in "Advanced Detachment."

While the selfish interests of the African working class proved to be in contradiction with the aims of colonial white power, they were in contradiction with the interests and aims of the black petty bourgeoisie as well. We noted again in "Advanced Detachment":

> *An inconsistent though generally materialist philosophy of "black nationalism" began to emerge out of the aims of the African working class. Black nationalism began to reject the idealist and obscurantist philosophy of the liberal black petty bourgeoisie. Martin Luther King's "dream" of a better day in America as a consequence of the moral regeneration of whites of the oppressor nation was challenged by the "nightmare" as defined by Malcolm X. The African proletariat, facing objective reality in America raised the demand for Black Power to determine our own black reality.*[7]

Indeed, the black power slogan-demand captured the reality for the entire African nation within the U.S. and the world. Inside the U.S. during this period every African community was literally on fire with rebellion and anti-colonial resistance. It was an anti-colonial demand that challenged the limitations of the call for equality and rights within the colonial relationship.

The Black Power demand gave a taste of political power to the masses of African people everywhere.

As we continued in "Advanced Detachment,"

6 Ibid., p. 288.

7 Ibid.

> *For the new generation of fully mobilized African workers that was thrust onto the scene as the main social factor in U.S. political life, its aspirations were far from being met by gaining legal democratic rights. The attempts by the petty bourgeoisie to moderate the Black Liberation Movement, to decelerate it and direct it towards liberal bourgeois democratic sops, were met with cries of "burn baby burn," in Los Angeles and "Black Power" in Mississippi.*
>
> *At this point the independent aspirations of the African working class became clear. This new clarity fueled efforts to build independent political parties by and for the colonially oppressed African population....*[8]

We explained further in the 1998 presentation that we call "The Wolf and the Double-Edged Blade," published in Omali Yeshitela Speaks:

> *Our movement emerged as an anti-colonial movement at the moment the issue became one of power. When African workers said "Black Power," they united with struggles like the ones being led by Che Guevara throughout Latin America and Africa.*
>
> *By 1967 we saw the rise of the Black Panther Party, which took the struggle even further. The Black Panther Party was immediately and explicitly informed and influenced by Malcolm X, who told us that since it's legal to have a shotgun, every African should have one in his or her house....*
>
> *With the emergence of the Black Panther Party we saw tremendous anxiety in this country. So much so that J. Edgar Hoover, who was then the*

8 Ibid., p. 291.

executive director of the FBI, which is one of the secret political police agencies in this country, characterized the Black Panther Party as the "greatest threat to the internal security of the United States since the Civil War."

Not Gaddafi, not Saddam Hussein, not the Russians but ordinary African working class folk, most of whom lived in housing projects and had to use public transportation to get from one part of the city to the other. That's a statement about where power can be found: in the masses of African workers and poor people, who, given organization and ideological clarity, can achieve anything. That's the thing that Hoover and the FBI recognized. Unfortunately not too many of our leaders today recognize that....

We know that the Black Revolution, once unleashed, gave rise to virtually every other progressive entity that sprung up in this country. It was the Black Revolution that took white women out of the kitchen and homosexuals out of the closet. It was the Black Revolution that energized the movements of other oppressed peoples, including Indigenous people in this country. It was a powerful and profound movement that shook this country to its very foundation....

This is why the government put in place a program to cut down and undermine the Black Revolution and assassinate our leaders. They created what we refer to as "counterinsurgency."

Counterinsurgency uses every form of attack: psychological warfare, actual armed struggle, economic warfare....

> *The name of the government's counterinsurgency against the Black Revolution was COINTELPRO, short for Counterintelligence Program. COINTELPRO was the program used to assassinate and imprison our leaders and destroy our organizations....*[9]

Imperialist violence sets back our anti-colonial struggle

The COINTELPRO objectives spelled out in this August 25, 1967 memorandum sent by the FBI to field offices throughout the U.S. is telling in its slander, lies and efforts to criminalize and set the Black Revolution up for violence and assault:

> *The purpose of this new counterintelligence endeavor is to expose, disrupt, misdirect, discredit, or otherwise neutralize the activities of black nationalist hate-type organizations and groupings, their leadership, spokesmen, membership, and supporters, and to counter their propensity for violence and civil disorder.*
>
> *The activities of all such groups of intelligence interest to the Bureau must be followed on a continuous basis so we will be in a position to promptly take advantage of all opportunities for counterintelligence and inspire action in instances where circumstances warrant. The pernicious background of such groups, their duplicity and devious maneuvers must be exposed to public scrutiny where such publicity will have a neutralizing effect. Efforts of the various groups to*

9 Yeshitela, "The Wolf and the Double-Edged Blade," *Omali Yeshitela Speaks*, pp. 93-94.

> *consolidate their forces or to recruit new or youthful adherents must be frustrated.*
>
> *No opportunity should be missed to exploit through counterintelligence techniques the organizational and personal conflicts of the leaderships of the groups and where possible an effort should be made to capitalize upon existing conflicts between competing Black Nationalist organizations.*
>
> *When an opportunity is apparent to disrupt or neutralize black nationalist, hate-type organizations through the cooperation of established local news media contacts or through such contact with sources available to the Seat of Government [Hoover's office], in every instance careful attention must be given to the proposal to insure the targeted group is disrupted, ridiculed or discredited through the publicity and not merely publicized.*[10]

The political structures within which the U.S. domestic anti-colonial struggle was being waged came under siege. In the mid-60s, the Student Nonviolent Coordinating Committee (SNCC) briefly became the center of anti-colonial resistance within the U.S. In the meantime, with the rise of African national consciousness of the African working-class-led movement, other anti-colonial organizations began an outright challenge to confining the African struggle to Civil Rights or rights within the colonial-capitalist system.

Among these were the Junta of Militant Organizations (JOMO) and the Black Panther Party. The African People's Party (APP) and the Provisional Government of the Republic of New Afrika (RNA) were others. These organizations and

10 Churchill, Ward, and Jim Vander Wall. *The COINTELPRO Papers: Documents from the FBI's Secret Wars Against Domestic Dissent*, pp. 92-93. South End Press, 1990.

the Revolutionary Action Movement (RAM) were influenced ideologically by Malcolm X, who had left the original Nation of Islam (NOI) in a split that divided that group between religious obscurantists, philosophical idealists and the growing materialist-influenced, revolutionary ideology and practice being promoted by Malcolm X.

The masses of African people were part of the wave of anti-colonial struggle sweeping the planet. The chains of colonial domination were being shattered everywhere. Kenya! Korea! Ghana! Congo! Viet Nam! Cuba! Grenada! Algeria! Oakland, California and St. Petersburg, Florida!

The colonial-capitalist ruling class had been defeated politically and ideologically within the U.S. and throughout the world. Part of that defeat was to be seen in the creation of independent political organizations—the Pan Africanist Congress of Azania is an example. But there was also the Kenya Land and Freedom Army (Mau Mau), Zimbabwe African National Union, Black Panther Party, Student Nonviolent Coordinating Committee, New Jewel Movement of Grenada, JOMO and African People's Socialist Party.

Many others developed in Africa and worldwide. Their main significance lay in the fact that they represented the intention of the colonized to seek solutions for ourselves outside the structures and political and ideological framework of the colonizers. They had won the support and participation of the broad masses of the hundreds of millions of colonized Africans and others determined to end our relationship with foreign colonial domination.

Comrades! While many of our people have been convinced that our colonial oppression is due to "racist" whites or the colonizer simply not "liking" us, the fact is that the entire success of the colonizers—all the wealth, happiness and democratic rights enjoyed by them—require our colonization. In other words, there has always been a material basis for our oppression to which the colonial hatred and brutality owe their existence.

The colonial-capitalist loss of political and ideological authority over our colonized communities—the U.S. government's political and ideological defeat—left the colonizer with only one logical response: military attack. Extreme violence! This was true all over the world, but this was especially true within the U.S. Here our Movement inside the imperialist center, the headquarters of human oppression and exploitation, inspired the fighting peoples of the world and presented white power with an existential crisis.

Because the U.S. Front of the Black Revolution of the Sixties threatened the very foundation of world capitalism, the U.S. initiated this counterinsurgency, with no recognition of our political prisoners, no protocols for the treatment of our prisoners of war or features of what the colonizer recognized as "civilized" conduct, much less the admission that the assault on our Revolution was indeed a war.

Attacks on JOMO's efforts to build a statewide party

Our success in building the Party and the fact that our Movement survived the counterinsurgency that defeated the Black Revolution of the Sixties should not be interpreted to mean that we were untouched by the U.S. counterinsurgency.

In *Izwe Lethu i Afrika!*, the Political Report to our Third Congress, we summed up:

> *It was the resilience of JOMO and the Party that denied the counterinsurgency its ultimate victory. For although the Black Liberation Movement was destroyed as a movement, the birth of the Party in 1972 as a part of the revolutionary continuum was the birth of a political force that was clear on*

its mission to complete the Black Revolution of the Sixties.

Our Party was founded in May of 1972 by the merger of three previously separate groups. The primary organization of the three was JOMO, the Junta of Militant Organizations, based in St. Petersburg, Florida and Lexington and Louisville, Kentucky. The others were the Black Rights Fighters in Ft Myers and the Black Study Group of Gainesville, Florida.

JOMO was the dominant organization by virtue of its political experience, its longer history and its urban working class base and character. The Black Rights Fighters was essentially an organization of migrant farm workers and organizers, and the Gainesville Black Study Group was an organization of community-based students and intellectuals.

Both the climate of political terror directed at the Revolution and our own inexperience prevented the use of a founding Congress or some other publicized mass meeting to bring the Party into existence.

Earlier JOMO efforts to build a revolutionary party in 1969-70 had been successfully blocked by the U.S. counterinsurgency. Even as the brutal U.S. colonial war was being directed at our movement, JOMO had organized regular monthly meetings of progressive African organizations throughout the state of Florida. It was precisely because JOMO was able to recognize the need to defend our Revolution that it saw the monthly meetings as leading to the creation of a statewide party.[11]

---

11 Yeshitela, *Izwe Lethu i Afrika*, p. 31.

The June 15-29, 1970 issue of *The Burning Spear*, JOMO's political organ at the time, reported on that month's meeting:

> *...Several Black organizations ended their fourth statewide Black Caucus since March on June 6. As a result of the fourth caucus several things happened.*
>
> *It was decided that JOMO and* The Burning Spear *are the official information and communication apparatus for the state movement.*
>
> *The need and name for a Black political party in the state was established. Details are to be worked out at the next caucus, scheduled for Miami. The name of the party is the African Nationalist Progressive Party.*[12]

The following long selection from *Izwe Lethu i Afrika* is important for what it reveals about the serious, anti-democratic and terroristic measures used by the U.S. bourgeois colonial state to crush our Movement and attempt to derail our efforts to build a statewide party. We recounted:

> *However, at the July Miami meeting, one of the meeting participants whom JOMO came to suspect as a government agent provocateur, successfully fought from an anti-Party, ultra-leftist position to block the group from consolidating JOMO's party-building effort.*
>
> *Then at the following meeting held in Daytona Beach, the provocateur, in violation of the June decision determining* The Burning Spear *as the group's organ, brought an African news reporter from the colonial white ruling class Miami Herald to the meeting. The consequence of this was an*

12 *The Burning Spear*, June 15-29, 1970.

article in white ruling class publications throughout Florida on the morning following the meeting which told of sinister efforts by members of the Black Liberation Army who were holding secretive meetings, planning to "kill whitey."

The fact that the provocateur admitted authoring the article because he "felt we need the publicity," and that the group refused to expel him for this blatant and dangerous provocation meant that the government was successful in having the statewide meetings die on the vine. Later a listing for the nonexistent African Nationalist Progressive Party in the Miami telephone directory gave the address and phone number of the provocateur.

Such was the repressive political atmosphere during the period.

In fact, on January 10, 1973, within eight months of the Party's founding, Lawrence Mann, a member of the Central Committee, Party co-founder and leader of the Black Rights Fighters, was assassinated by automobile wreck. This act disrupted the effectiveness of our efforts to consolidate other members of the Black Rights Fighters into the Party.

Then, in May of 1973 the government arrested and re-imprisoned me at Florida State Prison on the old mural charge[13] *that I was initially arrested*

13 In December 1966, in one of the first black power actions of the 1960s, Chairman Omali Yeshitela, then known as Joseph Waller and local leader of the Student Nonviolent Coordinating Committee, courageously tore down a hideous, anti-African mural that had hung in the St. Petersburg, Florida city hall for 30 years. Chairman Omali was given a felony conviction in a political trial, serving two and a half years of a five-year prison sentence for "destruction of public property" and "grand larceny." On May 2, 1967, barely four months after the mural was torn down, the Black Panther Party initiated its renowned protest by carrying guns at the California State Capitol building in Sacramento.

and imprisoned for as a SNCC member in December 1966. However, our young Party was able to mount a fierce resistance to my re-imprisonment and force the government to release me within two months....

But the government was not finished. After having attacked our newly-founded party at two of its three legs—Fort Myers with the murder of Lawrence Mann and St. Petersburg with my arrest and re-imprisonment—the colonial bourgeoisie attacked the Party in Gainesville in June 1973.

This attack came in the form of a concerted effort to chase Katura Carey, a Central Committee member and Party co-founder, out of the city. Born and reared in Virginia, Carey was fired from her job as a school teacher, having been isolated by outright FBI slander which accused Carey of keeping a cache of weapons. The FBI also established a campaign of terrorizing Carey's neighbors in the rural community where she lived.

This effort was led by the FBI and a North American [white] former principal at a predominantly African high school, who had become a city commissioner. This city commissioner, who had functioned in the military as a counterinsurgency expert and had written manuals on counterinsurgency which were in the local public libraries, used counterinsurgency expertise and connections and his position as city commissioner to launch his attack on Carey....

The consolidation of the Party through a merger based primarily on quiet meetings between the leaders and members of the three merging groups instead of through a publicly announced Congress was mostly determined by the terroristic colonialist counterinsurgency. And even when the merger occurred without a Congress, the white ruling class colonialist state wasted no time in attempting to destroy us. But we survived and in many ways we thrived, although not without contradictions.

The threat by then-U.S. Attorney General John Mitchell to destroy the Black Panther Party before the end of 1969 had been realized for all practical purposes. Indeed, it is important to remember that the Black Panther Party was the main target and bore the brunt of the colonialist counterinsurgency, the primary factor of the Panther's demise.

This was the period of the government assassinations of several Black Liberation Army fugitives, the near-assassination and arrests of Assata Shakur and Sundiata Acoli as well as other anti-colonial African patriots of the Black Liberation Army such as Herman Bell, Albert "Nuh" Washington and others.

The U.S. government aimed to systematically decapitate the revolutionary sector of our movement. George and Jonathan Jackson were executed by government agents, 43 rebelling prisoners and their captive guards were massacred in Attica prison, and more than 40 African prisoners were wounded by government troops at Florida State Prison, acts which had successfully followed the incarcerated Revolution into the prison and set upon it with genocidal efficiency.

Although it was also a target of the vicious counterinsurgency of the sixties—suffering government infiltration, agent provocateurs, helicopter and armored vehicle attacks on our community base, massive arrests, beatings and assassination attempts directed at me as its leader—JOMO was able to survive and lead the work to build the African People's Socialist Party in 1972.[14]

U.S. government counterinsurgency imposed deadly drugs on us

Ultimately, the colonial rulers imposed an illegal capitalist drug economy on the colony after denying African participation within the legal capitalist economy.

After the rebellions of the '60s swept U.S. cities, urban African communities throughout this country were consciously and strategically decimated by the colonial-capitalists through "urban removal" programs, that tore down long standing African economic, cultural and residential centers, efforts that often included building freeways and sports arenas through African neighborhoods.

The urban removal programs of the sixties paved the way for the now pervasive gentrification seen in most cities today. A goal of gentrification is to disperse concentrations of African people in urban areas, a goal consistent with the counterinsurgency.

In the 1960s the U.S. government that was carrying out vicious colonial occupation and war against the people of Viet Nam began flying opium from Southeast Asia in CIA planes to the U.S., simultaneously creating counterinsurgency programs against two critical anti-colonial fronts: Viet Nam and the U.S. internal or domestic African colony.[15]

This is why as soon as pro-democracy and anti-colonial African leaders such as Martin Luther King, Malcolm X and Fred Hampton were assassinated by COINTELPRO an epidemic of heroin hit our communities hard.

14 Yeshitela, *Izwe Lethu i Afrika,* pp. 32-35.

15 See: McCoy, Alfred W. *The Politics of Heroin: CIA Complicity in the Global Drug Trade.* Lawrence Hill Books, 1972.

By the early 1980s, following the victory of the Vietnamese Revolution over the U.S. imperialist military, the U.S. was again waging counterinsurgency, this time against the liberation movements in Nicaragua and Central America. Meanwhile it expanded its counterinsurgency against our domestic African colony far beyond the COINTEL Program with the mission to salt the earth of the entire African domestic colony in an attempt to make sure that it would never rise up again.

Our Party was the only force that correctly exposed the fact that the epidemic of the deadly, addictive, laboratory-created cocaine derivative called "crack" that profoundly ravaged our communities for two decades was a continuation of colonial war against us.

After the victory of the Sandinista Revolution in Nicaragua in 1979, the U.S. military sent massive amounts of munitions and training to undermine it and the Salvadoran Revolution. The training and arming of these proxy forces called the Contras was being funded by profits from crack sales in African communities by the Central Intelligence Agency and other arms of the U.S. imperialist state.

Indeed our Party educated Gary Webb, a reporter at the *San Jose Mercury News,* who used his position to expose that the U.S. government was responsible for crack cocaine in our communities. San Jose is part of the greater Bay Area of Northern California where for years from our base at the Uhuru House in Oakland we led marches and campaigns exposing that "The White House is the rock house and Uncle Sam is the pusherman."

In 1994 I was invited by African students to speak at San Jose State University where I responded to some doubting students:

> *Are you saying you don't believe that the U.S. government would actually put drugs in the*

> *black community? I will tell you this: This is the government that did slavery. If it did slavery it will do anything! They [the Contras] would be at Hull's*[16] *ranch to receive weapons coming on airplanes. The same airplanes would be loaded up with cocaine and brought back to this country, sometimes to Homestead Air Force Base in the state of Florida.*
>
> *This is in congressional records. The Tower Commission talked about this. They don't say what happened to the cocaine after that but they didn't keep it at Homestead Air Force Base. I want to tell you it's in San Jose; Oakland, California; Tampa, Florida and the rest of it!*[17]

In 1996 Webb published a lengthy, well-documented article in the *Mercury News* that later became the book, *Dark Alliance: The CIA, The Contras and the Crack Cocaine Explosion*, which exposes the fact that the U.S. government did indeed impose crack cocaine into African communities and funneled millions of dollars of drug profits to the CIA-backed Contras.

In his Author's Note, Webb states: "*Dark Alliance* does not propound a conspiracy theory; there is nothing theoretical about history. In this case, it is undeniable that a wildly successful conspiracy to import cocaine existed for many years, and that innumerable American citizens [sic]—most of them poor and black—paid an enormous price as a result."[18]

The cocaine economy functioned as poisoned meat thrown to a starving population. As in any colonial situation, the

16 John Hull, whose Costa Rica ranch was used by the CIA for drug and arms smuggling.

17 As recorded in the video, "Who Gave the 'Messenger' the Message?" *Race for the Times*, raceforthetimes.com/who-gave-messenger-message.

18 Webb, Gary. *Dark Alliance: The CIA, the Contras, and the Crack Cocaine Explosion.* p. XIII. Seven Stories Press, 1998.

economic activity is closely controlled and monitored by the colonizer. It is the colonizer that determines whether there will be colonial economic activity and what it will look like. Clearly the drugs imposed on the domestic colony, with an estimated annual value today at a half a trillion dollars, were there because the colonial state wanted them there. The absence of any legal economic life prevailed because the colonial rulers wanted it that way.

The drug economy served to demoralize and criminalize our community and provided a scapegoat for the neocolonial African petty bourgeoisie to avoid charging the colonial rulers for the conditions we face. This also allowed the petty bourgeoisie to distinguish themselves as the "good" negroes, who like the white colonial society, were being undermined and brought down by the African working class, the primary target of the drug offensive.

In the wake of the government-imposed drug economy, the U.S. began passing laws that enabled the colonial state to round up millions of African workers who had recently been organized to revolution and put them in prison, eventually building the largest prison population in the entire world.

Massive prison building projects were established all over the U.S. as white communities vied and fought for prisons to be able to provide colonizer nation white workers well-paying jobs at the expense of tens of millions of colonized African people stuffed into these concentration camps as their families and communities profoundly destabilized. Atrocities were and are carried out in the prisons, which created an economic boon to the white population.

African communities were under siege, facing literal martial law with set curfews amidst helicopters flying overhead as scores of repressive U.S. government organizations, deadly SWAT teams and police programs were set up in our oppressed and impoverished neighborhoods. Police programs such as

"Weed and Seed," "Hope VI" and vigilante neighborhood watch groups, among countless others, were established in African working class communities all over the U.S.

African children were farmed out to white women who earned small fortunes as foster mothers who tortured and in some cases mutilated our children in violation of the Convention on the Prevention and Punishment of the Crime of Genocide.

One such case around which the Party waged a powerful campaign was that of Yvonne Eldridge, a white woman from Walnut Creek, CA, a suburb of Oakland. Eldridge made over $10,000 a month housing scores of African children from the foster care system whose parents were victims of the U.S. government's imposition of crack cocaine in the African community.

Eldridge consciously made the children ill, killing at least three African babies and submitting at least eight others to abuse, including cutting intravenous cords and reporting nonexistent symptoms to doctors who collaborated by performing surgery to remove the infants' organs.[19]

Struggle led by the Party forced the state to finally indict and bring Eldridge to trial.

It took terror and opportunism to return to class peace

Political debate within our oppressed communities was neutralized by assassination and other forms of counterinsurgency, including the inundation of drugs in the African community.

Quoting from "Advanced Detachment" again:

> *It took an all out urban war against the black working class in the sixties for a return to imperialist class peace and the reinstatement of the façade of*

19 "Woman honored as foster mother guilty of abuse," *Los Angeles Times*, June 6, 1996.

> *the two-party system supposedly representing the class interests of all people.*
>
> *This war saw African workers stand up alone not only against armed police organizations, but even armed military forces usually reserved for foreign U.S. intervention. In Detroit this included the 82nd Airborne Division. In urban areas throughout the U.S. military tanks and an assortment of other sophisticated armaments were deployed against the unarmed black working class communities....*
>
> *The U.S. ruling class used its military power, its state power, to defeat the independent, revolutionary capacity of the African working class, the only internal social force that made it necessary to defend the capitalist social system. The African working class was the only social force inside the U.S. that was capable of challenging the bourgeoisie for power, the fundamental question in any revolution.*
>
> *For all these years subsequent to the military defeat of the Black Revolution of the Sixties the bourgeoisie has expended a tremendous amount of energy and resources in keeping the African working class politically disoriented, disorganized and unable to come together organizationally in its own class interests.*[20]

The whole of the North American colonial community of intellectuals hungrily jumped on the anti-African bandwagon. A concerted effort to use the consequence of the drug economy to prove the pathology of the African community became a goal of colonial academia.

---

20 Yeshitela, "Advanced Detachment," *Omali Yeshitela Speaks*, pp. 296-297.

Hillary Clinton made her infamous statement calling African children "superpredators" in 1996, following on the heels of her husband's 1994 counterinsurgent Crime Bill which implemented the "three strikes, you're out" clause targeting African people and installed 100,000 new cops on the streets of African communities all over the U.S.

Petty bourgeois, pro-independence black nationalists from a variety of organizations joined in on this attack on the African working class, in some instances actually supporting the colonial occupying military forces in their attacks on the colonized population in the name of "taking back" our communities.

At least one organization, the Provisional Government of the Republic of New Afrika (RNA), made participation in the U.S.-led "war against drugs" a part of its strategy to weasel "reparations" from the white rulers, "because we can use the money" to give RNA's drug-fighting "efforts a boost." [21] Like other apologists for the colonial terror being inflicted on our community, these black nationalist would-be leaders defined the U.S.-imposed drug economy and its aftermath as "self-inflicted."

Our Party took on a deep—and we should add futile—struggle with the RNA and other so-called pro-independence organizations for more than five years! We struggled that the African Revolution cannot move forward without defeating the counterinsurgency—the most important question of that period—and that we must defend the besieged African working class.

Our book, *Black Power Since the '60s,* which is a chronicle of those struggles, notes:

21 Yeshitela, *Black Power Since the '60s*, p. 45.

We initiated this discussion, this struggle against opportunism as part of a process to solve the outstanding problems of the Revolution....

The vicious counterinsurgent colonial war that defeated the Black Revolution of the Sixties continues to immobilize our revolutionary process today. We must overturn the counterinsurgency as a condition for moving our Revolution forward.

Hence our current fixation on the counterinsurgency. For while there are a handful of anti-colonial African organizations, some of which might actually do political work, it will take revolutionary work to liberate us. It is simple as that. And revolutionary work is that work which correctly sums up and acts upon the period in which we exist and struggle. But for this to happen effectively and consistently, such work must be informed by advanced, revolutionary theory.

For years now the African People's Socialist Party has been attempting to win the U.S.-based African anti-colonial movement to the significance of the U.S. counterinsurgency. We have held tribunals, forums, symposiums and mass mobilizations to expose the counterinsurgency....

The articles from The Burning Spear *which make up this book expose the actual participation of two groups, the Provisional Government of the Republic of New Afrika and the Nation of Islam, in so-called anti-drug counterinsurgent activity. But others have also participated in one way or another as well.*

The Nation of Islam, under the leadership of Minister Louis Farrakhan, initiated a campaign of so-called Dope Busters which achieved notoriety with a televised beating of a so-called drug pusher in Atlanta, Georgia. The New Afrikan People's Organization initiated some sort of "Take Back the Streets" campaign, based on the assumption that violent African youth gangs or drug pushers control the streets of our colonized communities and not the militarized colonial police who are the first line of counter-revolutionary resistance to our struggle against colonialism.

We of the African People's Socialist Party have argued that while we must struggle to achieve control of our communities as a part of the struggle against domestic colonialism, the activities of these groups bow to the definition of the primary contradiction in our community as defined by the colonial white ruling class—especially since none of them is involved in campaigns to "bust" the slumlords or the cheating avaricious merchants or violent white vigilantes. None of them has campaigns to take back the streets from ski mask wearing police thugs who violate our communities daily.

This coincidence of interest with the campaigns and definitions of the white ruling class and media validates the counterinsurgent activities of the colonial ruling class and state. It validates the counterinsurgency itself, notwithstanding the hollow protestations of the groups to the contrary.

The approach of our Party has been to identify the counterinsurgency and all its obvious components as the primary contradiction and to attempt to win all in our oppressed colonial community who can be won to struggle against the counterinsurgency, including the government importation of drugs into

> *our community and the vicious war against our people in the name of a war against drugs.*
>
> *This approach makes the government the enemy and calls on everyone, including the penny-ante drug dealers to unite against the government in every way, including a cessation of distribution and usage of drugs. The other approach makes the African youths the enemy and unites with a government campaign against them.*[22]

As our Party has summed up, the African working class was demoralized and under intense ideological and political assault, exacerbated by our apparent "voluntary" participation in the illegal drug economy that had been organized by the U.S. government and made possible in part by the counterinsurgency war that had effectively neutralized the most influential, organized components of the anti-colonial struggle.

It was this "voluntary" aspect of the drug war that made the counterinsurgency so effective. It gave the appearance of the victim being the perpetrator—even to the victim. Nevertheless there was a common refrain within the African colony that recognized, "we don't have the planes and ships to bring the drugs into our community." This popular statement echoed countless speeches, *Spear* articles by myself and demonstrations held by Party-led organizations over many years.

Neocolonialism key to the success of the counterinsurgency

Kwame Nkrumah, the first president of independent Ghana introduced the term neocolonialism to the world. In

22 Ibid., pp. 5-7.

his 1965 book, *Neocolonialism, The Last Stage of Imperialism,* Nkrumah wrote:

> *Neo-colonialism is also the worst form of imperialism. For those who practise it, it means power without responsibility and for those who suffer from it, it means exploitation without redress. In the days of old-fashioned colonialism, the imperial power had at least to explain and justify at home the actions it was taking abroad. In the colony those who served the ruling imperial power could at least look to its protection against any violent move by their opponents. With neo-colonialism neither is the case.*[23]

While we don't necessarily disagree with this statement, it does not get at the heart to the critical fact that neocolonialism is carried out by the African petty bourgeoisie.

As we explained in the Political Report to the Sixth Congress of the African People's Socialist Party, *An Uneasy Equilibrium: The African Revolution versus Parasitic Capitalism:*

> *[O]ur Party has been able to advance the understanding of neocolonialism, giving it a class character and identifying the African petty bourgeoisie as the social base from which it springs. Throughout the world when the movements for liberation grew to an extent that masses rose up with the blood-curdling cry of "kill the white man" it became no longer tenable for white power to exercise its rule directly.*
>
> *Indirect rule, neocolonialism, white power in black face became necessary. The mass struggles*

23 Nkrumah, Kwame. *Neo-colonialism, The Last Stage of Imperialism*, p. xi. International Publishers, 1966.

> *for liberation necessitated an obvious transfer of political power from the white colonizer to the black colonized. This serves to obscure the fact that the white colonizer continues to dominate the colonized through control of the economy and hence control of the politics of the colonized.*
>
> *Neocolonialism is the concept developed by Kwame Nkrumah to define the new face of colonialism. Nkrumah taught how the continued control of African economies allowed for indirect rule by the same powers. However, it was our Party that defined African neocolonialists according to their class character. It was we who recognized the role of class in the implementation of neocolonial rule. This had not been previously understood.*[24]

In our 1991 pamphlet, "Dialectics of Black Revolution: The Struggle to Defeat the Counterinsurgency in the U.S.," we showed how the U.S. government deepened the counterinsurgency against the African Revolution using neocolonialism:

> *With the defeat of the Black Revolution of the Sixties, the strategic target of the counterinsurgency shifted to include the entire African population, with emphasis on the African working class—employed and the increasingly enlarged unemployed. An essential component of this counterinsurgency is a drug economy, imposed on our economically dependent colonized community by the U.S. government. Accompanying this is the cynically deployed "war on drugs" used to justify a near-*

24 Yeshitela, Omali. *An Uneasy Equilibrium: The African Revolution versus Parasitic Capitalism*, p. 219. Burning Spear Publications, 2014.

> *total abrogation of the national democratic rights of African people that we fought and died for.*
>
> *To facilitate the criminalization of the African community, the counterinsurgency also utilizes a neocolonial policy which elevated thousands of Africans as elected officials and administrators. This has served to deflect consciousness of a defeated black revolution and gives a false sense of African "progress."*
>
> *Neocolonialism acts as a cover for the counterinsurgency either through the silence of these officials or through their actual hands-on participation in the attack on our people. Such was the case with the 1985 bombing of an African community in Philadelphia under the direction of an African mayor, Wilson Goode.*[25]

In our book, *Black Power Since the '60s*, in the chapter, "The Counterinsurgency Against Our People and the Response of the Black Movement," we provided the example of Washington, DC as a template for U.S. counterinsurgency with the complicity of the neocolonial class:

> *On April 10, 1989 the U.S. capitalist white power government revealed the newly-unfolding form of the government's counterinsurgency against our people's just struggle for freedom and repossession of the material wealth stolen from us by 400 years of slavery and foreign domination.*
>
> *April 10 was the day that William J. Bennett, the national drug policy director or drug czar [under then-U.S. president Ronald Wilson Reagan], flanked*

25 Yeshitela, Omali. "The Dialectics of Black Revolution: The Struggle to Defeat the Counterinsurgency in the U.S.," p. vi. Burning Spear Uhuru Publications, Second Edition, 1997.

by Secretary of Housing and Urban Development Jack Kemp and Richard Thornburg, U.S. attorney general, outlined an incredible state of martial law for Washington, D.C. that is public consolidation of a general campaign directed toward the domestically colonized African population.

Bennett's plan, which effectively nullified the election of the sleazy, neo-colonialist Marion Barry administration and returned the D.C. government to direct white control, calls for the deployment in Washington, D.C. of a so-called Metropolitan Area Task Force consisting of representatives from the Drug Enforcement Administration, FBI, U.S. Marshal's Service, Department of Defense, U.S. Attorney's Office, Internal Revenue Service, Immigration and Naturalization Service, Bureau of Alcohol, Tobacco and Firearms, U.S. Customs Service, Park Police, D.C. Metropolitan Police Department and state and local police agencies from Maryland and Virginia.

The immediate effect of Bennett's action was a legal coup d'etat as a means of countering one profound security problem for world capitalism led by U.S. imperialism; namely: the seat of international white power, the U.S. capitol, sitting in the middle of a population that is 70 percent African and extremely hostile toward the U.S. colonial government and its domestic and foreign policy.[26]

In a sense, Bennett's attack on African people in Washington, D.C. is testimony to the growing limitations of neocolonialism as the main strategy

26 Note that African people are only 47 percent of the population of Washington, DC in 2019, after being a majority in the city for more than 50 years, proving again that the gentrification by white people in urban African communities serves well the aims of counterinsurgency.

> *for U.S. imperialism in its war against African people.*
>
> *The fact is that the authority of the black puppet regimes established by white power in cities throughout the U.S. is wearing thin for the millions of oppressed and literally starving African working and poor people.*
>
> *The neocolonialism, more appropriately called 'Negro-colonialism' by some Party members, became a chief component of the counterinsurgency against our struggle following the defeat of the Black Revolution of the Sixties.*
>
> *Hundreds and thousands of well-trained, generally educated individuals, who together make up the worst kind of social scum, were recruited to the service of white power in the form of black elected officials, administrators and policy initiators such as civil rights groups and personalities. Their job was to act as political covers for white power by allowing it to assert itself against our people through themselves or their programs.*[27]

Our Party has made it clear from the very beginning of our existence that the African petty bourgeoisie as a class will always betray the African Revolution which must be led by the African working class with fierce adherence to its interests.

As we laid out in our 1981 book, *Bread, Peace and Black Power: Political Report to the First Congress of the African People's Socialist Party:*

> *This epoch of struggles and victories over neocolonialism and dependency represents the leading revolutionary tendency in the world today.*

27 Yeshitela, *Black Power Since the '60s,* pp. 15-16.

> *It is an epoch which finally thrusts humanity upon the threshold of world socialism, for it challenges the very foundations upon which world capitalism is built. This epoch of struggles and victories over neocolonialism and dependency directly threatens the primitive and non-capitalist accumulation of capital upon which world capitalism was constructed and without which it cannot survive in its present form.*[28]

The neocolonial strategy of the imperialist powers continues to serve the colonizers today, if not so well.

Only our Party, the Vanguard and Advanced Detachment, never stopped defending, engaging and upholding the interests of the African working class while neocolonial politicians and celebrities such as Jesse Jackson viciously attacked them. In later years Bill Cosby joined in the attack on African workers.

Today, thanks to the counterinsurgency, there are an astounding 2.3 million people in U.S. prisons—a 500 percent increase since the 1970s, when our Party was founded. This is in the context that the U.S. population has only increased by 48 percent in that time period.[29]

Colonized African and Indigenous people inside the U.S. officially account for 37 percent of the US population, yet we represent 67 percent of the prison population according to The Sentencing Project. We should note that those African prisoners who register as "mixed race" are now counted as white, allowing the U.S. government to give the appearance that the number of African prisoners in the U.S. has declined in recent years.

---

28 Yeshitela, Omali. *The Struggle for Bread, Peace and Black Power: Political Report to the First Congress of the African People's Socialist Party*, p. 5. Burning Spear Publications, 1981.

29 *The Sentencing Project*, sentencingproject.org.

African men, colonial subjects, are nearly six times as likely to be incarcerated as white men, and federal courts imposed prison sentences on African men that were 19 percent longer than those imposed on similarly situated white men between 2011 and 2016.

In 2015, 48,043 children were in U.S. juvenile prisons, of which 44 percent were African. There are about 1600 children in the U.S. serving life sentences without parole, 80 percent of which are colonized African children.[30] The U.S. is the only country in the world that sentences children to life in prison.

One of every eight people imprisoned in the entire world is an African man in the U.S.

This is significant not only because the large populations of China and India must be factored into the equation, but also because the entire billion strong population of colonized Africans throughout the world is factored in.

It is abundantly clear that the leap in prison incarceration within the U.S. is a direct result of the U.S. counterinsurgency that crushed the Black Revolution of the Sixties. A host of designer laws created especially for our movement and people were initiated and virtually every politician running for political office, often including Africans, ran on a platform of a public policy of police containment of the African community.

White people feigned ignorance of the war against African people

While it was clearly a war against our struggle for liberation from a hostile and alien foreign domination that is usually recognized as colonialism, the North American population, resting upon a parasitic foundation, was able to feign ignorance of the murderous assault against our Movement.

30 Ibid.

As we wrote in the Main Resolution to the First Party Congress published as *A New Beginning: The Road to Black Freedom and Socialism* in 1981:

> *In the U.S. imperialism was constructed off the enslavement of African people and the near-decimation of the Native population. This system has been the cornerstone of world capitalism since the Second Imperialist World War, which means among other things, that the resources, the wealth, the near slave-labor of the vast majority of the peoples of the world have been the basis for the development, not only of the wealth of the ruling class but of the entire North American society. Consequently the bases of opportunism within the U.S. are very deep.*[31]

White people were an objective component of the U.S. counterinsurgency, especially the "whites who love us," as they were characterized in Occupied Azania by Robert Sobukwe, a primary leader of our struggle there. These whites were the leftists, including Marxists and other socialists and communists, who made regular forays into our communities from the comfortable and generally safe libraries and cafes where they usually resided. They all expressed sympathy for our plight and cause, but not enough to get off our backs or to unite with our fight for self-determination.

With few exceptions they did not recognize that the socialism or communism they claimed to seek was to be found in the struggle for the liberation of our people. Instead they sought to show us the errors of our ways and introduce us to the "science of revolution" that required Africans and others

31 Yeshitela, Omali. *A New Beginning: The Road to Black Freedom and Socialism*, p. 29. Burning Spear Publications, 1982.

colonized within current borders of the U.S., to submit to the leadership of the colonizers that they called "workers."

Many of these white Left opportunists also politically supported and financially backed neocolonial politicians who were beginning to be elected to office in great numbers throughout the U.S. after the defeat of the Black Revolution.

The white opportunists rejected their responsibility to win the white "workers" to be organized under the leadership of colonized Africans who were on the front lines of the anti-capitalist wars within our colonized spaces. Nor did they see a responsibility to organize the colonizer population, white workers and otherwise, against the obvious war that was being waged against our leaders and organizations that were often being televised for the world to see.

Objectively, their role was no different from the strategy outlined in the August 1967 COINTELPRO memorandum to prevent anti-colonial coalitions from developing, to prevent our organizations "from gaining respectability" and to "prevent the long-range growth" of our Movement.[32]

As we summed up in our 1984 article, "A Political and Economic Critique of Imperialism and Imperialist Opportunism," white opportunism subsequent to the counterinsurgency that destroyed the African Revolution of the Sixties raised its ugly head:

> *Many of the radical white intellectuals who had previously lent ideological support to the Black Revolution found themselves conveniently rethinking their positions to bring them more in line with the tepid traditional politics of the Old Left radicals who had always ignored the plight of black people. As anticipated by some black organizations, the hippies took baths, cut their hair*

32 Churchill and Vander Wall, *The COINTELPRO Papers*, p. 110.

> *and often became successful lower-level capitalists, liberal Democratic politicians or overt right-wing, anti-black reactionaries.*[33]

African Internationalism enabled our Party to survive the counterinsurgency

The leadership that enabled our Party to survive those turbulent years of open U.S. government warfare was reflected in our political theory and our efforts to solve the problems of the Revolution. We did not, like some cultural nationalists, conjure up esoteric explanations within which our reality had to fit. We have always been practical revolutionaries. Our foray into theory was made necessary by the shortcomings in the inadequate explanations and solutions that we had inherited after the defeat of our Revolution.

Most of us who occupied the camp that we identified as pro-independence because of our determination to liberate ourselves from white colonial state power and become self-governing, were generally incapable of providing a scientific explanation for our relationship to each other as Africans and to our white oppressors.

For many years, stretching back to the sixties, we recognized our condition as being colonized within the U.S. as we obviously were in Africa and other places. From the beginning it has been clear to us that the problem of African people inside the U.S. and everywhere is not racism, the ideas in white people's heads.

During the 1960s, important books were written by African scholars affirming our colonial status. More importantly, our political leaders were using the colonial analysis as guides for our general movement within the U.S.

---

33 Yeshitela, Omali. "A Political and Economic Critique of Imperialism and Imperialist Opportunism," *The Road to Socialism is Painted Black*, p. 153. Burning Spear Publications, 1987.

Malcolm X, Frantz Fanon, Albert Memmi, Eldridge Cleaver and others within the Black Panther Party used this analysis that we are a colonized people within the U.S. It was an analysis embraced by what became the Uhuru Movement as far back as the SNCC and JOMO period.

The understanding that African people live under colonialism inside the U.S. and everywhere we are located is critical for us to be able to defeat the U.S. counterinsurgency and wage and win an anti-colonial war for the liberation of our homeland and people around the world.

We were in many ways blindsided by the colonial-capitalist war against our youthful movement in the '60s, coming at the very moment that we defined ourselves as colonial subjects struggling for power. With the military defeat of our Movement, the U.S. government also used a massive propaganda war telling us that we are victims of "racism" rather than a colonized nation of people fighting for liberation.

The colonial analysis rescued us from the impotent "racism" position forwarded by a sector of the African petty bourgeoisie, which implied that our problem was that white people did not like us. This analysis kept us in the very slavish position of struggling to win favor with the colonizer. This was true notwithstanding the fact that some liberals, even some associated with the black power position would begin to talk about "institutional racism," to explain why the system itself worked against the interests of African people.

Those who were not blinded by their profound desire to maintain their relationship to the U.S. empire were, with the slightest struggle, forced to recognize that the term "institutional racism" was simply used to obscure the colonial reality!

The struggle against racism was part of the ideological trap that kept our revolution based on efforts to reform or perfect U.S. imperialism. Even many black power proponents were defining ours as a struggle against racism *and* colonialism, using the terms interchangeably, a form of philosophical dualism.

As we showed in *An Uneasy Equilibrium,* the Political Report to our Sixth Party Congress in 2013:

> *The science of African Internationalism enabled our Party to avoid the ideological pitfalls that validate the assumption of the superiority of white people. Thus, we have never been diverted from our mission of capturing power and uniting Africa and our nation under the leadership of the African working class.*
>
> *Our Party brought science to our defeated African Liberation Movement at a time when it was generally bogged down in racial and cultural nationalism that indulged in candlelit ceremonies, religious obscurantism and nostalgia for an often imaginary African past. Through African Internationalism we were able to discover the material basis for the exploitation and oppression of Africans and others in this world....*
>
> *We determined long ago that characterizing our movement as a struggle against racism was a self-defeating waste of time. What is called racism is simply the ideological foundation of capitalist imperialism. Racism is a concept that denies Africans our national identity and dignity, rather than defining the system of our oppression. It relegates us to the Sisyphean task of winning acceptance from, and often becoming one with our oppressors....*
>
> *Africans are not a race but a nation of people, forcibly dispersed across the globe. We have*

> *been pushed out of history by our imperialist oppressors...Our national homeland has been occupied in various ways for millennia. Our people have been captured and shipped around the globe as capitalist commodities. Our labor and land have been violently extracted to build the European nation and the international capitalist system. This is what determines our reality and the contours of the struggle in which we have been engaged for more than 500 years.*[34]

The African People's Socialist Party leads as the Advanced Detachment

People make revolutions but it is the Advanced Detachment that leads them. An anti-colonialist, socialist revolution must be led by the Advanced Detachment of the African or colonized working class.

Our people have always resisted colonial slavery, but the creation of the African People's Socialist Party provided African people and workers with our own revolutionary class-based Party, led by African workers and informed by advanced revolutionary theory for the first time in history.

It is because of the existence of our Party that our struggle continues today despite its setbacks and despite the vicious total war made against our people by the U.S. government in the U.S. and by imperialist forces throughout the world.

Our Party has always understood that *real* national liberation can only be achieved through the leadership of the African working class. This is why we were able to recognize the counterinsurgency that, while directed at our total struggle, gave strategic primacy to an attack on the African working class.

---

34 Yeshitela, *An Uneasy Equilibrium*, p. 59.

It was *only* the African People's Socialist Party that initiated the campaign to identify and defeat the counterinsurgency that enveloped our nation and immobilized our Movement.

The defeat of the Black Revolution of the Sixties helped to define the task of our Party: Solve the problems of the Revolution. Complete the Black Revolution of the Sixties.

Central to this task, as can be seen in this chapter, was the urgency to expose and defeat the U.S. government's colonial counterinsurgency, the program that destroyed our Movement. Had we not taken on this work relentlessly over a period of decades our struggle to unite and liberate Africa and African people everywhere might have been set back for a hundred years or more.

For years we fought a persistent battle to win the unity of the U.S.-based anti-colonial movement with our efforts to expose and defeat the deadly counterinsurgency.

This struggle by the Party also forced upon us the task of determining why the anti-colonial movement could not unite with our efforts overturn the counterinsurgency despite all its destructive implications and the attempts by our Party. As we have shown, their stance was based in petty bourgeois unity with a neocolonial outcome and a fear that the African Revolution, led firmly by the African working class, could actually win our liberation and defeat U.S. imperialism!

Our struggle to expose and defeat the counterinsurgency is also the explanation of why the Party has advanced the African Revolution. Instead of moving backwards in history, attempting to build movements based primarily on the fight for democracy or a replay of the Civil Rights Movement under colonial capitalism, we continued to tenaciously pursue the revolutionary trajectory for *total* liberation.

Instead of raising empty slogans proclaiming to the colonialist-capitalist ruling class and state that "black lives matter," our Party has continued to develop a coherent theory and political practice. We equipped the African nation and essentially the oppressed peoples of the planet to be able to move from the last era of revolutionary struggle to usher in a new period in which revolution is becoming the main trend in the world again.

We summed up all the contradictions of the Black Revolution of the Sixties that allowed it to be set back by the U.S. government counterinsurgency.

This struggle deepened our understanding of colonialism and it helped us to understand opportunism within our own movement and the opportunism of the white colonizer Left even more.

This brief and incomplete summation of the counterinsurgency is possible only because we are adherents of African Internationalism. We have built a Party of professional revolutionaries organized under democratic centralist principles. We have carried out our strategy from the very beginning to prevent the isolation of the African Liberation Movement by building the African Socialist International that gives our Revolution a strategic character everywhere it is located—in Africa, the U.S., Europe, Australia, etc. No longer will an African in Haiti, in Congo or the North Side of St. Louis, U.S. struggle alone. The African Socialist International with the slogans, "Touch one! Touch all!" and "One Africa! One Nation!" has brought our dispersed nation together.

We have single-handedly rebuilt an anti-colonial movement and have successfully fought and won ideological and political recognition of the fact that African people are colonized wherever we are. We have single-handedly defended and extolled the leadership of the African working class. We have identified the previously unrecognized class struggle raging within our overall struggle for national liberation.

We have won solidarity for the African liberation struggle within the U.S. and globally, especially from other oppressed peoples. Through African Internationalism and the African People's Socialist Party it is now recognized that our struggle is intertwined with the struggle of our Mexican, Indigenous and Palestinian comrades and all the oppressed peoples of the Earth.

We have tapped into the Achilles heel of imperialist white power with the creation of the African People's Solidarity Committee, which extended the African Revolution into the citadel of U.S. imperialism. APSC and the solidarity movement are actively winning growing sectors of white people to practical unity with the Party's demand for reparations.

We have created dual and contending power that includes our own African working class media and a myriad of economic institutions which form the incipient socialist, anti-colonial economic foundation of the liberated African nation.

We created a mass organization with the fundamental task of exposing and defeating the counterinsurgency as far back as 1985. In 1991, that organization became the International People's Democratic Uhuru Movement, which has fought against police murder, mass imprisonment and every manifestation of colonial violence while promoting the strategy for political power and independence.

Our summation of counterinsurgency goes beyond the recognition of the involvement of the colonial state in the form of police, courts and the prison system. It also recognizes the role of counterinsurgent psychological warfare and the imperialist narrative in causing confusion within the African nation about our collective identity. We have scientifically and incontestably given definition to our dispersed African nation longing to be free and reunited. This collective identity is absolutely necessary for any liberation struggle to achieve a successful, united anti-colonial victory.

We solved the problems and attempted to overturn all weaknesses, contradictions and vulnerabilities of our revolutionary movement of the previous period. As the Vanguard, the Advanced Detachment, the African People's Socialist Party is ready. This time we are going to win. Indeed, we *are* winning!

IV. The deepening crisis of imperialism

The tipping point of the uneasy equilibrium

The unending wars waged by the U.S. from one end of the Earth to the other are evidence of the crisis of imperialism. Perhaps the greatest example of imperialist crisis today, however, can be found in the White House, the seat of U.S. governmental power. Every day, there is a new scandal associated with the regime of U.S. president Donald Trump.

A host of explanations is being advanced by the thinking representatives of the white ruling class for why the Trump administration continues to be embroiled in crippling controversy.

The struggle being waged against his regime by other sectors of the white ruling class is extraordinary.

The Trump regime is not fundamentally different from the Obama regime that preceded it. It is certainly not a departure from the predatory colonial-capitalist campaign of Hillary Clinton, his 2016 Democratic party opponent, whose loss to Trump sent shockwaves through the white ruling class elite.

We have said all along that the electoral process is simply a vehicle for nonviolent struggle by contending sectors of the colonial-capitalist ruling class for control of the state for their own profit-making advantage. Nothing clarifies this fact more than the 2016 U.S. presidential campaign and Trump's election.

The state is the organ of coercion utilized by the ruling class to protect the system of colonial capitalism. It is clearly the police, courts, jails and other repressive institutions. It is also the military and the various intelligence components associated with it. The state is the FBI, CIA, NSA and the assorted secret police agencies about which most people know nothing.

The state has existed since society split into irreconcilable classes, into groups locked into a relationship of the exploited and the exploiters, where the exploiters live at the expense of the others. The state is older than the U.S. In ancient Rome and Greece, the state protected the interests of the slave owners over the slaves. In feudal Europe it upheld the interests of the nobility over the peasants and serfs.

The European imperialist invasion of Africa, Asia and the lands now known as the Americas created a new *capitalist* social system. Now the state was no longer simply an instrument of coercion directed at protecting and maintaining the power of a social system *within* the boundaries of specific European territories.

The capitalist state created structures that protected and projected the interests of the bourgeoisie in far away places. This was a bourgeoisie made possible by the primary features of what Karl Marx termed the "primitive accumulation of capital," the genesis of the capitalist system itself.

The capitalist state was a consequence of Europe's imperialist assault on Africa and the rest of the peoples of the world. It has always had a global capacity flowing from its parasitic and predatory origin. Contrary to the notion that "globalization" is a new historical phenomenon, capitalism was born as a world system; the capitalist state is an international state power.

Without bourgeois elections, the ruling elites would be reduced to fielding their own private armies to advance their interests. They would be nothing more than the warlords that we see in some countries that have not achieved or developed the slavery-funded sophistication of bourgeois democracy most often found in European countries.

The bourgeois electoral process was designed to protect the colonial-capitalist system from destruction by internecine war between capitalist predators competing for resources and markets. In this way the electoral process functions as a component of colonial-capitalist state power.

The 2016 U.S. presidential election was also a white ruling class contest for control of the colonial-capitalist state. It was a contest that was clothed in bourgeois idealism designed to obscure the intention and interests of the minority white ruling class in order to win mass support from white people. The ability of the white masses to vote for their ruling class masters shrouds the dictatorship of the white rulers. This ability to vote has come to define democracy in the U.S. and for much of the white capitalist-dominated world.

The 2016 U.S. presidential election was a clear indicator of the growth of the crisis of imperialism. The fact that there were 17 Republicans contending for the nomination of their party and six major contenders for the Democratic party nomination, a total of 23 altogether[1], revealed a fractured white ruling class incapable of choosing a popular representative of its splintered economic interests.

The campaign occurred in a world that is being defined by the struggles of oppressed peoples whose subjugation is a condition for the success of the overall parasitic capitalist project. While U.S. politicians put their political programs forward as determinants of world history, all the presidential contenders were being driven by imperialist crisis that continues to threaten the stability and existence of colonial capitalism.

Trump breaks up Atlanticist bloc

In the Political Report to our 2016 Plenary we spoke of this crisis through the voice of one of the leading imperialist

1 There would have been 24 candidates, but the Democratic party refused to allow the participation of Chicago-based Willie Wilson, an African millionaire who met all the qualifying requirements, only to be forcibly escorted out of his attempts to participate in the Democratic party primary debates.

thinkers of the time. Zbigniew Brzezinski had recognized the crisis of imperialism for years.

In his 2007 book, *Second Chance: Three Presidents and the Crisis of American Superpower*, Brzezinski proved prescient in his explanation of the ruling class split into a myriad of self-serving components fighting for shares in an imperialist pie shrunken by the world's peoples desperately struggling to take back their lives and resources from a blood-drenched imperialism.

Says Brzezinski:

> *Global political awakening is historically anti-imperial, politically anti-Western and emotionally increasingly anti-American. In the process, it is setting in motion a major shift in the global center of gravity. That in turn is altering the global distribution of power, with major implications for America's role in the world.*
>
> *The foremost geopolitical effect of global political awakening is the demise of the imperial age. Empires have existed throughout history, and in recent times American paramountcy has often been described as a new global empire....*[2]

The contenders for the presidency during the 2016 elections were confronted by the reality described here by Brzezinski. They represented different sectors of the white ruling class. As Trump declared at every opportunity, they were hirelings of big money. Their individual political programs advanced during the campaign represented the different positions of their big moneyed employers who needed control of the U.S. state to realize their aims.

---

2 Brzezinski, Zbigniew. *Second Chance: Three Presidents and the Crisis of American Superpower*, p. 205. Basic Books, 2007.

But despite the fact that individual blocs of capital always fight to advance their own interests and were doing so in the 2016 U.S. presidential election, they have usually struggled within a generally agreed upon framework. Since the mid-1940s when the U.S. and much of Europe coalesced around a general strategy to counter the growing influence of the Soviet Union, the U.S. took the lead in creating what became known as the Atlantic bloc, whose proponents are known as Atlanticists.

The North Atlantic Treaty Organization (NATO) was the most obvious political and military manifestation of the Atlantic bloc. It also involved economic and security components that bound the liberal anti-communist white rulers into a common strategic trajectory for world domination.

U.S. leadership through the Atlantic bloc included the World Bank, the International Monetary Fund, the United Nations and an assortment of other related institutions, including international trade and economic bodies. Also a part of this bloc was an international court system that obeyed U.S. edicts, although the U.S. refused to recognize its authority as applicable to itself—an example of rule without regard for law, otherwise known as dictatorship.

The United Nations inherited the role previously assumed by the League of Nations, another U.S. brainchild that failed to win support within ruling circles after being advanced by U.S. president Woodrow Wilson following the First Imperialist World War.

This role was as unifier and peacekeeper among predatory imperialist white powers that have historically gone to war over division of the colonial-capitalist spoils among themselves.

Like the League of Nations, the United Nations was to function as a supranational agency that assured *peaceful, nonviolent* European control of the world's oppressed, colonized peoples.

The entire Atlanticist arrangement was designed to advance the interests of capitalists and the capitalist system by containing Soviet Russia. Another goal was to smother Germany's historical proclivity for violent domination of Europe that had resulted in the two previous imperialist wars to divide the world. The Atlantic bloc was created to ensure peaceful, white, collaborative domination of the colonized peoples upon whose exploitation the entire parasitic capitalist order depended.

For some time now the Atlanticist arrangement has been fraying. The decline of the Atlantic bloc was hastened by the 1991 collapse of Soviet Russia, whose existence was the impetus for its founding and the invention of the imperialist "Cold War."

U.S. collaboration with Europe on most questions now became increasingly unnecessary since the U.S. no longer had to compete for European loyalty with a now severely crippled post-Soviet Russia.

With the Soviet Union gone, Russia was no longer an ideo-political and economic contender in Africa, Asia, the Middle East and other regions of the world.

What had been considered a "bi-polar" world had suddenly become a "unipolar" world with U.S. imperialism unquestionably at the helm.

But all this changed. Lenin's declaration that the capitalist would sell someone the rope to hang him with was realized by the mad rush by all the European capitalists to take advantage of a presumed hapless China. The capitalists invaded with the intention of capturing the more than one billion Chinese as a lucrative market.

To the dismay of the European and U.S. capitalists, China instead became a major economic and political power whose success has come at the expense of the absolute hegemony of the U.S. and European capitalism in general.

The collapse of the Soviet Union meant that Soviet opportunism could no longer exert influence over the struggles of the oppressed. Many groups that were stronger in the Middle East and other places because of Soviet support for struggles against U.S. and imperialist white power lost their influence to indigenous movements.

This has unleashed massive anti-colonial resistance by Islamic-led movements fueled by poverty and repression by domestic U.S. and European puppet regimes, a history of European insults and humiliation and deeply held memories of the European Christian Crusades that provided a religious-based explanation for their struggle.

There is no little irony in the fact that the modern Jihadist movement was organized, funded and trained by the U.S. under the regime of U.S. president James Earl Carter. It was Carter's national security advisor Brzezinski who saw this as an anti-Soviet strategy to drain Soviet Russia economically by creating Russia's own "Viet Nam" in Afghanistan where there was a progressive Soviet-supported government in place.

It was the folly of Carter and Brzezinski to think that in the minds of the Jihadists, the U.S. white nationalist state would not also be seen as the imperialist infidel that had brought the Islamic world to its knees. It would not be long after the defeat of the Afghanistan government before the Jihadists would also turn their guns on the U.S., other imperialist powers and imperial craven domestic minions. This is what the CIA calls "blowback." In other words: what goes 'round comes 'round. This method continues to be used repeatedly by the CIA.

Colonialism, direct and indirect, which is the economic base of the global colonial-capitalist system, was in a state of flux along with all the reliant political and economic arrangements tethered to it.

The cozy relationship U.S. president Trump appears to want with Russia; the open near-declaration of war with the

G-7 group that presumes to collectively control the world's economy; the rocky courtship of China that involves the move toward rapprochement with the Democratic People's Republic of Korea; and the ongoing internecine wars within ruling circles that stretch around the globe, are evidence of a major shift in the political and economic alignments that have defined much of the world for the last 70-plus years of imperialist world domination.

The near absolute 500-year-old control of the world by "the white man" is on a shaky foundation that our Party has described as an uneasy equilibrium. The dominant world colonial-capitalist social system responsible for white wealth and security, and the brutal oppressive impoverishment of the rest of us, sits on the foundation of a profound, earth-shaking war between the colonial past and a post-colonial, increasingly visible liberated future.

Struggle within the white ruling class escalates

We of the African People's Socialist Party are contenders on the world stage. We are conscious, organized participants in the struggle of the oppressed and colonized. Our resistance is responsible for starving the bloated white nationalist colonial-capitalist system to the point of desperate division. This has resulted in every white man for himself. Today we see a scramble for new economic and political relations to stave off collapse of respective parasitic European economies within the shrinking system.

Indeed, this is a crisis of imperialism. It is also a moment where the possibilities of a new imperialist world war are greater than ever. Extremely significant economic interests are at stake. Bloodthirsty imperialist predators are willing and capable of mobilizing the oppressed of the world to fight other oppressed peoples to their collective extinction in the interests of protecting imperialism.

Trump's moves to normalize relations with Russia, China and Korea are being met with efforts to derail negotiations by an assortment of political forces, even within the Trump administration. The U.S. North American imperialist state, connected internationally with state institutions of imperialist powers of other countries, is generally committed to an Atlanticist strategy, with a huge political and military economy revolving around it.

There are Atlanticists within the Democratic and Republican parties and also within the Trump regime whence several attempts to block Trump's move with Russia, China and Korea have originated. The efforts by Trump's vice president Michael Richard Pence and U.S. national security advisor John Robert Bolton to scuttle the U.S.-Democratic People's Republic of Korea summit are examples.

The Atlanticists do not represent some kind of mysterious secret society. They are openly written and spoken of often in authoritative bourgeois media outlets, including political opposites like *The Wall Street Journal* and *The New York Times*.

They represent a very important economic agenda that was organized around the post-Second Imperialist War trajectory to protect and advance capitalist interests redefined by the outcome of the war. Almost all the economic and political relationships in the world were organized around, influenced or driven by the intra-capitalist hegemonic authority of the Atlanticists.

The Atlanticists have historically defined the security interests of imperialism. The influence of the Atlanticists reaches down into the retirement funds and job security of the hired killers that make up the officers and ranks of the U.S. military, the FBI, CIA, NSA, local cops and other terrorist organizations of the imperialist gendarme .

The Trump candidacy sounded so outlandish to many because his articulations challenged the long-held Atlanticist assumptions fed to the general public and regurgitated by every "legitimate" political hack on both sides of the ocean.

What soon became clear after the 2016 U.S. presidential election is that the intra-capitalist struggle for control of the state was not resolved. Trump, an outlier who contended in the electoral process without economic and political support from, and general unity with, the Atlanticists, had become at least nominal custodian of the U.S. colonial-capitalist state.

This is crisis on steroids. Not because Trump was an anti-capitalist or anti-colonialist, but because he was not bound by the strategic trajectory that held the capitalists together even when they were in friendly contention. Trump's ascension to the presidency and his actions since then represent the first all-out assault on the very foundation of Atlanticism, which, again, achieved its rationale and definition in opposition to Soviet Russia.

Trump has attacked the relevance of NATO and the United Nations, engaged in flirtations with Russia and has demanded that the traditional U.S. allies begin to pay their way militarily and renegotiate their trade relations with the U.S. These are not merely the egotistical rantings of a billionaire simpleton. They represent an attempt at a major reorganization of international white power and America's place in it.

While the split among the ruling class during the 2016 presidential election exposed the differences among the Atlanticists, it revealed that the Trump regime was an existential threat to their collective well-being under the existing setup. They had all determined to make it impossible for Trump to govern—at least up to now.

The unity of Trump's opponents is increasingly fragile, as Trump provides payoffs to individual sectors of the opposition, such as monumental tax breaks for the wealthy and all of occupied Jerusalem for Jewish capitalists and others who benefit from the reorganization of the Middle East under imperialist domination.

Also, the contradictions within the Atlanticist arrangement have been understated by the ruling class for some time now. Trump has driven the contradiction to the surface and with it a realignment of political and economic forces within the U.S. Some forces are growing or receding in significance and others, like Trump himself, have been introduced to pronounced, respectable significance for the first time.

Hence the intra-capitalist war for control of the state continues unabated.

Trump wages war against organizations of the state

Each U.S. presidential election retains residual state influence from previous regimes. Some, like the Bush regime, have gone so far as to create their own, separate intelligence organizations. There is also talk of Trump creating an intelligence organization headed by colonel Oliver North. North played a similar role for the regime of U.S. president Ronald Wilson Reagan during the illegal war against the Sandinista government in Nicaragua and in the CIA-orchestrated drug importation and distribution within the U.S. domestic African colony.

However, Trump has waged an outright public war against organizations of the state that are not under control of his regime. The most obvious example has been Trump's furious fight with the FBI, CIA and other intelligence fronts after they all embellished or distorted the story of improper Russian intervention in the 2016 election.

It has been suggested by some that Trump is motivated by a private economic arrangement he has in Russia or by fear of exposure by Russian intelligence agencies of licentious activities during a pre-election visit to Moscow. Trump may also recognize that the effectiveness of his enemies in undermining his ability to govern is directly connected to the perception they have created that his election victory was a consequence of Russian intervention.

Whatever the case, his openness to a potential U.S.-Russia partnership has caused no little consternation among the Atlanticists who stand to lose trillions of dollars and political control in Europe and, increasingly, in the Middle East because of Russian re-ascendancy on the world stage. Even Obama's failed "Asian pivot" from Europe to contend with China's growing economic and political influence, appears not to have shaken the Atlanticists as much as Trump's threatened embrace of Russia, characterized by U.S. pundits as "our adversary."

As this Political Report is being written, the Trump regime is under investigation by a "special counsel" for allegations of collusion with Russia in the 2016 presidential election. There is an obvious attempt by a collaborative bourgeois effort to undermine Trump's ability to govern and to remove him from office if necessary. Some have even suggested involvement by the British MI6 intelligence arm in the exposure of Trump's alleged collusion with Russia.

There are daily allegations, some without any legal basis, of impropriety by Trump and/or those close to him. Along with the manner in which Trump waged his campaign, this serves to tarnish the well-constructed fiction of U.S. governmental high-mindedness and presidential integrity.

The fact that Trump campaigned as an "outsider" meant that he had to campaign against the "system" itself, the system that had disillusioned so many people through the obvious duplicity of traditional politicians. Trump campaigned against the system that is no longer able to stanch the struggles of the world's peoples whose oppression allows ordinary white colonizers the psychological benefit of "whiteness," even when the economic benefits are not so obvious.

Trump has continued to wage a fierce fightback against his colonial-capitalist contenders. Even as his attacks on the intelligence agencies within the U.S. are causing obvious unease for some imperialist apologists, Trump has also worked incessantly to destroy the myth of a "neutral," "disinterested" bourgeois media working for the benefit of all the people. Trump's term "fake news" has become accepted lingua franca, even within the respected media platforms of the ruling class.

This intra-ruling class airing of "dirty laundry" is tarnishing and undermining the carefully constructed bourgeois myth of a noble white power working in the general interests of the world's peoples. The old adage, "Your actions speak so loudly I can't hear a word you say," is conspicuously applicable here.

There are no good guys in this struggle, neither the Democratic nor Republican parties.

Not the Democratic party disguised as the millions of white women who are declaring "me too," but who are, more than 160 years later, still unable to answer the question posed by Sojourner Truth, "Ain't I a woman [too]?"

Not the Democratic party disguised as thousands of high school students marching against gun violence as long as the police murder of Africans and the U.S. murders of colonized peoples of the world are not mentioned.

Not the Second Amendment defenders nor the Democratic and Republican protectors of the FBI who are outraged at alleged Russian intervention in "our elections," the "finest example of democracy" as long as it does not include an African church in Birmingham, Alabama.

The reputation of the office of the U.S. presidency and the most highly respected institutions of the U.S. are being sullied beyond repair. Nevermind that Trump is currently successful in carrying out many of his programs with an electoral base hovering at 40 percent or below, or that his capitalist opponents are too cowardly to make a frontal assault on the citadel. The fact is that there are millions of people within the U.S. and abroad who, while not organized to make a meaningful fightback, are nevertheless disgusted with the U.S.

DPRK alters global balance of power

The Trump regime has touted the U.S. meeting with Kim Jong-un, leader of the Democratic People's Republic of Korea (DPRK) as a major triumph, supposed evidence that his threatening anti-Kim antics drove the Korean leader to the negotiating table.

Almost everyone, including Trump's opponents and those made uneasy by the meeting, agree that it was Kim's desperation in the face of Trump threats that is responsible for the June, 2018 Singapore meeting. If there are some who cannot see through this obvious lie it is because they are not aware that the DPRK had always called for direct negotiations with the U.S. It has been the U.S. that has refused to meet with the Korean government, not the other way around. Since its failure to capture all of Korea during the colonial Korean war, the policy of the U.S. has been to deny the legitimacy of the DPRK that came to power through revolution led by a worker's party.

At the undeclared conclusion of the war, the U.S. began a process of pumping billions of dollars and capitalist investment into the Republic of Korea or South Korea. The U.S. wanted to show the superiority of colonial capitalism over a self-identified communist government under the authority of indigenous non-white working people. Thousands of U.S. troops have occupied South Korea since the end of the war, where they participate with troops from the Republic of Korea in incessant aggressive war games practicing the invasion of the DPRK.

The presence and role of China in the current developments of U.S.-Korean relations must not be understated. China has its own interests and will doubtlessly work to advance them. There has been much speculation as to whether the U.S. can threaten and bully China with economic sanctions and the like. One thing that we do know is that military intervention of Chinese troops in the Korean war prevented the U.S. from total domination of the Korean peninsula.

China recognizes that the thousands of U.S. troops stationed in the Republic of Korea and other components of the aggressive military presence in the region are there as part of an outdated China containment policy of the U.S. government. It is hard to imagine that China would look kindly at a U.S. assault on Korea that would open a direct military land line to China.

The U.S. and DPRK are engaged in direct talks now because the Koreans have changed the power relations in the Asian Pacific region and especially on the Korean peninsula. Indeed, the Koreans have altered the power relations in the world. After months of publicly testing nuclear warheads despite U.S. threats, the DPRK has demonstrated its nuclear capacity and a delivery system that can even reach the U.S.

All the people of Korea want the reunification of their land and nation. All are aware that Trump's prior threats to obliterate "North Korea" would mean a threat of existence of all of Korea, the south included. Most people are aware that at this point in history, a U.S. attack on Korea would not be a one-sided attack and that while the North could not match the U.S. in quantity and quality of arms they could certainly deliver a devastating military response that would involve the entire Korean peninsula and much of Asia.

In other words, the U.S.-Korean meeting represents a major policy shift on the part of the U.S.—not the Democratic People's Republic of Korea. Therefore, if fear was a factor in making the meeting happen, it was not the fear by the Democratic People's Republic of Korea.

Whatever the immediate consequences of the meeting, one thing is certain: the world has changed considerably and it will not go unnoticed by the oppressed that the U.S. no longer has absolute hegemony in Asia and the world. If developing Korean muscularity can push the U.S. imperialists back, there will be a great rush by others to attain a capacity to resist U.S. imperial terror.

The advent of China and Korea as major players in the world is further evidence of the retreat of absolute white power that defines the world today. It was only a few years ago that the phrase, "not having a Chinaman's chance," reflected the semi-colonial and economically deprived status of China in the world. The fact that China is boldly intruding on economic and political terrain that white nationalist imperialists have previously assumed their prerogative is part of the growing global trajectory of the oppressed to push European colonialism out of our lives and out of existence.

Crisis abounds!

The European Union, once perceived by some as a big-economy competitor of the U.S. is currently in disarray. The departure of England from the group and others threatening to do the same compounds the implication of the unremitting economic and political crisis of Greece, the threat to the integrity of Spain's presumed national identity and the Eurosceptic government that has come to power in Italy.

War continues to undermine the stability of the Middle East. Yemen, an ally of Iran, strategically located at the mouth of the Red Sea shipping lane has endured ruthless slaughter and starvation of its population by a U.S.-Israel-supported war by Saudi Arabia. The voluntary self-censorship of U.S. and European media serves as a function of the war.

The U.S. war that destroyed the Iraqi government of Saddam Hussein has resulted in the growing influence of Iran in that region. The U.S., Israel and Saudi Arabia have combined to combat Iran in a variety of ways that include the war against Yemen and the economic quarantine of Iran.

After five years, the U.S.-initiated war against Syria that stemmed from the counterinsurgent intent to overthrow the regime of Bashar Al-Assad continues to be fraught with a major potential for imperialist world war. Under Trump, the U.S. and Israel have attacked Syria to target Syrian-allied Iranian troops, also risking military confrontation with Russian troops deployed in Syria.

Contributing to the crisis of imperialism is the fact that China has initiated a major economic project designed to further challenge the Atlanticist arrangement. The $100 billion Asian Infrastructure Investment Bank (AIIB) created by the Xi Jinping administration already has commitments from at least 21 Asian countries. Australia, Indonesia and South Korea were noticeably absent from the deal after severe pressure from the U.S.

Many of the members of the AIIB are countries of the Chinese-led Belt and Road Initiative (BRI). These major Chinese economic projects that necessarily encroach on the heretofore domination of the world by Euro-American capital, contribute to the overall crisis of imperialism.

At the same time other countries find themselves looking for options outside the Atlanticist sphere of control. Even the ongoing scandal in South African politics involving former president and African National Congress (ANC) leader Jacob Zuma revolves around charges of corruption conveniently leveled at Zuma by equally corrupt officials opposed to his apparent coziness with Indian and possibly Chinese capital.

In Africa, at least one government has been overthrown by France because of an attempt to initiate a new deal with China that would free Ivory Coast from the clutches of historical French colonialism. Hugo Chavez of Venezuela and Mu'ummar Qaddafi of Libya are two of the leaders who were undermined and/or killed because of attempts made to escape domination of the U.S. military-backed dollar, still the leading world currency.

Imperialism continues to exist. Colonial capitalism continues to be the dominant social system on Earth. However, there is an uneasy equilibrium where the struggle of the oppressed and colonized peoples of the world calls into question everything that shaped the political and economic features of the world. This crisis has reached its tipping point.

The crisis of imperialism is characterized by extraordinary volatility that is also reflected in the politics and consciousness of the peoples of the world. Europeans and especially "Americans" are experiencing distress. The growing alcoholism, drug addiction, suicides, mass killings and a host of social afflictions and "diseases of despair" have caused an unusual spike in the death rate of white people, especially middle-aged white men in the U.S.

On the other hand, this volatility is represented by growing struggles of colonized peoples, boldly challenging their relationship to imperialist white power. This is happening globally and within the U.S. among Africans in the imperialist center.

The imperialists are struggling to find their place during this crisis. All kinds of new possibilities are opening up for our Revolution. Central to all our possibilities is the growth of the organization, capacity and influence of our Party, the key resource available to our forcibly dispersed colonized nation.

New alliances will also present themselves to our struggle as the old alliances among the imperialists are dying and/or reorganizing themselves.

In the past when certain fissures emerged within the imperialist camp, our movement was able to form important relationships with the governments of Cuba, Algeria and Congo Brazzaville, among others. Viet Nam and China also played a key support role to anti-colonial freedom fighters. Even some bourgeois nationalist governments of Africa and the Middle East were willing to leverage their power by aiding the struggle of Africans in the U.S. and throughout Africa during an era when the Soviet Union also represented a counterbalance to U.S. power.

As the balance of power continues to shift and the crisis deepens, the coming years will bring to light the possibility of new allies and alliances which embrace the African anti-colonial struggle.

Whites fear "fascism" while ignoring everyday terror of colonialism

There are some liberals who would have us engaged in an unrelenting fight against "fascism" that they see in the utterings and actions of Trump. However, we never forget that we are colonized and that "democratic" colonialism is still colonialism. The fascism feared by whites and liberals looks very much like the colonialism Africans have experienced in this country for centuries.

Europeans are accustomed to the experience of bourgeois democracy which hides the dictatorship of the bourgeoisie. For colonized people the dictatorship of the bourgeoisie is raw and obvious all the time, through the violence of the state and the general white population, as well as the arbitrary denial of the civil and democratic rights of the colonized. What Europeans call fascism is the point when the dictatorship of the bourgeoisie experienced all the time by Africans and other colonized people challenges the veneer of bourgeois democracy enjoyed by white people.

The liberals would have us turn our backs on the liberation of our people and the colonized peoples of the world to come to the rescue of liberal, democratic colonialism. The struggle against fascism serves a sector of the white ruling class and colonial society but for African people it only maintains our self-defeating fight to make white people like us and to stop the police from killing and imprisoning us.

The struggle against fascism is, in many ways, similar to the fight against racism, in that it is a struggle to find a safe place within colonialism. It is a struggle that protects the colonial-capitalist relationship that we have with imperialist white power. It is a struggle that unites us with one sector of colonial power against another and it does absolutely nothing to destroy colonialism.

This is reminiscent of now-deceased activist and poet Amiri Baraka, when he expressed concern in 2008 that African and/or "left" refusal to support Obama's election would open the door to fascism in a way similar to the rise of Hitler in Germany during the 1930s.

First of all, many Africans have recognized over the years that what happened to European Jews at the hand of Nazi Germany follows on the heels of an accepted, normalized practice of genocide against African, Indigenous, Arab and Asian peoples for hundreds of years by Europeans in the process of imposing slavery and colonialism on the majority of humanity—the process of building parasitic capitalism.

The tendency to compare our situation with fascism in Nazi Germany and elsewhere is erroneous and outrageous when considering the murder, terror, torture and exploitation that Africans have endured at the hands of our white, "democratic," colonizers for the past 600 years.

It is worth noting that with all the terror and brutality Africans have faced since our introduction to European democracy, it took the emergence of Mussolini and Hitler and the attack on the rights of white people for a special designation called fascism to suddenly become necessary.

Aimé Césaire, the African leader based in Martinique and mentor to Franz Fanon, wrote in 1955:

> *First we must study how colonization works to* decivilize *the colonizer, to* brutalize *him in the true sense of the word, to degrade him, to awaken him to buried instincts, to covetousness, violence, race hatred, and moral relativism; and we must show that each time a head is cut off or an eye put out in Vietnam and in France they accept the fact, each time a little girl is raped and in France they accept the fact, each time a Madagascan is tortured and in France they accept the fact, civilization acquires another dead weight, a universal regression takes place, a gangrene sets in, a center of infection begins to spread; and that at the end of all these treaties that have been violated, all these lies that have been propagated, all these punitive expeditions that have been tolerated, all these prisoners who have been tied up and "interrogated, all these patriots who have been tortured, at the end of all the racial pride that has been encouraged, all the boastfulness that has been displayed, a poison has been instilled into the veins of Europe and, slowly but surely, the continent proceeds toward* savagery.
>
> *And then one fine day the bourgeoisie is awakened by a terrific boomerang effect: the gestapos are busy, the prisons fill up, the torturers around the racks invent, refine, discuss.*

People are surprised, they become indignant. They say: "How strange! But never mind—it's Nazism, it will pass!" And they wait, and they hope; and they hide the truth from themselves, that it is barbarism, the supreme barbarism, the crowning barbarism that sums up all the daily barbarisms; that it is Nazism, yes, but that before they were its victims, they were its accomplices; that they tolerated that Nazism before it was inflicted on them, that they absolved it, shut their eyes to it, legitimized it, because, until then, it had been applied only to non-European peoples; that they have cultivated that Nazism, that they are responsible for it, and that before engulfing the whole edifice of Western, Christian civilization in its reddened waters, it oozes, seeps, and trickles from every crack.

Yes, it would be worthwhile to study clinically, in detail, the steps taken by Hitler and Hitlerism and to reveal to the very distinguished, very humanistic, very Christian bourgeois of the twentieth century that without his being aware of it, he has a Hitler inside him, that Hitler inhabits *him, that Hitler is his* demon, *that if he rails against him, he is being inconsistent and that, at bottom, what he cannot forgive Hitler for is not* the crime *in itself,* the crime against man, *it is not* the humiliation of man as such, *it is the crime against the white man, the humiliation of the white man, and the fact that he applied to Europe colonialist procedures which until then had been reserved exclusively for the Arabs of Algeria, the "coolies" of India, and the "niggers" of Africa.*[3]

3 Césaire, Aimé. *Discourse on Colonialism*, pp. 35-36. Présence Africaine, 1955.

When "proto-fascist" repression did appear in the U.S. the 1950s in what is called the "McCarthy Era" with a reign of terror backed by popular support from the general white population, chasing the Communist Party underground and almost into extinction, it was the colonized African population whose struggles for democracy kept the society open.

Ella Baker, Fannie Lou Hamer, Rosa Parks and an army of Africans living near starvation and suffering every imaginable deprivation, were the forces that not only defeated U.S. fascism but forged new definitions of democracy onto the agenda of the U.S.

Africans would still be on plantations, buck dancing for a slimy, non-fascist democratic white nationalist social system and every white person who so demanded had those aforementioned Africans trembled from the fear of fascism.

The designer character of the term is even more obvious when we search for a definition of fascism. While there are many, including some identified as "scientific" or Marxist, it is clear that there is not a satisfactory a priori definition.

Fascism has become a pejorative, something that defines some traits of the phenomenon once it appears, but fascism is incapable of being defined scientifically in a way that would help us to know it before it arrives.

It is notable that the ubiquitous murder, imprisonment and police containment of the African population is never defined as fascist. These conditions are seen by the white population as normal.

It is only when the features of the normal existence of the colonized begin to intrude into the existence of whites or "the larger society" the term "fascism" comes into play.

At that point the colonized are called on to choose between fascist colonialism and non-fascist democratic colonialism.

Amilcar Cabral, a leader of the revolutionary movement to defeat Portuguese colonialism in Guinea Bissau, West Africa stated, in response to a Portuguese leftist position that defeat of fascism inside Portugal—something the Portuguese Left saw as primary to their interests—would come with the defeat of colonialism, led by African liberation movements in Portuguese colonies that:

> *We must reaffirm clearly that while being opposed to all fascism, our people are not fighting Portuguese fascism: we are fighting Portuguese colonialism.*
>
> *The destruction of fascism in Portugal must be the work of the Portuguese people themselves: the destruction of Portuguese colonialism will be the work of our people.*
>
> *While the fall of fascism in Portugal might not lead to the end of Portuguese colonialism—and this hypothesis has been put forward by some Portuguese opposition leaders—we are certain that the elimination of Portuguese colonialism will bring about the destruction of Portuguese fascism.*
>
> *Through our liberation struggle we are making an effective contribution towards the defeat of Portuguese fascism and giving the Portuguese people the best possible proof of our solidarity. This factor is a cause of pride to our people, who hope for the same solidarity from the Portuguese people...*[4]

Like Africans in what was then Portuguese Africa, Africans in the U.S. and around the world are also fighting against colonialism.

---

4 Cabral, Amilcar, *Revolution in Guinea*, p. 23. Stage 1, 1974.

This is something that Baraka and the anti-fascist alarmists have not understood.

The concern expressed about fascism is one that would keep the struggle for our liberation locked into a "fight against fascism" by supporting one or another of the "non-fascist" ruling class parties or personalities.

The "fight against fascism" is a fight to maintain the capitalist-imperialist status quo.

Our Party must deepen the crisis of imperialism

Our Party, the Advanced Detachment of the African working class, the Vanguard of the African Revolution is unimpressed by the bleatings of the Democratic and Republican parties and the liberals of all nationalities hiding in their shadows. Both bourgeois parties had already fallen into such disrepute that Trump was not an illogical choice for white people to elect. Not to mention that, among the Democrats, the contending "outsider," Bernard Sanders, presented the greatest challenge to the party's anointed establishment leader, Hillary Rodham Clinton.

The majority of the people in the U.S. are not members of our African People's Socialist Party or Movement. In fact, the majority does not know of our existence, but the greatest chance of the people knowing who we are and why they should stand with us is our willingness to take advantage of the disarray among the leading institutions of the colonial white ruling class. We must draw the line by taking clear, non-opportunist, African Internationalist positions that expose the system and show the way forward in an unambiguous way.

While some liberals are protesting his castigation of the secret political police organizations and the bourgeois colonial media, Trump's revelations are useful in exposing the rot of this social system born of slavery, colonialism and genocide.

All the peoples in the U.S. and the world are thirsty for real leadership to show the way forward, out of the morass of bourgeois lies and deception that pushed them to Trump and the white nationalist Democratic party Left in the first place.

Trump makes daily, open attacks on the "deep state." The term "deep state" refers to the permanent, hidden bodies of ruling class decision-makers whose long-term plans are unaffected by changing administrations. Through use of this term, Trump has introduced the question of the state to the millions of people worldwide who never knew of its presence by name. This has forced outright denials of the existence of the "deep state" by paid "experts" of ruling class media outlets and the new Central Intelligence Agency head during his Senate confirmation hearing.

Our Party's exposure of the role of elections to provide a means of nonviolent struggle for control of the state by contending sectors of the ruling class will now fall on better-informed ears. The point is, Comrades, we must move forward with our criticism of colonial capitalism without cessation. The white ruling class inadvertently continues to assist our exposure of the true nature of parasitic capitalism and the colonial domination of African people within the U.S. and abroad. We must continue to build the capacity of our people to resist.

Indeed, these are dangerous times. They are dangerous because of the depth of the crisis of imperialism. As always, our Party, the Advanced Detachment will not join the herd in fighting to protect the system by struggling against fascism or racism.

History has taught us that the biggest guarantee we have for any kind of democratic opening is to be found through struggle to limit the influence of the colonial-capitalist state in the affairs of our people—political and economic power in the hands of the African working class. For colonized people, *this* is a measure of democracy.

Our power is in the masses of African workers, in the heart of the colonies throughout the U.S. and the world. We must build here, among the unorganized and barely-organized masses of African workers who, under the leadership of our Party, will set the terms for a revolutionary response by the entire African nation that will bring the crisis of imperialism to a head, to a revolutionary conclusion.

In the African colonies, the message of our Party about the "rigged" elections will have a more receptive audience than ever. The FBI program targeting "Black Identity Extremists" is further evidence of the U.S. counterinsurgency carried out by intelligence agencies, also known as the "deep state" exposed by the intra-capitalist struggle surrounding the Trump presidency. The high public disregard for the foul, garbage-spewing media outlets of the colonial bourgeoisie gives us the opportunity to elevate and expand the influence of the Party's media outlets.

The future of our people can only be guaranteed by the success of our Party in leading our colonized nation throughout the world in an organized struggle to deepen the crisis of imperialism. We do this concretely by constructing a real capacity among the people to wage an unrelenting, unwavering fight against colonialism. We build a popular resistance and hatred of alien and foreign domination, a resistance to colonialism. We build the institutions of dual power that our Party has been constructing for nearly two generations. We create the ideological, political and territorial spaces for the masses to join in the building of dual power even without the direct intervention of our Party.

Comrades! Sisters and Brothers! Our Party has been waging this struggle against colonial capitalism for almost 50 years now. We are the only organization that has fought consistently to complete the Black Revolution of the Sixties. We do this not as an abstract project based on a collection of position papers representing a thousand different political trends and tendencies. We are part of a historical continuum that has been busy solving the problems of the Revolution from which theory was developed and confirmed through practice. You can tell the effectiveness of African Internationalism by the accomplishments of our Party.

It is our practical experience in advancing our struggle among the African working class that enables us to go into the trenches in the fight against the Trump regime, the latest manifestation of colonial world power.

Comrades! Sisters and Brothers! The new world we are fighting for is possible within our lifetime. It is up to us, Africans and other oppressed and colonized peoples of the world, to achieve the political clarity and organizational capacity to provide the revolutionary leadership required by colonized nations and workers to overturn this system in critical flux.

We must bring about the new world without oppressors and the oppressed, exploiters and the exploited—a world in which African workers have power over our lives and future.

Our Seventh Congress is the contribution the African People's Socialist Party is making to this end.

V. African Socialist Internationalist dual power versus New Afrikan opportunism

Throughout our entire history, the African People's Socialist Party has always believed that the strategy of building dual and contending power is key to achieving our overall aim of liberating Africa and African people everywhere. The strategy of dual power is tied to the consolidation of the African nation and the struggle against colonialism.

Forty-one years ago last April, we introduced the concept of dual power into the African Liberation Movement with a paper titled, "The Political Aspects of Building a Mass Movement–The Tactical and Strategic Objectives for Black Liberation."

The paper became influential within our Movement and throughout the African liberation struggle in the U.S. It was printed in installments in *The Burning Spear* and also published as a popular pamphlet.

The paper was written for the 1977 Black Organizers' Conference at the University of Massachusetts Amherst, which was attended by many notable figures of our independence movement of the time.

They included Robert Williams, the first president of the Provisional Government of the Republic of New Afrika; Reverend Charles Koen from Cairo, Illinois; Ella Baker, creative genius of the Student Nonviolent Coordinating Committee, as well as representatives from the Institute of the Black World and others. Also in attendance were representatives of the Afrikan People's Party and its founding member, Akbar Muhammad Ahmad, organizer of the conference and a heroic figure of our liberation movement in his own right.

Known in the Party as "Tactics and Strategy for Black Liberation," the document has since guided the Party's work. The strategic objectives spelled out in the document have also influenced other organizations within the liberation movement. Increasingly we are hearing various groups and personalities beginning to espouse the strategic concept of dual power today.

In the "Tactics and Strategy" paper, we laid out these strategic objectives:

> *...One of these objectives must be THE CREATION OF DUAL, OR COMPETING, OR CONTENDING GOVERNMENTAL POWERS (emphasis in the original). That is to say, to the degree possible, our movement must assume the real and actual responsibilities of government for our people....*
>
> *If we can do this in practice, we will have plunged a wooden stake into the heart of the imperialist blood-sucking vampire of the world. For it is not only true that U.S. bourgeois democracy, which is capable of being so defined because of its ability to obscure its class dictatorship, cannot exist in the face of such mass rejection, but to the degree we can effectively build competing state power, we actually negate the power of the U.S. North American state.*[1]

The "Tactics and Strategy" paper was one of the many efforts made by our Party to introduce a scientific approach to the entire African Liberation Movement in that period when

1 Yeshitela, Omali. "Tactics and Strategy for Black Liberation," pp. 20-21. Burning Spear Publications, 1982.

the U.S. government defeat of our movement left it generally bogged down in cultural nationalism and superstition.

Over the years this paper has continued to guide our Party's work. Five years after its conception we elaborated on the principles of the "Tactics and Strategy" paper in the Political Report to the First Party Congress in Oakland in 1981, published as *The Struggle for Bread, Peace and Black Power*:

> *The real question is the demand for political independence, for self-determination—moving off the premise that Africa is the national homeland....*
>
> *As to how this self-determination will be realized, this will depend on several factors: the aspirations of the masses here, in Africa, and elsewhere during the critical development of our Revolution; the actual unfolding of the revolutionary process within the U.S., and the ability of the Party to contribute to the construction of the African Socialist International.*
>
> *The African People's Socialist Party has called for the creation of dual power within the U.S. as a strategic objective for winning liberation. This call presupposes the transformation of every oppressed community within the domestic African colony into revolutionary soviets*[2] *for political independence, African liberation and socialism.*
>
> *...Moreover, since the land question in this instance has been demoted from the height of theory and properly raised to a political and strategic question, it allows us to develop political alliances and relationships with the Native people,*

2 "Soviet" was the word used in the Russian Revolution to describe the workers councils that formed the basis of socialist governmental power.

> *the North American working class*[3] *and others during the unfolding of the revolutionary process in developing a strategy regarding the struggle for land distribution and socialism.*
>
> *This line of the Party represents the proper approach to the question of land and nationality. It is a line born out of a dialectical approach to our history and present conditions in the real world. It is a line which targets imperialism thoroughly as opposed to some neo-Zionist assumptions which often presuppose an answer which does not destroy imperialism. It is a line which, if adhered to, will surely lead to victory, the defeat of U.S. imperialism, and the socialist revolution. Comrades, this is African Internationalism ... the theory of the international African working class.*[4]

We are African Internationalists. In all our work, we realize that our struggle locally, wherever we are, is a component, a front, of the struggle to liberate all 12 million square miles of our conquered and oppressed, resource-rich African homeland.

---

3 The Party understands today that it was slavery, genocide and theft of the land from the Indigenous people that resulted in the emergence and development of both the capitalist white ruling class and the white working class. Today our position is that sectors of the North American population who want to disengage from their role as colonizers of African people can only do this through being organized in solidarity with African liberation. It is not a matter of "alliances" but principled solidarity, which means joining the African People's Solidarity Committee, the white organization under the leadership of the African People's Socialist Party that operates as a component of our strategy for winning national liberation. The Party understands that the African working class is the true working class and that the class question in the whole world is located in the colonial question.

4 Yeshitela, Omali. *The Struggle for Bread, Peace and Black Power: Political Report to the First Congress of the African People's Socialist Party*, pp. 48-49. Burning Spear Publications, 1981.

Every African living in colonial captivity must be able to recognize the significance of the struggle within each community as one of the many strategically-located launching pads contributing to the victory that will enable Africa to feed, clothe, house and protect Africa and African people worldwide for all eternity.

Land of U.S. stolen from the Indigenous people

Critical to the genuine understanding of dual power is the fact that we have always recognized that the land occupied by what is now known as the United States of America was stolen from the Indigenous people in a brutal and genocidal war that has not ended. We have always maintained that *Africa* is the national homeland of African people who have been divided and forcibly dispersed throughout the world.

We have never accepted any opportunistic theory that presupposes that our forced colonial enslavement on the land of the Indigenous people has somehow transformed us into some kind of hybrid nation with a claim to it. However, neither are we Pan-Africanists who simply claim Africa as our homeland without having any responsibility to fight U.S. imperialism where we are—in the U.S. and elsewhere.

The struggle for dual and contending power by Africans within current U.S. borders under the leadership of our Party is a revolutionary method of fracturing the territorial integrity of the U.S. white settler state. It is also a means of seizing the political, ideological, organizational and economic platform necessary for the practical exercise of incipient black state power.

This understanding enhances the Party's presence throughout the African colony. Our local offices, as discussed in Chapter VI, become the instruments for exercising power *and* influence within our colonized nation from bases among the African working class, the real source of revolutionary power when organized in its own independent revolutionary Party.

We contribute to the defeat of imperialism, the liberation of Africa and the toiling masses of the world by fighting where we are for genuine dual power as part of the strategy for total African liberation. We must make every colonized African community ungovernable by the colonial state. This is what dual power means. It can also be described as d-u-e-l power, a struggle for actual black state power at the expense of the white nationalist U.S. state.

We are materialists. We understand that power occupies space: territorial, ideological, political and organizational. It has been this recognition of the practical requirement for territory that has befuddled and compromised some of the "honest opportunists" whose worldviews are limited by imagination and influenced by petty bourgeois class interests.

Our position stands in opposition to those who adhere to what is known as the "Black Belt South" line, which purports that several U.S. southern states with a high concentration of Africans constitute the land base of a "Negro nation." This is sometimes characterized even today as a "New Afrikan" nation when its borders are defined as five contiguous states in the South.

Those who adhere to the Five-State position are opportunists because they liquidate the struggle for Africa in favor of a presumed short-term victory of a limited land conquest. Often it is these opportunists who are most eager to characterize our Party's struggle for dual power, to transform every African community into fighting soviets for the liberation of Africa and Africans worldwide, as hypocritical. Indeed, misery does love company.

Our point is that the struggle for dual power and the Five-State position are diametrically opposed. We begin with the recognition that this land mass under the illegitimate authority of the U.S. colonial settler state is the land of the Indigenous people, period. For us the question of dual power is the means by which we, Africans on this stolen land, are able to establish actual political bases from which to more effectively make the struggle to win our liberation as a step toward the total liberation and unification of Africa and African people.

In *The Struggle for Bread, Peace and Black Power* we dedicated two chapters to this question:

> *The theoretical question concerning land is significant as it identifies the land base which must be liberated in order to achieve our historical mission of national liberation and national consolidation. That land base is obviously Africa. It is within Africa that the question of nationality is to be resolved. The Black Belt South position and all its variations attempt to graft a bourgeois inclination onto our movement through the use of the national question in a manner which can only mean that our struggle is purely one to achieve land ownership.*
>
> *A genuine revolutionary nationalist struggle for land is a struggle which is designed to remove the blocks which prevent the historical process of liberation and national consolidation from occurring. These blocks are the various forms of colonialism which prevent Africa from being liberated and united under socialism. These forms of colonialism utilize the various Western and U.S. economies to suck Africa dry and to extract super profits*[5] *from African workers through employment of the*

5 Today we understand that what is called "super profits" are the normal profits extracted from African people. What is normal under colonial capitalism is what happens to African people and colonized people, not what happens to white workers.

> *Western and U.S. state apparatuses in destructive opposition to the weakly-formed or non-existing African state apparatuses. The colonial conditions of African people in the U.S. are an extension of the colonialism in Africa which began with the European scramble for Africa immediately following the cessation of the slave trade.*[6]

It is important to note that the discussion of what has been called the "national question" by Marxists and other militants was mostly used to limit the struggles of Africans and other colonial subjects. *Our* entry into this discussion was another case of responding to the material conditions we suffer in the real world and how these conditions are affected by the crisis of imperialism as it represents itself today.

The ridiculous assertion that some portion of the land within current U.S. borders is the national homeland of African people has serious implications for our struggle. It is a position that unites with the U.S. government attack on the Indigenous people who continue to struggle based on the theft of their land and relegation to concentration camps known as "Indian reservations." It also deflects the struggle of African people from our mission to liberate and unite Africa and Africans the world over.

This assertion makes ours a struggle for land possession as opposed to the revolutionary overthrow of world capitalism that stems from the enslavement of Africans and the theft of the land of the Indigenous people. Again, we make an uncompromising statement that the land of the Americas is the land of the Indigenous people.

We also recognize that struggle within current U.S. borders and other places within the Americas is an obligation of the African Revolution. Again, we must fight for revolution

---

6 Yeshitela. *The Struggle for Bread, Peace and Black Power*, p. 47.

wherever we are located. Specifically, our forced location in the Americas means that the African Revolution itself has a front in the Americas, not only in the U.S. but in the Caribbean, Brazil and throughout Central and South America.

In other words, Africa is our national homeland, but we are also part of the Revolution of the Americas. The struggle of the Indigenous people is our struggle also. This recognition sets a principled basis for the combined, strategic relationship between African and Indigenous peoples against white settler colonialism.

African people are one nation forcibly dispersed around the world

Our Party, using the historical materialist method of investigation and analysis, concluded that black people within current U.S. borders are Africans, an integral part of a forcibly-dispersed nation. National oppression and subjugation is not something that is resolved through integrating into the system of the colonizing nation. It is resolved through emancipation from the grasp of our predatory, parasitic colonizers.

The recognition of Africans globally and within the U.S. being one nation is longstanding. One hundred years ago, African nationality was summed up in the declaration by Marcus Garvey: "Africa for Africans...at home and abroad." Garvey's Movement was embodied in the Universal Negro Improvement Association and African Communities League (UNIA-ACL) with its millions of members stretching across the globe.

It was the largest material manifestation of the recognition by black people worldwide that, indeed, we are one nation of people dispersed around the world through violence and coercion.

In a report from the New York chapter of the UNIA-ACL at the First International Convention of the Negro Peoples of the

World in 1920, New York delegate Mrs. Sarah Branch stated: "We are tired of being called Negroes. We are not Negroes. We are Africans. [Applause] We want to be called Africans. God gave us the name Ethiopians, and we want to be called Ethiopians or Africans. Negro is simply a pet name that the white man when he went to Africa and stole our foreparents gave us. Let us all in this convention with one voice cry out, 'We will not be called Negroes any longer, but Africans!'"[7]

However, we cannot overlook the fact that there is a large sector of African people around the world that finds itself endowed with false national consciousness imposed by our colonial oppressors. We exist as hyphenated people everywhere: We are Afro-Germans, Black-Brits and Afro-Americans, Afro-Colombians, etc. On the continent of Africa, we have assumed the identity associated with the European-controlled-and-named territories created for exploitation of our people and resources.

We are one Africa and one nation. The Party's analysis of our unified African national identity is one of the most significant contributions we have made to the African Revolution. This is why the entire chapter on the African nation from *An Uneasy Equilibrium* is definitive and is included in this Political Report. It is the responsibility of every cadre to fully understand and be fluent in our position on the African nation.

Our salvation depends on our rejection of the false national consciousness imposed on Africans by colonial capitalism. Our struggle has always been for power and self-government. This is one of the reasons why it is necessary to abandon the liberal fight against racism, an idea in white people's heads. We must fight for our liberation as a nation.

7 Hill, Robert, Editor. *The Marcus Garvey and Universal Negro Improvement Association Papers, Volume II.* p. 517. University of California Press, Berkeley, 1983.

African Internationalism contains the only definition of the emergence of the modern nation that makes any sense, not just in general, abstract terms, but in the context of the world in which we live and struggle to end our oppressive relationship with colonial capitalism.

This definition of the African nation is also the basis for understanding the merger of the interests of the colonial ruling class and the white working class, both of which were born of colonial slavery. This is also an elaboration of the declaration by our Party that class struggle in the real world is concentrated in the struggle against colonialism. Otherwise there is no way to make sense of the deep unity to be found between the white ruling class and the white working class.

This theoretical understanding disproves the assumption by Marx and most European and European-influenced communists that there is a historically-determined material basis for the unity of what they describe as the international working class against the international capitalist rulers. The contrived confusion of the Europeans—Marxists included—on this question lends to ideological and political stupefaction.

It is confusion fueled by class interests. It is confusion that once honestly confronted must necessarily lead to the proper conclusion that any struggle for communism or historical progress must submit to the leadership of the African working class-led national liberation movement. Anything else results in nothing more than white rights gained at the expense of the rest of us.

The essential class contradiction here is between the total white oppressor nation and the colonized rest of us, African workers included.

The masses overwhelmingly chose Garvey

What is often referred to as the "national question" by Marxists and other leftists, especially within current U.S.

borders, only became a "question" because of the need for ammunition to discredit the Garvey Movement.

With the 1922 arrest of Garvey, assisted by the Communist Party USA along with W.E.B. Du Bois and others who had ideological differences with him, the material evidence of the universality of the African nation was temporarily obscured. Thus in Africa and around the world today we are still known as Ghanaians, Somalis, Ivorians, Cameroonians and other imaginary, contrived nationalities such as New Afrikans in the U.S.

These false identities rob our Revolution of its inherent power and are further evidence of the correctness of our political line. Only African Internationalism solves the problems associated with having to come up with hundreds of separate identities (more than 50 in Africa alone) to win what should be a single struggle for national liberation.

African Internationalism teaches us that black people everywhere are part of a single African nation with the responsibility of opening up fronts for the total liberation of Africa and African people worldwide.

While African Internationalism solves the issue of African nationality, it does not deny that Africans, like all peoples, have other identities as well. We are attached to different ethnic groups; we have diverse religions, speak different languages and identify with different regions in Africa and the world. African Internationalism shows us, however, that our primary identity is as Africans! This helps us to achieve strategic loyalty—loyalty to the greater good for all our people regardless of religion, ethnicity, language and other identities of lesser significance.

In the U.S. this gives us the additional ability to overcome the psychology of "minority" politics. It connects our Revolution to the more than one and a half billion other Africans locked in the same struggle.

It also exposes the neo-Zionist nature of the Black Belt South line introduced in the 1920s into our movement by the Communist International and Communist Party USA to attack Garvey in the first place.

The Black Belt South claim that black people colonized in the U.S. have been transformed into a new nation meant that the Communist Party could vie for the membership of Africans whose unity with Garvey revealed such a strong aspiration for African national identity and unification. In fact, it was the Garvey Movement and the demand by Africans for national liberation that forced the Communist Party USA to admit that there *was* such a thing as an African nation within the current borders of the U.S.

It was only in 1928, nine years after its founding, that the CPUSA spoke of our people as a nation.

The discovery of a "Negro nation" in the Black Belt South was made in a miserably unsuccessful attempt to recruit Africans into the Communist Party. The communists were intimidated by the power of the worldwide Garvey Movement. Nevertheless, the contrived Black Belt South position never organized Africans. CP organizers complained that Africans were not coming into the party despite its new slogan calling for self-determination for the "Negro nation."

As one account stated, the Black Belt South position "did not receive wide support from African Americans [sic], either in the urban north or in the South...While the party continued to give lip service to the goal of national self-determination for blacks, particularly in its theoretical writings, it largely ignored that demand in its practical work."[8]

The Party's position has actually been tested in the real world. There was a time when the African masses had the opportunity to choose between the Black Belt South line,

---

8 "The Communist Party USA and African Americans," *Wikipedia.org.*

integrationism or assimilation and the movement of Marcus Garvey. The test with Garvey was made by the CP-supported African Blood Brotherhood and the Pan-Africanist project of W.E.B. Du Bois. The masses overwhelmingly chose Garvey.

This unwillingness of Africans to join the Communist Party was interpreted by some to mean that Africans did not want self-determination. This was joy to the ears of the handful of African CPUSA members who were apparently attracted to the Communist Party because it represented a militant assimilationist politic that satisfied their own personal aspirations.

The concession of black nationality by the Communist Party USA spoke of our "right to self-determination," a "right" that would be granted by the new post-revolutionary socialist state under the leadership of the industrial (white!) workers. The Africans would be recognized as a nation that could realize self-determination through the authority of a multinational (white) workers' state.

According to the CPUSA, Africans would improve our conditions of existence essentially through the historically white nationalist trade unions, which were united with their bosses in keeping African people unemployed or underemployed. The unions physically fought us as "scabs" when we sought work while white workers were on strike, demanding African workers maintain solidarity with sectors of the oppressor nation conveniently identified as workers.

While we were to be slaves of trade unionism, the real *political* leadership of our people would come from the multinational, colonizer-controlled Communist Party. We would fight for higher wages and better working conditions under colonialism, but the colonizer-controlled Communist Party would handle the critical political questions. After the revolution, Africans in the Black Belt South could achieve the "right to self-determination" according to the whim of the white workers who would now become the new colonial ruling class. Socialist colonialism!

Black Belt South position is opportunist, comparable to Zionism

African Internationalism recognizes the African working class as the primary force for revolution, the force that will finally bring real communism to the world, benefitting Africans and all the toiling masses. African Internationalism informs us that the African working class must have its own, independent, revolutionary Party. Only such a party can guarantee the self-determination of the African nation and determine what the African nation is, based on the needs, aspirations and objectively and scientifically defined interests of African people.

The Black Belt South concept was an opportunistic contrivance when it was created nearly a hundred years ago. It continues to be philosophical opportunism today in its new designation developed by the Provisional Government of the Republic of New Afrika. The "New Afrikan" designation is also gladly accepted by some U.S.-based African communists.

This is a political line comparable to that of the European settlers who have claimed the land of the Palestinian people, originally under the guise of white socialism, renaming it Israel and themselves Israelis. The whites who occupied Southern Africa made the same claims to our land there. In South Africa, the Dutch colonizers even renamed themselves Afrikaners. In what is now called the "Americas," Europeans gave themselves a similar designation as "Americans."

The theft of land in each instance by European settlers was central to exploitation and oppression that have yet to be overcome. In South Africa, what is being called liberation is simply domestic neocolonialism. In reality, the land and resources are controlled by a handful of whites that effectively transformed a handful of petty bourgeois Africans into managers of resources mostly owned and controlled by white power.

In Israel, or Occupied Palestine, the white nationalist settler colonial state also functions as a military outpost for the U.S., itself a settler state. Israel has violated every semblance of international law through expanding violence against Palestinians and incessant annexation of Palestinian and Arab lands.

Ours is a just struggle. We do not have to create a political line that inadvertently legitimizes the theft of Palestinian land by European settlers. Since the beginning of the work on this Political Report, the Israeli Defense Forces have, on one occasion, publically murdered 60 unarmed Palestinians and wounded more than a thousand to reinforce their colonial control. This is how Zionism looks. It is necessary whenever there is an illegitimate annexation or theft of the land of the oppressed.

In the same way, the Black Belt South line places our movement for the liberation of our people in objective unity with the ongoing oppression of the Indigenous people within current U.S. borders. This remains true notwithstanding the offensive claim by black Zionists that the genocide of the Indigenous people has sufficiently reduced their population to such an extent that it would be impractical to concede the land to them. This is a position that settler colonizers always use to justify the occupation and theft of the land and resources of others.

We reiterate: the African People's Socialist Party stands in unwavering solidarity with the Indigenous people of the Americas in the struggle for their land.

We recognize that Indigenous people include the Spanish-speaking residents south of the stolen southern border of the U.S. who are known by an assortment of names because of European colonization of the landmass known as the Americas.

Our Party's uncompromising solidarity with the Indigenous people is the only way our struggle can have integrity. We are not their enemies. We will not add the extra burden onto their already Herculean struggle of having to defend themselves from an incursion of Africans contending with other settler colonialists for possession of their land.

With our Party's position, our relationship with the Indigenous people can work out all the questions concerning the dispensation of the material and human resources created on this stolen land by colonially enslaved Africans.

Because of African Internationalism the integrity of our national liberation struggle under the leadership of the Party of the African working class will not be sacrificed on the altar of the false god of New Afrikanism. African Internationalism also makes it unnecessary for our people and our struggle to labor in isolation from each other anywhere on Earth.

Africans must fight for Africa no matter where we are

The fact that we are One Africa! One Nation! means we can fight for the liberation of Africa wherever we are. In Germany and other places in Europe where we are located, it is no longer necessary to define our struggle as a fight to be accepted as Europeans. Nor, for that matter, are we without options in the U.S. Because we understand the true nature of our struggle for national liberation, we can be in all these places and fight for the liberation and unity of Africa, our Motherland, as our common strategic objective.

With African Internationalism and the African People's Socialist Party, our people and movement don't have to assume we have to find some kind of compromised future in hostile and foreign lands. We are empowered to fight for

Africa no matter where we are and no matter what short term struggles are dictated by our immediate physical location.

To accept a designation as New Afrikans or as Bahamians or Black Brits is to doom our struggle to failure. It is to ignore the fact that our oppressive conditions of existence everywhere stem from the initial European attack on Africa that condemned Africa to a critical loss of population and a state of poverty, violence and ignorance. It is to ignore the fact that our condition and status, wherever we are, owe themselves to the initial attack on Africa that placed our national homeland under the boot of foreign, imperialist domination.

Even if we were to concede to New Afrikans the possibility of liberating an isolated five states in the U.S. as our national homeland, how does that contribute to ending the imperialist-imposed misery on Africa and the rest of the African world? The Five-State "solution" is an attempt to solve the problems of Africans in the U.S. at the expense of the liberation and unification of Africa and all Africans under revolutionary working class leadership. This is one reason we say that the Five-State solution is philosophical opportunism which, by the way, can only result in opportunist practice.

The Five-State position would have us voluntarily create a nation surrounded by highly armed, imperialist thugs that are notorious for murder and brigandage throughout the world. The purpose of revolution is to surround the enemy, not to be voluntarily surrounded!

Our presence in the U.S. and other places of forced dispersal denies Africa the benefit of our physical presence as producers for Africa. Our refusal to recognize the critical strategic objective of uniting Africa and Africans worldwide, denies Africa the wealth and value that we have created for white power throughout the Americas and the world.

This is why the African Internationalist demand for reparations is a response to the initial imperialist attack made on Africa and must be seen as a revolutionary demand.

Any economic advancement or "catch-up" for Africa will require Africa's ability to wage revolutionary struggle within the U.S. and the other centers of imperialist development rooted in slavery and colonialism.

A revolutionary objective of the African Revolution must be to return to Africa the stolen value wrenched from Africa. This is the revolutionary pursuit of reparations. We will do this from every front of the African Revolution, especially the U.S. and Europe. But also from Canada, Australia, South Africa and everywhere else we have, either directly or indirectly, created life for Europe and other exploiters at the expense of African development.

Comrades, the African Socialist International (ASI) is a practical, material manifestation of our philosophy of African Internationalism. It is the African People's Socialist Party writ large throughout the world. It is living proof of the failure of imperialist white power to permanently separate Africans from our resources and our identity as a single people.

In *An Uneasy Equilibrium,* the Political Report to the Sixth Party Congress in 2013, we clarified:

> *Developing the African Socialist International (ASI) is the strategic heart of our work and one of our greatest challenges. The African Socialist International is our organization of African People's Socialist Party formations on the ground every place in the world where African people are located.*[9]

9 Yeshitela, Omali. *An Uneasy Equilibrium: The African Revolution versus Parasitic Capitalism,* p. 282. Burning Spear Publications, 2014.

This is the strategic heart of our work because it addresses both the root of the contradictions confronting Africans worldwide and the road to our liberation as the African nation.

As the worldwide organization of the Party, the ASI manifests the reality of the African nation including Africans on the continent of Africa and those forcibly dispersed throughout the world. Today it is only the African Socialist International that concretely provides the dispersed African nation with a common identity.

The ASI arms the international African working class with the revolutionary science and organization to fight successfully for our liberation everywhere we are located. Through the ASI we are organizing the Advanced Detachment of the African Revolution throughout the world. We are providing the organizational, ideological and political training that we require to win.

During the height of the anti-colonial struggles in Africa in the 1960s the then-Soviet Union chose what it determined to be the "Authentic Six"[10] anti-colonial organizations. These were organizations that the Soviet Union provided with ideological, political, military and other kinds of training and material resources.

That left other anti-colonial organizations to have to contend not only with direct imperialist white power, but also with the "Authentic Six" whose strength was often determined by support from the Soviet Union, which was motivated by its own material and policy interests.

With the ASI, Africans ourselves can determine the legitimacy of revolutionary anti-colonial movements and organizations based solely on *our* self-defined interests. These interests include the leadership of the African working class

10 The "Authentic Six" included the MPLA in Angola, PAIGC in Guinea and Cape Verde, ANC in Occupied Azania, SWAPO in Southwest Africa, ZAPU in Zimbabwe, FRELIMO in Mozambique.

and opposition to all borders separating Africans in Africa and elsewhere. With the ASI we can measure the legitimacy of any anti-colonial movement or organization by its commitment to the total liberation and unification of Africa and African people worldwide under the leadership of the African working class organized in its own independent African People's Socialist Party.

The European assault on Africa played the critical role in the development of capitalism and global white power. For more than 600 years, since Portugal began the capture and commercial sale of African people in the 1400s, Europeans have been joined by others in the ongoing looting of Africa that has survived despite the formal end of colonial slavery. Colonialism continues up to now. Lorries, trains and ships are removing wealth from Africa in an unending process that contributes to the upkeep of capitalism at the expense of the life and wellbeing of African people in Africa and worldwide.

Capitalism was born and will die in Africa

Today, the U.S., all of Europe, Israel, Canada and other European settler states, along with China, Japan, India, Turkey and any other ambitious would-be capitalist power, are concentrated in Africa like leeches enjoying a feeding frenzy.

This concentration of strategic, global capitalist interests in Africa is immeasurably important for the defeat of capitalism as a world system. A "single grenade" will destroy the entire system! Africa was the critical factor in the advent of capitalism.

Comrades! Sisters! Brothers! Amafrika! The African Socialist International allows Africans to play our historically pre-determined role to destroy imperialism. Capitalism, born through imperialist intervention in Africa, will die in Africa! The ASI provides Africa the tool to slay colonial capitalism and liberate all of Africa and the oppressed and exploited of the world from the forcibly imposed cruelty that has imprisoned humanity for the last several hundred years.

The British colonizer Cecil Rhodes understood the significance of Africa to imperialism way back in the 19th century. Rhodes became the single individual most responsible for the white stranglehold on Southern Africa, where territories known as "Rhodesia" and South Africa were conquered with high-tech weapons of the day that allowed the white colonial interlopers to murder thousands of Africans in a single afternoon before sitting down for dinner with champagne and roast beef.

In 1917 V.I. Lenin quoted Rhodes on the significance of imperialism for the development of Europe. While this quote by Lenin spoke of imperialism in general, the role that Rhodes played in Africa makes clear the significance of Africa in his plans. Says Rhodes:

> *I was in the East End of London (working class quarter) yesterday and attended a meeting of the unemployed. I listened to the wild speeches, which were just a cry for "bread, bread!" and on my way home I pondered over the scene and I became more than ever convinced of the importance of imperialism.... My cherished idea is a solution for the social problem, i.e., in order to save the 40,000,000 inhabitants of the United Kingdom from a bloody civil war, we colonial statesmen must acquire new lands to settle the surplus population, to provide new markets for the goods produced in the factories and mines. The Empire, as I have always said, is a*

> *bread and butter question. If you want to avoid civil war, you must become imperialists.*[11]

Years earlier, writing in Volume I of *Capital*, Karl Marx explained the advent of capitalism quite simply:

> *The discovery of gold and silver in America, the extirpation, enslavement and entombment in mines of the aboriginal population, the beginning of the conquest and looting of the East Indies, the turning of Africa into a warren for the commercial hunting of black-skins, signalised the rosy dawn of the era of capitalist production. These idyllic proceedings are the chief momenta of primitive accumulation.*[12]

Africa has always been central to the development and maintenance of capitalism. This is why Africa will also be central to its destruction. Quoting Marx further we made this statement in *One People! One Party! One Destiny!*, the Political Report to our Fifth Congress in July 2010:

> *Hence, we understand that a key function of the revolutionary struggle for the permanent defeat of imperialism and to liberate Africa and her scattered children is the reunification of African people worldwide into a revolutionary, proletarian nation.*
>
> *"It is slavery that gave the colonies their value; it is the colonies that created world trade, and it is world trade that is the precondition of large scale industry." These words by Marx recognize the role of the plunder of Africa in the establishment of capitalism and carry within them the suggestion*

11 Lenin, V.I. *Imperialism, the Highest Stage of Capitalism*, p. 93. Foreign Language Publishing House, Moscow, 1952.

12 Marx, Karl. *Capital: A Critique of Political Economy, Volume 1*, p. 751. International Publishers, New York, 1967.

> *of what it will take to destroy the capitalist world economy. The Africans who gave value to the "colonies" are now the oppressed and exploited inhabitants of the colonies that are sometimes referred to as nations.*[13]

The Political Report to the Fifth Congress reads further:

> *Our revolutionary struggle for liberation, unification and socialism in Africa, throughout the "colonies" and other areas of the world to which we have been forcibly dispersed in the construction of capitalism will prove to be as significant in the defeat of the capitalist social system as the slave trade was in its advent.*
>
> *The socialist liberation and unification of Africa and African people under the leadership of the African working class will be the central factor in the defeat of world capitalism and will provide the material basis for the advent of world socialism.*
>
> *African Internationalism, which demands the total revolutionary liberation and unification of Africa and African people worldwide under the leadership of the African working class, is informed by this scientifically sound dialectic.*
>
> *Hence, the African Internationalist struggle for the liberation and unification of Africa and African people is at the same time the key factor in the achievement of socialism as a world economy. It is the way forward for those Marxists and other socialists who are confronted with the false*

13 Yeshitela, Omali. *One People! One Party! One Destiny! The Political Report to the Fifth Congress of the African People's Socialist Party-USA*, p. 53. Burning Spear Publications, 2010.

> *conundrum surrounding the question of "socialism in one country."*
>
> *As capitalism was born as a world economy with its basis in the enslavement and dispersal of African people, leading to [as Marx wrote] "considerable masses of capital and labor power in the hands of producers," so, too, will socialism be born as a world economy in the process of reversing the verdict of imperialism.*
>
> *Hence, socialism will not be born in one country, but in many countries that are tied to the defining economy of a liberated Africa and people under the revolutionary leadership of the African working class.*
>
> *This is why a fundamental task of the African revolutionary is the consolidation of the proletarian African nation.*[14]

Although there are some Africans—"communists" and otherwise—who do not understand the significance of the statements of both Cecil Rhodes and Karl Marx, the U.S. government and other capitalists on-the-make have a very clear understanding of the critical role that Africa plays in the development and survival of capitalism. This is increasingly being revealed by heightened imperialist military activity in Africa, where at least a third of the entire world's known reserves of mineral resources lie beneath its soil.

U.S. expands military presence in Africa

The French have military forces that are active in at least 14 different French neocolonies, but the most noteworthy imperialist military presence in Africa is that of the U.S., which has created a special command force that is solely dedicated

14 Ibid.

to the entire continent. The Africa Command or AFRICOM has the responsibility for crushing any independent political or military activity that might threaten U.S. domination of Africa.

AFRICOM is also in Africa as the muscular threat to China and other challengers to U.S. hegemony on the African continent that is the birthright of Africans the world over.

Nick Turse is a prolific writer reporting on U.S. military intervention in Africa. He has played an important role in exposing what he refers to as a massive "shadow war" on the Continent. In an article for *Vice.com*, Turse wrote:

> *Six years ago, a deputy commanding general for U.S. Army Special Operations Command gave a conservative estimate of 116 missions being carried out at any one time by Navy SEALS, Army Green Berets, and other special operations forces across the globe.*
>
> *Today, according to U.S. military documents obtained by VICE News, special operators are carrying out nearly 100 missions at any given time—in Africa alone. It's the latest sign of the military's quiet but ever-expanding presence on the continent, one that represents the most dramatic growth in the deployment of America's elite troops to any region of the globe.*
>
> *In 2006, just 1 percent of all U.S. commandos deployed overseas were in Africa. In 2010, it was 3 percent. By 2016, that number had jumped to more than 17 percent. In fact, according to data supplied by U.S. Special Operations Command, there are now more special operations personnel devoted to Africa than anywhere except the Middle East—1,700 people spread out across 20 countries dedicated*

> *to assisting the U.S. military's African partners in their fight against terrorism and extremism.[sic]*
>
> *"At any given time, you will find SOCAFRICA conducting approximately 96 activities in 20 countries," Donald Bolduc, the U.S. Army general who runs the special operations command in Africa (SOCAFRICA), wrote in an October 2016 strategic planning guidance report.*[15]

The number of U.S. military forces in Africa and their activities has grown considerably since this article was written. Several months following this article, four U.S. Special Operations forces were killed in Niger in an apparent firefight that has never been satisfactorily explained to the world, much of which was surprised to learn that U.S. troops were fighting in that area of the globe.

U.S., French, Israeli and even NATO forces are in Africa in a more pronounced way only because they are more reliable arms of the imperialist state than the neocolonial forces the imperialists have normally depended on.

These forces are the armies of the African neocolonial flunkies that brutalize and control African people to facilitate ongoing imperialist looting of Africa that has been going on for more than 500 years. The neocolonial governments are themselves arms of the white nationalist imperialist state. Their purpose is to protect the colonial status quo that bleeds and starves Africa and our people for European benefit.

The European colonial powers continue to depend on looting a prostrate Africa for their benefit. The U.S. holds the commanding height in this process because of its superior military capacity and economic strength. However, China, India and even Turkey have joined in on the feeding frenzy. And, like Cecil Rhodes, they all expect to either rescue

15 Turse, Nick. "The war you've never heard of," *Vice.com*, May 18, 2017.

themselves from dimming fortunes or project themselves up the ladder of imperialist significance through further, deeper exploitation of Africa.

The state of Israel is another example of a white colonial power thrusting itself into history at the expense of others, in this case, Palestinians.

Let them all deploy in Africa! Every capitalist power in the world. Again, it is in Africa, the place of its birth, that capitalism will die. To paraphrase a statement attributed to African mothers contending with wayward children, we will say to world capitalism, "We brought you into the world and we will take you out!"

African resources are critical for the successful functioning of the most advanced capitalist countries. According to the "Mineral industry of Africa" entry on *Wikipedia.org*, in addition to containing 30 percent of the Earth's remaining mineral resources Africa's bounty includes 89 percent of the planet's gold, 92 percent of platinum and 87 percent of coltan, along with petroleum, titanium, cobalt, copper and uranium. There are also fish, timber, tobacco, cocoa and many agricultural products.[16]

This only touches the very tip of the resource mountain that is the 12 million square miles of Africa. But it is enough to illustrate that when influenced by a strong, organized Party of the African working class, the ability of Africa to shut down capitalist production worldwide is real!

The ASI will choke capitalism's resource lifeline

Only the ASI, rooted in the African working class throughout Africa and globally, will be able to coordinate our struggle for liberation, choking off capitalism's resource lifeline, stopping production in every critical area.

16 *2005 Minerals Yearbook Africa*, U.S. Geological Survey, 2007, https://minerals.usgs.gov/minerals/pubs/country/2005/myb3-sum-2005-africa.pdf

We are also the workers in the mines and on the docks. We drive the lorries and trains ferrying away Africa's resources to Europe, the U.S. and elsewhere.

Organized through the ASI we can force the colonizers to fend for themselves.

They will have to fight their own parasitic wars.

They can clean their own toilets and houses. They can have and tend their own children, cook food for themselves and even learn to sing and dance and make music and do all the things they have been able to take for granted because of the ever-present, multi-talented African colonial servant, sometimes called "citizen" during periods of colonial generosity.

African workers are everywhere. The only thing that is missing is organization. And the African Socialist International is fast solving this problem.

Obviously we will have to overturn every aspect of neocolonialism that allows for indirect rule of capital by a local or domestic African managerial class, white power in black face.

These preening neocolonialists are pissing on the graves of Garvey, Lumumba, Nkrumah, Sankara, Winnie Mandela, Dedan Kimathi, Sobukwe and the host of other patriotic African men and women who attempted to rescue Our Africa and our people from the hellish existence forced on us by colonial capitalism.

Through the ASI the African working class must fast organize to become the new ruling class of Africa. We must prepare to govern in the interests of Africa and its majority working class and poor peasantry.

This is the significance of the ASI. We provide the revolutionary organization of the African working class throughout the African continent and beyond. We will provide the ability for Africa to engage the capitalist in a continental-wide guerrilla war.

Located throughout Africa and the world, the ASI has the ability to draw the imperialists deep into the Continent, surround and harass them, close enough to neutralize their technological superiority and, as the Vietnamese taught us, "grab them by the belt" in a ground war. Malcolm X told us and the Vietnamese showed us, the white man can never win a ground war when faced with ideologically steeled, patriotic, determined and organized revolutionaries.

Moreover, African Internationalists are everywhere Africans are. As we stated in the Manifesto of the African Socialist International, written and adopted at a 2000 ASI Conference in London, eighteen and a half years ago:

> *African people throughout the world are rising up. We have entered into the new millennium in motion, struggling to overturn the 500-year legacy of oppression and exploitation to which we have been subjected by a parasitic social system born at our expense.*
>
> *We are fighting to reclaim our destiny as a single people whose forced dispersal in a world defined by artificial borders has served to undermine our common identity and dilute our collective strength.*
>
> *We are everywhere! We are in Chicago, Illinois; in Florida, Texas, California and New York and throughout the United States in North America, as well as Toronto and Montreal in Canada. We are in Brasilia in Brazil, Caracas in Venezuela, Bluefields in Nicaragua, in Central and South America. We are in Trinidad, Haiti, Jamaica, Guadeloupe, Martinique, Dominica, The Bahamas, Cuba, Puerto*

> *Rico, the Dominican Republic, Barbados and all the islands of the Caribbean.*
>
> *We are in London, Birmingham, Manchester, Liverpool and Nottingham in England. We are in Paris, Lille, Lyons, Marseilles and Nice in France. We are in Brussels, Belgium; Amsterdam, Holland; Berlin, Germany; Rome, Italy; as well as Spain, Portugal, Russia, Turkey and all of Eastern Europe.*
>
> *We reside in the hundreds of millions in our ancient Motherland, which was the birthplace of humankind more than 150,000 years ago and which served as the cradle of human civilization more than 10,000 years ago...*[17]

This is our strength when organized under the leadership of our revolutionary Party armed with the only advanced revolutionary theory that speaks to the crisis of imperialism stemming from the growing changes in the parasitic economic base of international capitalism.

Africa and Africans are part of the world

African Internationalism and the African Socialist International free Africans from either political paralysis or inactivity. There are at least a million Africans living in Europe today, chased by violence and starvation, hopeless of any possibility for a decent life in Africa. Many attempt to secure some peace of mind by becoming cultural nationalists, extolling the virtues of African culture from afar, away from Africa. While some make a living from this cultural exhibition, others make cultural celebration a substitute for struggling for African liberation.

With African Internationalism, Africans are not limited to uniting with Africa by participating in support movements.

17 "African Socialist International Manifesto," 2000, *asiuhuru.org.*

We no longer need to focus on single issues such as disaster relief or opposition to the most recent African neocolonial election or European-organized coup. All Africans everywhere are now able to join with a common effort to liberate all of Africa from the deadly grasp of imperialism that colonizes us in Africa and in Berlin or Paris.

Comrades, African Internationalism is not only a theory of African people. Africa and Africans are part of the world. Our theory can be called scientific because it speaks to the liberation of Africans as part of the struggle of the peoples of the world in the international system of capitalism that came into existence through our colonial enslavement.

Our Party's understanding of the African nation requires that we build revolutionary dual power wherever we are located under the leadership of the ASI, in solidarity with the Indigenous people and other colonized peoples, to forward the strategy for the liberation of Africa and the emancipation of the toiling masses of the world.

This is our time!

The Party's presence in Africa, our Motherland, does more than anything else to validate our theory of African Internationalism within the African world and put to rest the petty bourgeois concept of the Black Belt South.

Today we should be suspicious of those whose ideological and political views cannot be implemented to the benefit of our people in the real world. The vision of Garvey's African Fundamentalism recognized Africa as our national homeland and the center of our future as a free people living in a highly developed society. This vision was made real through our own labor and implemented through the creation of a shipping line, factories, hotels, a host of other anti-colonial economic enterprises and features of dual power.

What is the program of the assimilationists? After more than 100 years we have yet to see anything. Their philosophy, based on integrating into the capitalist system of the oppressor nation, has never required them to delay their headlong rush to join with white colonial enterprises long enough to create an independent program of their own!

When challenged by Marcus Garvey about his program, or lack thereof, W.E.B. Du Bois answered, "The Pan-African Congress is for conference, acquaintanceship, and general organization. It has nothing to do with the so-called Garvey Movement and contemplates neither force nor revolution in its program. We have had the cordial cooperation of the French, Belgium and Portuguese governments and we hope to get the attention and sympathy of all colonial powers." [18]

Very telling!

The Pan-African concept continues to be the provenance of the African petty bourgeoisie.

It has always been used by the petty bourgeoisie to prevent the rise to power of the African working class that, allied with the poor peasantry, will create the new Africa that has full possession of its own resources, *human* and material, that have been used to fatten the coffers of imperialist white power at the expense of Our Africa.

African Internationalism is not something that relies on belief in some purely abstract theory. It is a theory of practice. In addition to our many dual power programs, the most visible evidence of this practice is the existence of the African Socialist International, the international Party of African liberation and socialism.

This is our time. During the era of Garvey, imperialism was strong, still on the ascendancy. Even so the UNIA made

---

18 Martin, Tony. *Race First: The Ideological and Organizational Struggles of Marcus Garvey and the Universal Negro Improvement Association*, p. 290. The Majority Press, 1986.

incredible advances in our struggle for liberation and national unification under the leadership of the organized African working class. Today, colonial capitalism is characterized by crisis that is spurred by near-universal, anti-colonial resistance and is undergoing a major, anxiety-inducing realignment of its gravitational center.

The struggle within the ruling class to alter the existing arrangement challenges the most powerful bloc of imperialist white power and reveals a major transformation in global capitalist relations that has within it the potential for another imperialist war to redivide the world.

The re-emerging resistance of oppressed peoples to colonial domination, the split among the imperialist rulers and the growth of the African Socialist International all deepen this crisis, this uneasy equilibrium.

This is one of the advantages we have over Garvey and the UNIA. History is our ally. This is our time, not to be squandered. These are the circumstances that demand that we live up to the requirements of the Advanced Detachment of the African nation, the Vanguard of the heroic African working class.

Arm the people with African Internationalism

Our most important task is to spread African Internationalism throughout Africa and the world. Arming the people with theory is the most important priority before us at this time. Even the development of organization must initially be designed to facilitate our spread of African Internationalism among the African working class, in every village, community, workplace, school and university, even prisons where our people are concentrated.

Where we have created organizations that are growing a political capacity we must organize study groups that can win African people to African Internationalism. This is the philosophy that promises Africa and Africans a future of prosperity free from colonial domination, direct or indirect. The African Internationalists who take on this responsibility are those who earn the right to be recognized as the Advanced Detachment.

Prior to our Seventh Congress we are organizing regional conferences, all over the world. In these regional conferences African people will come together under the leadership of the Party to discuss this Political Report, pass resolutions for the Congress that are relevant to the Africans within the region and, where appropriate, elect regional leaders of the Party to serve on our Party's Central Committee.

The regional conferences are also expected to develop plans and organization for spreading the Party throughout the region, whether in Southern Africa, Europe, the Caribbean, the U.S. or elsewhere.

The regional conferences will carry out the mandates of this Political Report for building the Party's political and organizational presence through the African Socialist International. The Seventh Congress will initiate the practice of our regional conferences as a permanent feature of spreading the ASI throughout Africa and the African world.

The development of the ideological, political and organizational capacity of our Party will provide us with the army of genuine revolutionaries, those who are most concerned with the rescue of Africa and our future from the clutches of imperialism. This is more important than the need of individual Africans to improve their immediate situation.

Some will be drawn to the Party because of our proven ability to create institutions that may solve some immediate problems, but the success of the Party will be determined by those Africans who can see a future for Africa and our people beyond their own personal pain.

The Party must not be seen as an NGO or ATM machine that can provide solutions within the existing colonial-capitalist system. Our dedication must be infectious; our philosophy, inspirational. This is what is so encouraging about the comrades building the Party in Occupied Azania (South Africa) and Kenya in East Africa. They have truly embraced the theory and are seriously engaged in taking African Internationalism out to the people in their regions.

We must organize resources to facilitate our political work in Africa. We must send some of our experienced organizers to work with these comrades for longer periods. Our Department of Agitation and Propaganda (DAP) must give special attention to the production and organized distribution of political education and training resources to Africa and throughout the African Socialist International regions.

The Department of Agit-Prop must also fight to build within each of the regional, national, provincial and local Party organizations. This deepened internal division of labor will maximize the spread of the Party and our philosophy. It will allow DAP to be in a state of perpetual reproduction throughout our structures. And, as we consolidate our ideological, political and organizational presence, we will also be organizing to govern through our strategy of creating dual and contending power.

It is also important for us to raise the profile of Comrade Luwezi Kinshasa, the Secretary General of the ASI and our Director of International Affairs. No one has done more practical, immediate work to build the Party in Europe. Although Luwezi is working without the direct benefit of the organizational infrastructure available to us in the U.S., he has organized in France, Belgium, Sweden and England, as well as in East, West and Southern Africa. His dedication, selflessness and ideological clarity are legendary within our Party and the Uhuru Movement. His writings on Africa are profound and prolific. He is a well-known and respected leader among the expatriate African population in Europe.

In *An Uneasy Equilibrium,* we laid out a detailed approach to developing the African Socialist International. It is an approach that has informed the work we have been doing since that time mostly under the leadership of Comrade Luwezi Kinshasa. We should continue to study and implement all the mandates laid out from all our congresses concerning the ASI.

Now, with the successful inclusion of the comrades in Kenya and Occupied Azania in the ASI work, we are in a much better place to lead the struggle for the total liberation and unification of Africa and African people under the leadership of the Advanced Detachment of the African Revolution.

We are successfully organizing the army of African Internationalist evangelists preparing to sweep through Africa and organize our people for the final offensive that will liberate Our Africa, emancipate the African working class and destroy the pedestal upon which rests the very foundation of colonial capitalism.

Only the Vanguard, the Advanced Detachment, can unite African people everywhere through the African Socialist International and bring victory to the African nation, the basis for the emergence of genuine world communism.

VI. The regional strategy

Putting dual power into practice

Our struggle against colonial capitalism must be rooted in the actual colonized territories that we occupy. This is the essence of dual and contending power. The victory of our Party will come as a consequence of our success in transforming every colonized African community into a conscious, active opponent of colonialism. We will take organization and ideological development to the heart of the African working class communities where the colonial contradictions are concentrated.

The reality of our theory of dual power will be made more obvious in this regional strategy that we will implement coming out of our Seventh Congress.

In the Political Report to the Party's 2017 Plenary, we began the discussion of the need for our regional work to function properly as a critical vehicle for the development of the Party and implementation of our political agenda.

Addressing the need for the Party to fight for our regional structure, the Political Report declared:

> *The leadership of our regional work based on the organizational structure of the "national" Party is something that has not been vigorously fought for within our Party. Again this is due in part to the limitations of our Party's National Secretary General.*
>
> *Nevertheless, the responsibility for leadership of the Party's regional work falls squarely on the shoulders of the regional leaders themselves. Going forward the Party must require a dedicated and demonstrably strict adherence to Party-building by the regional leaders. All of them. All the time.*

There are organizational manuals and organizational principles that must dominate the approach to this work and must be fought for in the strongest possible way. On a practical level we know the efficacy of our regional leadership by the number of cities and states that have the Party's presence. Our membership growth must reflect the numbers of the Party's journal, The Burning Spear, *sold monthly. The regional work must be reflected in the quantity and quality of regional participation in the Party's work and institutions.*

It will no longer be allowable for Party organizations to exist in name only. We must see growth and development. What is the quantity and quality of our membership? These are critical questions every committee or organizational leader will have to answer in order to validate their position and to continue in positions of leadership.

How can we explain, especially now when the people are actually clamoring for organization and resistance, why we have not grown our organizations and committees after years of existence?

What other practical means of measuring our regional work is applicable? This is even more important than our Plans of Action, which are meaningless if they are not actually used to guide practical work that we actually carry out. Practice is primary....

As fast as our Party is growing already, the development of our regional work and the presence of genuine regional leadership operating within the Party structures would provide our people and our Revolution with the army of cadres necessary to overturn our relationship with colonial capitalism forever.[1]

The regional structures must create organizational hubs from which Party growth and organization radiates.

For example, our European Regional Committee, currently led by Comrade Makda Yohannes from Sweden, has the responsibility for organizing the African People's Socialist Party Sweden. It is also responsible for organizing, building and leading the national Party, or Front, in the UK, France, Belgium, Finland, the Netherlands, Norway and all over Europe.

Similarly, the Caribbean Regional Committee, headquartered in The Bahamas, is not only responsible for building and leading the African People's Socialist Party in The Bahamas, but throughout the entire Caribbean region.

Continental Africa has also been divided up into geographical regions for the development and leadership of the different fronts of the Party existing within the various colonially-defined ill-formed territorial states.

The various Regional Committees provide the infrastructure for building and leading the Party all over the world. Regional leadership assumes the responsibility for spreading the Party ideologically, making African Internationalism the guiding worldview for the African masses within the region. The regional leadership puts the Party on the ground in the various neocolonial state territories and spreads the Party and our organizations throughout every village, city and province.

Coming up for a vote in this Seventh Congress is the restructuring and reduction of the number of Party regions within current borders of the U.S. Formerly, our regional

1 Yeshitela, Omali. *Putting Revolution Back on the Agenda: Political Report to the 2017 Plenary of the African People's Socialist Party*, apspuhuru.org/2017-plenary-political-report/

territories included the Southeast, Southwest, Northeast, Northwest, West Coast and Midwestern U.S.

Because some regions have a negligible African population within huge territories, we believe that our organizational and political work would be best served if we limited our regional designations to four: Northern, Southern, West Coast and Midwestern.

Too much of the regional Party work occurs without an overall plan. This must change and we must begin to view our regional work differently moving forward.

Building Party regions as political-economic hubs

Henceforth, each region must be recognized as a political-economic hub of the Party. Our regional political work must be forwarded as a manifestation of the economic trajectory of our Party toward self-determination. In other words, our political work is the anti-colonial representation of the struggle against economic dependency, the essential component of colonialism.

These regional political-economic hubs must inform our recruitment and membership drives and Party assignments. Our basic recruitment targets remain the same as laid out in the political reports to the past two congresses: African women, labor, students and prisoners. We must now be conscious of a real need to recruit and assign forces within the regions to facilitate the economic development, political promotion and protection of the institutions of our Party and Movement.

The economic component of the regional hubs of the Party, operating under the leadership of the Deputy Chair Ona Zené Yeshitela, whose office is responsible for all our economic work, would have the responsibility for building the Party's regional economic presence.

Each of the Party's regions must become custodians of the economic strategy of the Party for advancing this critical component of the anti-colonial struggle for self-reliance. Each of the regions would have the assignments of building the Party's economic work within its designated area of responsibility. In addition to the political work implicit in their presence, all our Uhuru Houses must become economic outlets for all the products from our related enterprises.

Currently, most of the Party's economic work is consolidated in specific institutions within the four regions being considered. The oldest Uhuru House community organizing center is located in Oakland, California in the Western region. Oakland is also the location of Uhuru Furniture & Collectibles and Uhuru Foods & Pies, two of our most successful economic enterprises that have been in place for three decades or more. Our economic institutions are also regular features at markets and fairs throughout the Oakland-San Francisco Bay Area.

St. Petersburg, Florida, in the Southern region, is also home to an Uhuru House and Uhuru Jiko, a commercial community kitchen that functions as an incubator for community enterprises. The TyRon Lewis Gym is also in St. Petersburg. Uhuru Foods & Pies has been a successful, longtime and highly respected participant in a local market there. The Southern region is also home to the Zenzele Consignment shop, an economic institution operated by the All African People's Development and Empowerment Project in Huntsville, Alabama.

Uhuru Furniture & Collectibles and the One Africa! One Nation! Marketplace are two important economic institutions in Philadelphia in the Northern region. In fact, Uhuru Furniture has been an economic and political fixture in the region for 25 years or more.

All of these institutions provide some employment and income to Africans within their respective regions. For example, in Philadelphia alone, scores of Africans have been able to create successful businesses from vending at the One Africa! One Nation! Marketplace. When including the numbers of Africans benefitting from their relationship to our economic institutions in Florida, they probably amount to many more in business creation and employment. Our economic enterprises are also anti-colonial political institutions that constantly win practical support for the issues confronting the international African community, especially those of reparations and anti-colonial economic development.

We are constantly reminded of the significance of these institutions. They are concrete manifestations of our theory and their implementation under the leadership of Deputy Chair's Office is an important example of the unity between the political and the economic. Now, the Party truism that "politics is simply concentrated economics," must be better understood and more consciously reflected in every aspect of our work.

We must build all our work, beginning with the regions, as reflections of our intent to seize control of the productive forces of the cruelly oppressed and exploited, colonized African nation. This is what is meant by the total liberation of Africa and African people worldwide. This is what is meant, ultimately, by winning self-determination. This is what is meant by the adage that there is no political self-determination without economic self-reliance.

Our political objective to liberate Africa and African people is a statement of our intent to achieve the economic capacity to produce and reproduce real life, something that cannot happen as long as Africa and Africans are forced to endure colonial captivity by foreign and alien powers—colonialism.

The leadership for all our work is located within the Central Committee. The Party will now confer legitimacy on the regional structures and work by learning to successfully integrate the work of the entire Central Committee to that end. Up to now, the Party's regional work has occurred in a vacuum of sorts, with an inferred assumption that the success of that work depended solely on the respective leading Regional Committee.

However, every regional leader sits on the Party's Central Committee that is responsible for carrying out the mandates from our congresses and planning much of our work. This helps us to understand that regional Party work is part and parcel of our international work.

The Secretary General also sits on our Central Committee, along with the Deputy Chair who leads the Party's economic work. All the leaders of our mass work—InPDUM, ANWO, AAPDEP, etc.—also occupy seats on the Central Committee.

Along with the Department of Agitation and Propaganda, headquarters of the production and distribution of Party ideology, the regional leaders and other Central Committee members are key to how the Party's integration of human and material resources will be achieved under the leadership of the Chair.

With the strategy of turning the regions into political and economic hubs, we will see an exponential leap in the production and distribution of Party and Party-related economic products and influence.

Similarly, the production and mass distribution of the Party's theory, especially through *The Burning Spear*, will make a major leap forward.

The success of the Party's regional work will depend on the success of each regional leader and committee. This is where the leadership to build Local Party Organizations and offices will be concentrated. Much of the Party's recruitment efforts will also be brought down to Earth within the *local* Party organizations and offices that must be built in *every* colonized community within the African nation.

Black Power Blueprint unites politics and economics in U.S. Midwest Region

Currently, the economic work we are most involved in promoting is the Black Power Blueprint. This is a major economic project that has brought inspiration to Africans throughout the U.S. and elsewhere. In a short period of time, a matter of months, Comrade Deputy Chair Ona Zené Yeshitela has driven this project, most often from the construction sites themselves, in the thick of dirt and dust in the torrid, sometimes suffocating, heat of the St. Louis summer without air conditioning and during the cruel, numbing cold of winter in temperatures that are often below freezing.

Politically, the Party has built a meaningful presence since the 2014 assassination of 18-year-old Mike Brown and subsequent generalized resistance of the African working class.

The African People's Socialist Party has been the only revolutionary organization of the African working class in St. Louis to have built an independent political presence to further the liberation of our people from the colonial chokehold that starves us of resources and freedom.

The headquarters of InPDUM is now located in St. Louis, where its President, Comrade Kalambayi Andenet, was born and raised.

Comrade Kalambayi, new to our Party and to political life, has brought with her the spirit of the African working class and exemplifies the leadership of real-life African women, as opposed to the airbrushed imitations offered up by the white ruling class and the African petty bourgeois collaborationists.

The African People's Socialist Party has a real presence in the St. Louis-Ferguson area. Our community meetings bring out regular people, children and high school students who have given their own twist to African Internationalist politics, taking them to their neighborhoods and the colonial schools.

Neocolonial office holders who have handed over all the resources of our colonized communities to the bankers and white colonial rulers of the city have begun to create paltry imitations of our Party programs. They are attempting to use the politics and economic success of the Party and Black Power Blueprint to endear themselves to our people. But they have a big problem. Politics is truly concentrated economics, and *their* politics ring hollow because they respond to the economic interests of the colonizer and not the colonized.

Our economic project is aptly named the Black Power Blueprint because self-reliance is key to self-determination, to the struggle against colonial subjugation. Ours is a blueprint that enthralls the entire colonized African population, a blueprint that is the possession of the much-maligned African working class. This is why it is supported by skilled African workers whom we have hired as contractors and who, because of their unity with the Black Power Blueprint struggle to uplift the African community, go above and beyond what a paycheck could ever bring.

Several of the contractors have given discounts on the cost of their labor and have even made financial contributions to the success of a project that they are able to see represent their interests as African colonial subjects.

The African contractors are beginning to see the Vanguard. They, like the residents of the neighborhood associations whose meetings we attend, have been won to the Black Power Blueprint because of what it obviously brings to our community which has been suffering political and economic quarantine and deterioration. It is the first glimpse of concrete development most have seen in ages. It is the *only* glimpse of concrete development that is initiated and led by the Advanced Detachment of the African working class anywhere in the world.

We have transformed a 9,000 square-foot, three story formerly-abandoned and once-deteriorating community eyesore on a main thoroughfare into a model of development in St. Louis. It is the site of our latest Uhuru House and the center of much of the Party's Midwest regional leadership.

We acquired two additional commercial buildings of similar size across the street from the Uhuru House. These buildings were demolished and, along with the two other contiguous lots we acquired, are being transformed into an event space, African community garden and One Africa! One Nation! Marketplace to address the cultural and material needs of this working class community.

We have acquired other properties to further economic and political projects under the leadership of the African working class. Among them is a massive building that was once a boat dealership, known as "the boathouse," on another major thoroughfare. This will become the site of Uhuru Bakery Cafe and the African Independence Workforce Program that will provide training and employment for Africans whose prior captivity within the colonial prison system prevents them from being hired and trained elsewhere.

We are practical revolutionaries. African Internationalism is a theory of practice. We have always struggled to make concrete our goals and objectives. We do, indeed, constitute the Advanced Detachment, the Vanguard and general staff of the African Revolution.

Export-import business will spread African revolutionary culture and build anti-colonial economy

Moving forward, we must use the economic and political base we have developed in the U.S. to enhance our regional work throughout the African world.

The Office of the Deputy Chair must give serious consideration to the establishment of an export-import enterprise that can begin with the import of African garments and fabric directly from the African continent. Eventually we will be capable of establishing factories where we can design and construct our own clothing for export to the U.S., Europe and the Caribbean, especially The Bahamas.

This enterprise can create economic development for Party organizations in Africa and the export of apparel and other accessories can lead to the creation of storefront economic operations in the colonized, economically dependent African communities in the U.S., Europe, the Caribbean and elsewhere.

Zenzele Consignment in Huntsville, Alabama and anywhere else it is established, can supplement its inventory through this enterprise, as can Uzi Clothing, InPDUM's institution, and Decolonaise, the African National Women's Organization economic front.

We should be able to distribute our imported African garments, supplemented with accessories, and other cultural and health-related products like shea butter, etc. Oils and incense, soaps and related products are inexpensive and should not take too much overhead. This enterprise could offer resources to support our local work and evoke the spirit of self-reliance within our resource-starved colonized communities right at the doorsteps of the people.

West Africa will be the location for our export-import jump-off enterprise. Right now, Ghana appears to be the likeliest place, but there may be other places in West Africa as well. I think our contacts and experiences in Ghana favor it as the regional center for our West Africa work. From Ghana, we can embark on economic activity throughout the region.

I do not have a suggestion of what kind of economic activity we can develop in Southern Africa. The strength of our Party work in Occupied Azania (South Africa) demands that we establish a regional office there. Much of our work there will have to be subsidized for a while, but I am confident that with consistent leadership we will build a formidable organizational and political presence in this strategically important, critical, location in Africa. I am confident that the unity of our Party forces in Occupied Azania will enable the Party to develop the regional presence necessary for our mission.

The Party's political work in Occupied Azania will also be informed by our determination to achieve economic independence and the actual capture of our existing resources. We must use all our creativity to develop other resources that are also linked to the struggle to build our Party and revolutionary mission. We must struggle to achieve an ability to print *The Burning Spear* in Occupied Azania.

At the time of the writing of this Political Report, we were also studying the plan of action for our economic development work in Kenya in East Africa. The Party's presence there appears to be growing in our organizational capacity under the leadership of a dynamic young woman who has accepted the overall strategy of our Party to build an independent political capacity to seize the power to make anti-colonial work successful in concert with the economic work of the entire African Socialist International.

We must also make decisions about our economic front in Europe. We will have a market for our African garments and accessories there, and possibly Uhuru Foods & Pies.

Some of our garments could be produced in Europe for export to the U.S. and other markets, especially The Bahamas.

Additionally, we are intent on *developing* a market within the colony itself. This means that we will be constant evangelists of revolutionary African culture.

We will take the best of traditional African clothing and artifacts and give them the modern youthful swag demanded by these times. The Uhuru swag will dissuade our young people from deserting our culture for popular expressions that are usually designed by Africans under colonial labels. The African community will be won to a greater appreciation of our African national identity and revolutionary cultural expression as exemplified by the clothing produced by this independent, anti-colonial economic institution.

The Bahamas is a tourist destination and there are relatively well-established marketplaces there, but few that provide Bahamian or African products. Nassau could be an important outlet for African products coming directly from the Continent if they can be acquired for an affordable price. The target for our products would be the African community in The Bahamas as well as the thousands of tourists who come to the islands for an exotic "black" experience.

Buy Black Power: building our independent African economy

Learning from our colonial capitalists, we will buy from each other and sell to everyone. Our slogan will be: "Buy Black Power." This takes us beyond the petty bourgeois Afro-neocolonialist demand for African people to "Buy Black," which might profit them but promises nothing to our people as a means of breaking out of the colonial prison we have inhabited for the last several centuries.

"Buy Black Power" does not only serve to promote our Movement products, but will encourage other merchants within our colony to promote and develop an anti-colonial commercial approach as well.

The Office of the Deputy Chair must also examine the possibility of using the Uhuru Houses and our local offices in each region within the U.S. and anywhere else possible, as distribution points for our food products. This is especially true of Uhuru Foods & Pies. In other words, our economic activities will expand exponentially through utilization of these regional hubs and the initiation of local distribution points. These products for distribution must include shea butter from ANWO, clothing from Uzi, clothing from Zenzele Consignment and Planet Uhuru apparel from the African People's Solidarity Committee. *The Burning Spear* newspaper and all our books, audio and visual products must also be distributed from these sites.

The Office of the Deputy Chair will have the responsibility of providing overall leadership for all the economic activity outlined here. It must develop its own system of training and support for all the economic work and provide strategic direction, leading to the creation of an independent, anti-colonial, international, socialist economy of liberated Africa and African people.

We want to create independent economic activity that is not simply inspired by an aspiration of individual wealth but that recognizes itself as a part of the struggle for self-determination. The Office of the Deputy Chair can begin training programs for Africans to initiate and participate in successful economic ventures as part of the overall anti-colonial economic work.

Our "Buy Black Power" programs will help to inspire our community from its deepest, most oppressed and exploited sectors, to political consciousness of self-reliance. This, along with all our community and neighborhood gardens, will begin the process of generalized, self-initiated economic development on the terms of the people. This is how we free ourselves from the predatory colonial merchants, bankers and their political minions.

Again, our basic point here is that we must develop an approach to organization that is centered in the regions that will have the responsibility of emanating outward throughout the states, provinces and cities with all our political and economic programs.

This is not an approach designed to minimize what is normally considered our political work. This is a critical, strategic *approach* to our political work, marrying it to the economic interests of the colonized African working class. In the political struggle to be free, we are also preparing to govern in an economically independent, anti-colonial socialist world that we are actively constructing.

Moving forward, these initial economic projects will develop to the point that we can grow other, more sophisticated economic activity that functions as a counterweight against gentrification and population displacement, and as an engine for the defeat of colonial dependency.

Our headquarters, working with our regions, will discover other opportunities for the kind of development currently exemplified by the Black Power Blueprint. Our One Africa! One Nation! Marketplaces can also be duplicated within each of the regions.

Increasingly, we will be able to work with a strategy organized from our headquarters that will enhance our capacity for creating food, clothing and shelter, independent of the colonial capitalists. "Buy Black Power" campaigns will flourish as part of our Black Power Blueprint projects throughout the U.S. and our bases of operation throughout the world.

This will be a demonstration of democratic centralism—democracy under centralized leadership—employed throughout our organizational structures.

Even in the arena of electoral politics we will be capable of concretizing our political demands in support of the economic interests of our people, whether this is through anti-colonial politicians we may support or through our own candidates.

The working class must have its own independent capacity. Our regional strategy concretizes this as nothing else we have ever done.

The Office of the Secretary General must pay constant attention to recruitment and assignment of forces for the development of the regions under the leadership of the Central Committee and the Chairman. For example, while our presence in Oakland extends back to 1980 when the Party was indisputably the primary political force there for many years, the African face of our Party has been missing there for some time now.

Uhuru Furniture & Collectibles and Uhuru Foods & Pies have been uninterrupted successful enterprises since the 1980s. Their presence has contributed to our political prestige in the area. We continue to promote and win support for our reparations work from these institutions. We also use them as platforms for promoting the various political campaigns our Movement is always waging.

We must begin to strategically recruit and place cadres in Oakland in order to carry out our regional strategy. Similarly, recruitment and assignments must target Philadelphia where we are working to assign Party cadres to lead our highly successful Uhuru Furniture & Collectibles. A local Party member has taken over direction of the One Africa! One Nation! Marketplace.

The recruitment and deployment of solidarity cadres will have to submit to the overall plan of the Party, including the regional strategy. In some ways this is already happening.

We have been able to reinforce some of our political work by assigning solidarity forces to locations strategic to our progress. One such place is St. Petersburg, Florida, our national headquarters. Another is St. Louis, Missouri.

We have also moved or kept solidarity forces to shore up and reinforce our economic work when necessary. Now our regional strategy gives us the best process for strategic recruitment and deployment of solidarity forces.

The solidarity movement is also recruiting in locations where the Party is not currently located. In some instances, this will mean we will simply utilize these forces to deepen our reparations work according to already-developed plans. We will also doubtlessly develop other tasks for solidarity forces in these locations along with Party and InPDUM development in those areas.

We have significant economic institutions in Philadelphia and Oakland in which solidarity forces have been working for many years. Now the Party must make the political determination to shore up our political presence in both these locations. Failure to do so will be to the detriment of the Party and the U.S. Front of the African Revolution.

The benefit of this plan is that it enables us to place *all* our economic work under one umbrella. Although the regions will achieve limited stand-alone capacity, all our efforts will work under the strategic leadership of our headquarters. Uzi, Zenzele, Uhuru Foods & Pies, Uhuru Bakery and Cafe, Uhuru Furniture stores, commercial kitchens and marketplaces will all have the benefit of centralized support that will make it unnecessary for any institution to depend *solely* on its own individual capacity. Our economic work will have greater strategic flexibility and resilience if ever attacked by the white ruling class colonial power.

History has taught us that once we begin to initiate this regional strategy with determination, we can be certain that we will open up many other doors for advancing our struggle for the total liberation of Africa and all her globally scattered children that constitute our nation.

Obviously, this regional strategy is not simply an economic one. This is not a task that the economic development arm of the Office of the Deputy Chair will take on by itself. This is an organizational and political strategy as well. It is in the custody of the entire Party leadership.

The recruitment and membership arm of the Secretary General will have to work closely with the ODC and entire Central Committee to lay out a strategy for recruitment and personnel assignment to meet the requirements of revolutionary Party-building for the Party internationally through our regional development.

InPDUM must open local offices in the African colony

In addition to the regional Party offices, InPDUM must open up local storefront offices in every region in order to deepen its relationship with the African working class. Like our regional Party offices, InPDUM offices should function as outlets for products from the economic enterprises of our Party and Movement until the local InPDUM branches are capable of opening stand-alone neighborhood storefronts, deep in the working class communities within the African colonies.

The colonial state knows more or less where we are located. Now the masses, upon whom our security and revolutionary success depend, need to be able to find us.

The existence of local community offices becomes material, practical evidence of our work. The offices become community meeting places for discussing and organizing around the critical questions assaulting our people daily, especially the working class. *The Burning Spear* and other Party and Movement materials can also be acquired at our offices.

Political posters in our offices contribute to mass political education by showing our unity with the oppressed peoples of the world and exhibiting our revolutionary credentials.

Running and raising the resources to operate local offices and providing community political education will contribute to the ideological, organizational and political development of Party cadres. This is key to our local Party forces becoming entrenched in the working class sections of the African colony that are traditionally overlooked by everyone except the colonial state.

Our local offices will be the centers of organized resistance. They will be the institutions within which the African working class will organize the implementation of the community gardens for collective efforts to feed our colonized communities. They will be the location for the work to build the African People's Free Childcare collectives, designed to initiate the socialist-inspired struggle for political, economic and social liberation of working class African women, too many of whom are immobilized by the sole responsibility of raising our children. The offices will become the centers for the development of black community control of the police and schools, centered in the leadership of the African working class.

The work within our communities and from the local InPDUM and other mass Movement offices will function practically as politically directed components of the Great Cultural Revolution that will facilitate our African Internationalist global Revolution.

The offices will also function as fortresses against gentrification. The very presence of conscious anti-colonialist Africans who are organized and in constant motion will function to dissuade the North American interlopers from invading our community. In fact, it was the rise of the revolutionary anti-colonial resistance in the 1960s that resulted in the "white flight" that emptied the "inner cities" of colonizers at the time.

It has only been since the quiet that has descended with the defeat of the Black Revolution of the Sixties that there has been a resurgence of white "investors," many of whom are ordinary white colonizers mining for cheap property at the expense of the collective wealth, potential political power and social cohesion of our colonized communities.

The fight against gentrification will also come through the development of Party economic institutions and others we inspire throughout the African colony. Employment and independent economic activity within the African colony will function to push back the vulturistic economic opportunists from the oppressor colonizer population. We will enhance the ability of our people to hold on to properties that are currently vulnerable to white takeovers.

Our local community offices will bring organization to our colonized people. The Advanced Detachment of the African working class, the Vanguard of the colonized African nation, concretizes our presence through a direct, immediate integration with the African working class even as the class is busy struggling to solve the problems imposed on our nation through a hostile foreign and alien state power.

In the 2016 Plenary Political Report, we spoke to the role of InPDUM in these defining words:

> *InPDUM is the Party's most important connection to the masses of our people. It is the Party's instrument for intervening in the mass struggles of our people with revolutionary science. InPDUM is the method through which Party cadres can root ourselves among the people and provide leadership*

> *for the thousands of Africans who, for any number of reasons, are not members of our Party.*[2]

Since InPDUM is the main, most dominant mass organization of the Party, it stands to reason that InPDUM should lead the pack in establishing local offices throughout the African colony.

We will influence and have access to the scores of thousands of African workers within the African colony, whether they are InPDUM members or not. This is what is meant by "reserve forces" for the Revolution.

Our development of the Party and InPDUM also coincides with the practical, revolutionary requirement of the Party, like any other genuine anti-colonial movement, to occupy, develop and defend territory. This includes ideological, political, economic, geographical and organizational territory.

Part of our work is to transform every community of the domestic African colony into citadels or strongholds of the scientific, African Internationalist worldview. Politically our communities must become conscious and organized participants in the anti-colonial resistance movement for the immediate defense of our people and communities wherever we are currently located.

The Report was clear that InPDUM must be the primary vehicle for building the presence of the Party throughout the colony:

> *Every member of the Party must join InPDUM and even if our primary work prohibits us from the fullest participation, our membership dues and participation in local meetings will give the organization greater capacity on many levels.*

---

2 Yeshitela, Omali. *Organize to Win! Organize to Govern! Political Report to the 2016 Plenary of the African People's Socialist Party*, apspuhuru.org/2016-plenary-political-report/

> *InPDUM, understanding itself to be an organization of the Party, must be the most zealous distributor of the Party's press, especially* The Burning Spear *for which it must also supply articles that will facilitate its organizing efforts.*
>
> *Our Party leaders must also be cognizant of the role of InPDUM as a major producer of a deep pool of potential Party recruits, a reserve force for the Revolution, where Africans learn organization and how to be organized. InPDUM must become the method with which we actually contend with non-proletarian forces for political, ideological and territorial influence and power.*
>
> *All communities within the colonized African territories must be followers of the Uhuru Movement. They must be transformed into anti-colonial bastions of resistance.*
>
> *In the final analysis we are in a struggle for political power over our own black lives. We will settle for nothing less. InPDUM, perhaps more than any other organization, must exude this determination and the confidence of its achievement.*[3]

The InPDUM local offices will reflect the general condition of the community and not the alienating institutions installed in the colony by colonial poverty programs and African petty bourgeois opportunists whose income is dependent on the ongoing impoverished conditions of our people.

These will be offices that radiate optimism for the future promised by our presence and the programs of self-reliance and self-determination that we provide. They will become the offices wherein the community may organize their own childcare and tutoring programs and where we can provide

3 Ibid.

immediate cultural upliftment, including African liberatory culture.

Our objective is not to simply set up offices and retail shops throughout our communities. This is a part of the decolonization project. This is part of the process of contributing to the further development of concrete dual power that includes the most meaningful capacity to feed, clothe and house ourselves—our self-determination, which has been robbed from the African nation since the advent of colonial slavery and capitalism. True liberation cannot be achieved without neutralizing the economic and political domination by the white nationalist colonial power that controls every aspect of our lives as a subjugated people.

True socialism is the conquest of state power and ownership and control of the means of production by the working class. As a Party of practical revolutionaries, we are constantly in the process of solving the problems of the Revolution and practically implementing our ideological conclusions. This is an example of how our Party is the Advanced Detachment, the Vanguard in the struggle to liberate and unify Africa and the African nation under the leadership of the African working class.

The implementation of this regional political-economic strategy will raise the struggle for dual power to a higher level. The deployment of Party members into their immediate locales will stabilize and dynamize this dual power work in a way that contributes to the transformation of our colonized African communities into fighting anti-colonial soviets. The distribution of *The Burning Spear* newspaper will function as the ideological and informational arm of our community.

Our local InPDUM offices will be the people's fortresses against colonial state power in the fight for self-determination, in the struggle for genuine anti-colonial democracy.

In so doing, we will rapidly escalate the struggle to contend with and ultimately defeat imperialist state power over our lives and resources.

VII. The state of the Party, part 1

Our Party is aware of our significance

The African People's Socialist Party has solved the most important contradictions of the African Revolution. Our existence is testimony that revolution continues to be on the agenda.

It is only we who have been able to fight to recapture the revolutionary trajectory by, first of all, recognizing and acknowledging its defeat. This is what enabled us to see that the election of Barack Hussein Obama represented neocolonialism and not a continuation of the revolution heroically fought by the most downtrodden and oppressed sectors of our colonized nation.

There are individuals who now safely extol the virtues of the Black Panther Party of the past, many claiming to have themselves been a member of it. They all conveniently forget, however, that the basis for the Panthers' significance and the enmity it earned from the white ruling class is the fact that it was intent on capturing revolutionary political power.

The defeat of the Black Revolution of the Sixties only punctuated the necessity of taking power if our people are to know real freedom. It is our responsibility to prepare to govern. This is not the same as presuming to give a "brilliant analysis" that can be showcased at conferences and talkfests.

There are some who proclaim that the defeat of the Black Revolution of the Sixties is evidence that political parties are outdated as vehicles for winning freedom. Some claim that what is needed are coalitions because there is no one organization that has all the answers, or swill to that effect. This is a typical petty bourgeois political line.

Political parties require the struggle for a correct line and ideology that unites the party; they require revolutionary principles of organization, revolutionary discipline and an internal assault on petty bourgeois inclinations of liberalism and subjectivism. As they have been doing lately, ruling class pundits tend to praise movements of the oppressed when they do not have obvious structured leadership.

Indeed the colonial-capitalist rulers of the world do believe in leadership. Their assassination and jailing of our revolutionary leaders of the past and their moves to slander and crush all traces of revolutionary leaders today testifies to this even more than the promotion of their chosen puppets who do their bidding.

We address the state of our Party quite aware of our significance as the continuation of the revolutionary leadership that the defeat of our Revolution was designed to eliminate. We recognize all the contradictions and weaknesses of our Party but we proudly remind the world and ourselves that our existence today, some 46 years after our founding, is a remarkable feat. The Party's continued existence confirms our historic role in refusing to allow the struggle of African people to die an inglorious death.

We are the only African revolutionary Party in the world that has assumed the responsibility to lead the struggle for our total liberation, the unification of Africa and African people, and socialism.

One reason we can claim the mantle of the Advanced Detachment for the African Revolution is the fact that we are among the few that realize the need for a vanguard and, having realized the need, set out to create that vanguard.

The Black Revolution of the '60s was thrust upon us during a time when, generally speaking throughout the world, our anti-colonial movement reflected the militant, nationalist aspirations of the African petty bourgeoisie. This fact is responsible for tremendous confusion both by militants of today and those from the period of the '60s.

Africans are oppressed and exploited as a whole people. This means we suffer *national* oppression and the entire colonized African nation is united in wanting to bring it to an end. For the petty bourgeoisie, freedom from foreign domination is the ultimate aim. And, while this is the aim of the African working class as well, the African working class cannot be satisfied by simply acquiring independence or national liberation as defined by the African petty bourgeoisie.

There is also a class struggle that is raging, sometimes below the surface, within the struggle for national liberation. The African working class must destroy the power of capital; the working class must fight for and win control and ownership of the means of production in order to bring about a transformation of the nationally liberated society that we seek. We must fight to control the means of production throughout Africa, the Caribbean, the U.S. and South America, wherever we are located.

In order to do this, the African working class must be armed with its own class party to take the struggle for national liberation to its successful conclusion for the benefit of the majority proletarian African nation.

Our Party is responding to this contradiction when we say that the global African Liberation Movement has realized its limitations when fought within imperialist-imposed borders. This is another way of saying that what is incorrectly called "national" liberation is not enough. "Flag" independence that ended direct colonialism in Africa and the Caribbean is not enough. We cannot declare liberation simply because there is no apparent direct white colonial domination of our people.

For national liberation to be *real,* liberation that results in an end to foreign domination, there must be socialist revolution with the achievement of state power by the African working class. This is the only way we can win genuine independence or national liberation.

African revolutionaries of the 1960s most often did not begin the struggle as revolutionaries. Revolutionary consciousness came about in the heat of the struggle for democracy under white power, the so-called Civil Rights Movement in the U.S. or for independence from direct white power in Africa or elsewhere.

We are not discovering revolution; we are *planning* revolution!

Today the African working class has its own Party. We are not *discovering* the need for revolution; we are planning for revolution. We are not struggling to learn all the lessons that were so late in coming to us in the 1960s. We are prepared and spreading the theory and practice of revolution throughout the African world "...at home and abroad."

We must keep this important truth in mind as we sum up the state of the Party today. The state of our Party is influenced by the requirements of history. We are the Party where once there was none. We are the Advanced Detachment of the African working class, and therefore the Advanced Detachment of the forcibly dispersed colonized African nation. Our class and our nation are better off as a consequence of the existence of our Party.

The character of our Party has been shaped by intense struggles within our ranks, throughout the U.S. and the world. We have engaged representatives of the imperialist ruling class in ideological and political struggle. We have experienced military assaults on our headquarters and suspected assassination of one of our most beloved leaders. Our phones have been tapped and our news organ has been intercepted, spoiled and otherwise made unusable. I have experienced jailings, prison and extreme harassment that included slander and police beating.

From this platform we have initiated some of the most important anti-colonial political campaigns in the U.S. The case of Dessie Woods in the 1970s that the white Left and other liberals wanted to turn into a bourgeois feminist campaign supporting the "right to self-defense" by "women in general" was fought by our Party as a struggle against colonial violence. While the former may have won greater support, especially from white feminists, it would have not advanced our struggle against colonialism and for Black Power. It would not have provided an explanation for the oppression of African women as *colonial* oppression just as the oppression of African men and children is colonial. Instead, we raised the slogan, "Free Dessie Woods! Smash Colonial Violence!"

In 1977 in Atlanta, Georgia, we used the Dessie Woods campaign to launch the first significant, pro-independence, anti-colonial mass mobilization since our military defeat in the 1960s. We organized the first mass march that ever took place in Plains, Georgia, the hometown of then-U.S. president James Earl Carter. We took militant demonstrations into Hawkinsville, Georgia, where Dessie Woods was tried by a vicious colonial court. Colonialism was so pronounced in Hawkinsville that some white plantation owners had their own private jails used to punish Africans.

The Dessie Woods campaign also established the conditions for much of the work to organize the African People's Solidarity Committee (APSC) in 1976, four years after the founding of the Party. The African People's Solidarity Committee, whose work revolves around "material solidarity" from the white community, has become the most outstanding manifestation of the correctness of our Party's revolutionary reparations demand.

Never before has the African Revolution extended itself into the colonizer nation population. Never before have the white ruling class and its minions had to defend themselves from the demand for African reparations from within its own previously sheltered and generally comfortable position on the pedestal of African colonial oppression.

For the first time in history, the demand for reparations is *more* than a demand. It is actually being accomplished, right now, by the African working class through white people of the colonizer nation whose unity requires submission to the leadership of African people through its Advanced Detachment, the African People's Socialist Party.

It confirms our theory of the role of white people as the colonizer nation based on the history of parasitic capitalist development resting on a foundation of the enslavement and colonization of African and oppressed peoples of the world. The unprecedented relationship of white people organized under our leadership is a critical component to our overall strategy to overturn the colonial-capitalist social system.

Our Party fought mass land reform battles in Oakland and waged major political contests with the domestic neocolonial government officials in defense of the African working class there. In 1986 we responded to the police-U.S. government bombing of African militants of the MOVE organization in Philadelphia with a national African Liberation Day demonstration under the slogan, "Reinforcements are on the way!"

We were determined to demonstrate to Africans in Philadelphia that they were not alone. We denied the vicious imperialists and neocolonialists their victory in terrorizing and silencing our struggle with the horrific murders of 11 men, women and children of MOVE and the bombing demolition of an entire colonized African community.

The work of our Party has never been limited to abstract theoretical screeds. We are practical revolutionaries and we recognize that the importance of theory for our Revolution is its testing and validation by practice. As the Advanced

Detachment, we are always developing our theory through practice. All the work we have done, and this is only a hint of what we have accomplished, is evidence of the efficacy of our theory. As we have repeatedly stated, African Internationalism is a theory of practice.

Since the 1980s we have led incessant struggles against police murder in Philadelphia and were central to campaigns in London against police violence against Africans. When our organizers were arrested in Sierra Leone, West Africa we successfully mobilized an international public response that forced the neocolonial state to retreat. We have organized multiple independent economic institutions, making us genuinely self-sufficient, and created a true foundation for dual and contending power in the hands of the African working class for the first time since the Marcus Garvey Movement a hundred years ago. And much, much more!

The activity of our Party since our Sixth Congress in 2013 has been characterized by the same rapid revolutionary pace for which we are known. Our Party is the only organization with a real revolutionary "work ethic." Everyone sees us as the ones who actually get things done quickly and efficiently.

Much of our work today is centered in the Black Power Blueprint project in St. Louis. Although hundreds of different personalities and organizations descended on Ferguson following the uprising of the militant young working class Africans, the African People's Socialist Party is the only organization remaining from the lot. The TV cameras, money and ruling class media are now gone, along with most of the personalities and organizations. However, colonial oppression still defines the lives of the African working class. Now we are there in St. Louis, the Advanced Detachment of the colonized African nation, the African People's Socialist Party.

The Black Power Blueprint represents a major advancement that has implications for the development of the African anti-colonial struggle all over the world. We have remained in St. Louis and we have organized a presence and movement among the working class of this community whose heroic resistance has re-energized African anti-colonial consciousness in a way not seen since the Sixties.

Our Party's long-standing influence on the continent of Africa

However, St. Louis is only one of many places where the Party is building or has built a revolutionary presence. The years of work we have done in Occupied Azania, presently known by its colonial name of South Africa, are now bearing fruit. After important groundwork done there by a Party delegation led by Comrade Luwezi Kinshasa, we have recently consolidated an organized presence comprised of enthusiastic, dynamic young working class Africans in several provinces.

Comrades Deputy Chair Ona Zené Yeshitela, ASI Secretary General Luwezi Kinshasa, Themba Tshibanda and myself spent two weeks from late March to mid-April working with the Party forces there. Under the leadership of Tafarie Mugeri, Party organizers are building in the working class townships to construct Party units there and promote an African Internationalist worldview. The Party in Occupied Azania organized and publicized our Azania visit as the "Africa Must Unite!" tour.

Our 2018 tour was not the Party's introduction to struggle in Occupied Azania, however. Our Party's history there dates back to the liberation struggle in Occupied Azania when African people were fighting the nakedly oppressive, racialized apartheid state only to win nothing more than a new form of imperialist rule under the formal African leadership of the African National Congress (ANC).

In fact, our relationship with the Pan Africanist Congress of Azania (PAC), which along with the ANC had been an anti-colonial, organized fighting force on the ground, enabled our Party to be an active participant in that struggle. We intervened, bringing African Internationalism to the debates that were conducted within the Azanian expatriate community in the U.S.

We expressed very strong, vocal and sometimes unpopular disagreement with the position to accept the proposed negotiated settlement, led by the ANC and its puppet Nelson Mandela, that established the settler neocolonial state that exists today.

We made a coherent argument in opposition to the negotiated settlement in those debates. Overwhelming evidence has confirmed the correctness of our position. As prophetically stated by Party member Omowale Kefing at the time, the African working class would be in worse shape in a post-liberated South Africa under the rule of the ANC than they were under direct, white nationalist, colonial rule. Indeed, this is the case.

Our participation in the debates was based on the work we were doing with the PAC, at the time recognized, along with the African National Congress, as one of the two legitimate representatives of Africans in Occupied Azania. Our unity with the Pan Africanist Congress of Azania included publishing the various pamphlets that contained the PAC history and program. Unlike the ANC that was the darling of the international white Left and European liberals throughout the world, the PAC had few resources with which they could publish their political materials.

We also united with the PAC in opposition to the ANC because the PAC claimed to believe in the unification of Africa. Like us, the PAC at that time opposed the ANC's so-called Freedom Charter that stated that South Africa belonged to everyone who lived there—both the colonized, oppressed Africans and the white oppressor colonizer population that had taken the land in a murderous European assault from which we have not yet recovered.

Though we were united with the PAC, we nevertheless criticized the PAC's self-designation as a "congress" as opposed to a party. Congresses, fronts and "conventions" disguise the leadership of the treacherous African petty bourgeoisie and the African working class has paid a bitter price for this all over the world.

The African working class *must* wage internal class struggle within our liberation organizations in order to build revolutionary vehicles to achieve the emancipation of the working class in the struggle for national liberation. Better yet, we must build branches of the African working class-led African People's Socialist Party wherever we are as components of the African Socialist International, as our comrades are doing.

We also questioned the inability of the PAC to define its differences with the ANC as class-based. It was clear to us that the ANC was a petty bourgeois formation, a glaring fact played out daily as ANC leaders became obscenely wealthy while much of the African working class is condemned to eke out a life of numbing poverty in hideous shantytowns called "townships" today.

Even *Bloomberg.com,* the voice of Wall Street financial interests, wrote at the time of Mandela's 2013 death:

> *The basic deal Mandela struck from prison with F.W. de Klerk [the colonial leader of the apartheid state at the time], and which was subsequently enshrined in the South African constitution, essentially guaranteed the existing property rights of white South Africans in exchange for an end to apartheid.*

> *Nelson Mandela sold out black South Africans. Now there's a sentence you won't have heard in the days since his death and that you won't be hearing at his memorial tomorrow. Yet it is incontrovertibly true that after centuries of being robbed of possibly the greatest mineral wealth the world has ever known, not to mention decades of being repressed by apartheid, black South Africans got almost no compensation for what should rightfully have been theirs when the old regime was swept away for the new South Africa.*[1]

With the science of African Internationalism, our Party understood, predicted and raised this more than 40 years ago. Because the ANC and Nelson Mandela were loved by the white Left and imperialism alike, however, we earned the wrath of colonizer liberals as well as opportunist African nationalists from around the world.

On one occasion, after the release of Mandela from a South African prison, our Party attended a conference in Libya. We experienced a strong reproach from Libyans and African attendees from within the U.S. after we refused to agree to conduct African Liberation Day mobilizations in the U.S. at which we would distribute poster pictures of Nelson Mandela together with Mu'ummar Qaddafi.

The only cause for anyone to be disappointed or surprised by our stance around Nelson Mandela and the ANC would be their ignorance of our history as revolutionaries fighting for the total, unambiguous liberation of all of Africa under the leadership of the African working class. We fought the ANC and other African opportunist opponents of genuine African liberation in Occupied Azania. We shut down efforts by white

1 Feldman, Noah. "Was Mandela Right to Sell Out Black South Africans?" *Bloomberg.com*, Dec. 9, 2013.

liberals to bring Bishop Desmond Tutu to Oakland to support neocolonial opportunist elected officials with whom we were locked in combat in the struggle to win housing for African workers there.

There was a time in the liberal Oakland-San Francisco Bay Area when our Movement was regularly denounced for exposing the opportunism of Mandela and the ANC currently responsible for the vicious repression of the African working class in Occupied Azania.

New young leaders grow our Party organization in Africa

Today, after our years of unfruitful work with the Pan Africanist Congress and constituent organizations, the African People's Socialist Party is on the ground. The African People's Socialist Party-Occupied Azania is real, further manifestation that our Party is the Vanguard.

The comrades in Occupied Azania are generally new to political life and organization. All are disgusted by the opportunism that characterizes so much of the political life in Azania under the leadership of the ANC ruling party that threatens the future of our people and our class. Our comrades were brought to the Party by their desire to overturn the ongoing colonial-capitalist exploitation and oppression of our people and our resources by the settler neocolonial state.

African Internationalism has helped these comrades overcome the confusion of many of our people in Occupied Azania and the world caused by the formal end of apartheid in 1994. Our Party's scientific approach helped these comrades understand that apartheid was only the *form* of the oppressive capitalist state. The end of apartheid left the same system of exploitation in place with the added assistance of a sector of the African petty bourgeoisie. This was simply settler neocolonialism, indirect rule, white settler power in black face.

The work and presence of our Party function as a criticism of the entire imperialist setup. We have always recognized that the South African state is an illegitimate entity that came into existence through the brutal, forcible expropriation of African land and resources by British imperialism and others. The land is ours. So too is all the value stemming from the land. We will not settle for areas where the shanties are located! The mining, corporate, industrial and agricultural sectors belong to us!

This is important to say because opportunists such as Julius Malema and other militants are moving the masses to occupy the lands where the shantytowns are "illegally" located, often on territory "owned" by white settlers. While the struggle for dual power as an anti-colonial, revolutionary strategy would doubtlessly include taking the land occupied by shanties, this must not be seen as an end unto itself. Poor Africans in possession of crowded townships, or even of the ownership deeds, is no substitute for the revolutionary capture of land and power by the African working class as part of the struggle to liberate Africa and African people everywhere.

At the same time, Malema is demanding nationalization of the mines and strategic resources, a demand that we recognize as simply a call to transfer ownership to the bourgeois state. For nationalization to be meaningful and helpful to the masses of our people and the African working class, there must be capture of the means of production by an African workers' state. Otherwise, the resources remain in the hands of the bourgeoisie which, under the existing arrangement, includes the South African or "white" settler bourgeoisie.

Such struggle must be part of an overall fight to advance the Revolution to the seizure of total power in the hands of the African working class. The shantytown dwellers must become a part of the new ruling class in possession of all the means of production, of which the land is an essential component.

In other words, the struggle for land on the Azania Front is a struggle for revolution.

Without their own revolutionary working class party capable of fighting in the selfish interests of our class, any of the initiatives sponsored by militant opponents of the existing setup can only benefit the African petty bourgeoisie, which is sometimes a very militant petty bourgeoisie. The African working class must have the benefit of its own working class party.

Our Party in Azania will be moving to incorporate into our ranks the African migrants from Zimbabwe who have been forced by colonial-capitalist-induced poverty to cross the colonial-capitalist-created borders to search for income. These Africans are some of the inhabitants of the crowded shanty dwellings created from scraps of tin, plastic, boards and other discards on vacant properties.

During the "Africa Must Unite!" tour, the Party visited the Alexandra Township that is inhabited by thousands of Africans, many of whom are from Zimbabwe. Alexandra, or "Alex" as it is called, is adjacent to the upper class Johannesburg neighborhood of Sandton and is under constant assault as an eyesore and reminder of an unfinished revolution.

African Internationalism teaches us that Africans living in Zimbabwe are part of the African nation. What separates all the people living in Occupied Azania are class interests and national oppression. We reject the colonial borders and as our capacity grows in Occupied Azania we will work to organize all of the destitute African workers throughout that country, the region and the great African continent into a powerful proletarian army under the leadership of their revolutionary proletarian Party.

Unlike the African petty bourgeoisie, our Party is not looking to build a movement to get Africans a bigger piece of the colonial-capitalist pie. We are determined to capture the entire kitchen, end colonial capitalism and eliminate the borders that separate the African nation and the African working class.

During our trip, the African People's Socialist Party Occupied Azania organized three meetings in Gauteng Province. The first was in Johannesburg and was well attended, especially by young people, some of whom were students who accompanied their professor, a Party supporter. Comrade Deputy Chair Ona Zené Yeshitela showed a video of our economic development project, the Black Power Blueprint, along with a film portraying the work and philosophy of our Party. The manager of the venue for this event was so impressed that he decided to join the Party. Interestingly, he is an African that was born in what the British named Nigeria.

The APSP-Occupied Azania also organized a very well-attended public meeting for the Party in Fochville. We were pleasantly surprised to see comrades we have known for many years there. One of them functioned as our security during an organizing trip to Kenya in April 2009.

Young people were prominent features in Fochville as well. All expressed the same disgust with the political establishment as in our first meeting. They recognized the fallacy of the so-called revolution that ended apartheid in South Africa, but left the minority white population in control of 87 percent of the land and most of the means of production. The discussion was very lively and we continued to make the call for the African working class to get organized in the Party and prepare to lead our own struggle in our own class and national interests.

The question of corruption was raised by attendees of this meeting as people are very conscious of the issue of former president Jacob Zuma and his connection with a prominent Indian capitalist. We explained that corruption is common with capitalism, but that the issue is not corruption. The issue is colonial capitalism whence all the corruption springs. Even non-corrupt capitalism, if such a thing were possible, could not work in the interests of the majority African working class.

Our final meeting was in Evaton West. Like all of our meetings this was a training meeting, this time primarily for people interested in coming into the Party. We were able to identify an assortment of contradictions that have to be overcome to make our work competent and grow our Party's capacity to build and make the Revolution so desperately needed by our people.

In Evaton West, our venue was without electricity, making it necessary to run extension cords for about 100 feet from a source at a home to the venue where the training was conducted. The lack of electrical power placed limitations on our training schedule, but we were able to unite the attendees with our Party and our objective to build in Evaton where there was already an existing Party unit at work. As in the other meetings, one of the most important trainings was led by Comrade Deputy Chair Ona Zené Yeshitela who conducted a workshop on developing plans of action (POA) that professionalize all of our work.

The comrades in Azania are busy organizing their leading Party bodies and planning for the Pre-Congress Conference in preparation for the Seventh Congress in St. Louis, Missouri, U.S.

"We want freedom in our lifetime" in Kenya!

Another dynamic, new front for the Party is in Kenya, East Africa. The Party's organization in Occupied Azania and Kenya are comparatively new to our ASI Africa Front and represent some of the most exciting of all our work on the Continent. At the time of this writing the Party has consolidated a functioning basic Party organization, led by M. Kask, a young African woman in her 20s.

This is an excerpt of Comrade Kask's plan of action to build the Party in Kenya. This was a dated plan even when it was written because she had already organized a Party unit, holding regular meetings and developing propaganda to build the Party while exposing the people's class enemies and national oppressor:

> *The proposed African People's Socialist Party-Kenya will be a component organization of the African Socialist International. It is our vision to be an organization that will comprise the Advanced Detachment of the African working class.*
>
> *In Kenya, there is dire need to split the African proletariat from the African petty bourgeoisie, to stop the latter from using poor African workers as cannon fodder in the fight between its neocolonial power factions.*
>
> *Tribalism and ethnic politics in Kenya are endemic. Unbeknownst to the poor Africans in Kenya, these divisive, myopic identities are a defence of neocolonialism and of the African petty bourgeoisie against African workers.*
>
> *They obscure the exploitation of all African workers by white imperialism and their black lackeys; they obscure the betrayal of Africa by the African petty bourgeoisie.*
>
> *We want freedom in our lifetime. This will require us to be revolutionaries and build the kind of organization that the African working class can trust to liberate them.*

The comrades in Kenya set for themselves many reasonable goals for the development of the Kenyan Front of our Revolution. The significance of the African Socialist International will deepen our capacity there. One of the goals set by these comrades is to formally register the APSP-Kenya as a legally recognized Party before the Kenyan general elections in 2022.

Also, in the words of the Kenyan comrades, "For 2018, M. Kask will represent APSP-Kenya. This will be done by providing documents that detail the political situation in Kenya and why Africans in Kenya need to unite with APSP. She will also attend the Congress via video link."

Our Party is active in other areas of Africa as well, including Sierra Leone, Ghana and to some extent Tanzania, Uganda and Nigeria.

There have been times in the past when we made significant but sometimes frustrating efforts in building on the ground in Ivory Coast and Sierra Leone. We also expended time, energy and material resources struggling to build the ASI in South Africa many years ago, which planted the seeds for our growth there today. There is no straight, linear trajectory to victory.

However, as a new generation comes of age in the deepening crisis of imperialism with no choice but to fight for its future, we can speak of the Party comrades in Kenya and South Africa with confidence. Our past experience and direct involvement in the revolutionary movements there help us to recognize the difference in these comrades who are really struggling to be cadres.

These young comrades have deeply internalized the theory of African Internationalism and show profound respect for the significance of the African People's Socialist Party as the Advanced Detachment of the African working class.

In May of this year Comrade Luwezi Kinshasa, working with European Party members, organized an African Liberation

Day event in Paris. The ALD re-energized the existing Party forces in Europe, spread the revolutionary philosophy of the African working class, built new Party organizations and pulled together the African People's Socialist Party's European Pre-Congress Conference in Paris.

This Pre-Congress Conference, like the ones scheduled for Africa, the U.S. and the Caribbean, will allow democratic input in the Party's Seventh Congress by much of the forcibly dispersed and colonized international African nation.

Our 2010 Party Congress set the terms for our work today

As we know, Comrades, much of the Party's work is presently concentrated in the U.S. The history and current mobility of our Party here helped to predetermine this reality. Most of our material resources and programs are located in the U.S., something this Congress will help to rectify by struggling to extend our institutional reach throughout Africa and the African world.

As this Political Report will reveal, our work is not without contradictions. However, what should be very clear to all is that our self-criticism is one made by the Advanced Detachment for errors and shortcomings that undermine our work as the general staff of the African Revolution and the Vanguard for our class.

The strategic tasks we set for ourselves as a Party go back beyond our Sixth Party Congress, which, by any measure was extraordinarily successful. In fact, it was our Fifth Congress in 2010 that set the terms for what our work would look like up to this point and by which we must measure the current state of the Party.

The goals set by our Fifth Congress and restated at our Sixth Congress called for work to escalate and professionalize our recruitment and to specifically organize African labor, prisoners, women and students. In response to the growing influence of the Christian church in Africa and among African expatriates in Europe, we also resolved to build the African Redemption Church as an arm of the workers' Party to combat philosophical idealism from within.

In addition, our Fifth and Sixth Congresses called for the development of all the departments of the Party, our infrastructure and all the committees and organizations of the Party, especially InPDUM, the All African People's Development and Empowerment Project (AAPDEP) and our Department of Agitation and Propaganda (Agit-Prop). We also placed a lot of emphasis on building the international Party, the African Socialist International.

Prior to our Fifth Congress we would establish resolutions and mandates that often went without being held accountable. Our "One People! One Party! One Destiny!" Fifth Party Congress changed this and initiated an internal campaign to change the culture of our Party to one that demanded a different kind of structural accountability.

Although there are some things that we did not complete from our two preceding Congresses, they did not fall through the cracks as before. Some of our goals have gone unaccomplished, including at least one that will have to be reconsidered, such as the African Redemption Church.

We will also have to consider the strategic implications of trade union work as a primary means of organizing African labor. Our initial intent was to build a genuine, international African Internationalist trade union that would be used to organize African workers throughout the world into a single association. Initially there was a trade union organizer in Occupied Azania who we thought would lead this project. That has not worked out and we will revisit this issue.

One thing is certain: our trade union work will go beyond the opportunistic approach of simply organizing workers to fight for higher wages and better conditions. African workers must be won to their historically determined mission to become the new ruling class. While trade union organizations can be the vehicle for economic improvement, the Party must be the *political* organization of the African working class if their work is not to descend into opportunist economism that only fights for economic reforms under colonial capitalism.

Agit-Prop, the heartbeat of our Party

A critical component of our Party's structure is the Department of Agitation and Propaganda, or Agit-Prop. It is a department that has always been in an uneasy state of development. The department has within its purview a host of invaluable assets. These include:

- Overall responsibility for the political education and ideological development of the Party, the Uhuru Movement and the entire forcibly dispersed colonized African nation.
- Overall cadre development.
- *The Burning Spear* newspaper; Party book production and distribution.
- Our two FM radio stations in St. Petersburg, Florida.
- All our social media sites and their content.
- Training our Party and Movement in the art and science of production and distribution of the ideas and views of the African People's Socialist Party, etc.

A large department with a large responsibility, Agit-Prop is often characterized as the heart of our Party because it has custody of how the Party is perceived and how it perceives itself.

Agit-Prop is a department of which our Party can be most proud. For the entire 46-year history of our Party, Agit-Prop has published *The Burning Spear* newspaper despite contradictions that still plague us even today. It has provided political education and propaganda development. In fact, the Agit-Prop of old created the foundation upon which we stand today. It is responsible for the historical struggle by our Party for ideological fidelity and clarity and the political cohesion of our Party and Movement.

The work and responsibilities of Agit-Prop have grown over the years, requiring an increasing level of organization and sophistication to advance our Revolution during the development of every period of struggle. It has not been easy and our capacity has always been partially determined by the quality of Party forces available to us during each period.

This period, however, has resulted in generally high-quality recruits. One of them is Comrade Akilé Anai, a child of the Uhuru Movement who assumed the role of Agit-Prop Director in November 2017 and has moved swiftly to attack all the contradictions holding back the work and development of the department.

Since her appointment to the post, Comrade Akilé has moved to bring the necessary level of organization and efficiency to this critical department. When she assumed leadership of Agit-Prop, there were at least 30 members of *The Burning Spear* production team alone. One of the first things Comrade Akilé did was to determine the legitimacy of everyone working or assigned to the department. How many of them are really members of the Party? How many of them are actually participating in the committees to which they are formally assigned? How many of them have gone through the Party's sponsorship process and are capable of representing the Party's African Internationalist principles? These were questions that had to be answered in order to determine the quality of forces available to her and the department.

An example of the progress made by Akilé is a summary report for the department in April 2018:

> *Since the last NCC (National Central Committee) meeting, the Department of Agitation and Propaganda has made exciting new developments, consolidating the organizational structure, really incorporating the manuals, trainings and science to build this department and make our work successful. We have received new members who are enthusiastic about the work and Agit-Prop has taken the political development of its forces seriously, implementing a strict sponsorship process.*
>
> *Much of the work has been centered around activating each member and assigning them to an area of work, ensuring that no force falls through the cracks. This period has also focused a lot on getting the work of* The Burning Spear *on track—in terms of production, distribution, finances and staffing.*

The rest of the report has the same character that demonstrates that Agit-Prop is in good hands with Comrade Akilé. The trajectory is extremely positive. The future of the department—including every component, from the radio stations to *The Burning Spear*, to Burning Spear Publications and the economic development arm of Agit-Prop—is bright.

The Department must now move our agitation and propaganda work beyond the ongoing production and distribution of information throughout existing organs like our Black Power radio stations and *The Burning Spear* newspaper. We must learn to speak to this moment in history where white nationalist expressions and sentiments abound. Africans are reflexively looking for an ability to express our national identity, if only in self-defense.

The Department of Agit-Prop must begin to promote African national identity in a thousand different ways. The Red, Black and Green national flag our people inherited from the thousands of Africans who voted for it under the Garvey Movement a hundred years ago must be promoted and all our members and communities must proudly display it—all the time. Agit-Prop must produce popular posters and other items that portray our African nationality, including postcards, greeting cards and buttons, among other things.

The most significant weapon in the arsenal of Agit-Prop will continue to be *The Burning Spear.* This is the tool that weaponizes every member of the Party with the power to take our politics, our Party and our Movement to every door, shopping center and political event in our colonized communities. *The Burning Spear* provides all Party members and Movement supporters with day-to-day work, independent from the tasks that may be assigned by our leaders.

The greatest victory in Agit-Prop will be the success in winning the Party and our organizations to take seriously the important task of winning the war of ideas on every street corner and available space within our oppressed colony. This is the work of the Party that will create the impenetrable anti-colonial unity necessary for our victory.

It is also important to remind the Director of Agit-Prop of its tremendous capacity for economic development. In fact it is accurate to say that, next to the economic work under the leadership of the Office of the Deputy Chair, this Department has greater potential for economic development than any other department or committee of the Party.

The Office of the Secretary General leads Party recruitment

The Office of the Secretary General is now occupied by Comrade Gazi Kodzo. This is an important development because the Party has experienced serious political and organizational difficulties with this office having been unoccupied for too long. With Comrade Gazi's assumption of the responsibility of the Office of the Secretary General, we abolished the National Office of Recruitment and Membership (NORM) and brought the responsibility of the office under the leadership of the Secretary General.

Since our Fifth Party Congress we have placed a lot of emphasis on recruitment. We initiated a recruitment process along with organizational protocols for the Party and the Uhuru Movement as a whole, including Uhuru Solidarity Movement. Comrade Gazi's organization of NORM was impressive and, along with his reach as a social media personality, resulted in a rapid growth in our membership applications.

At first most of our recruitment came through social media and other internet connections. This was helpful for bringing new forces into our Party and Movement, in some cases strengthening our infrastructure. This approach has had its limitations, however. Too many recruits were more impressed with an internet personality than with the Party and African Internationalism. Too often their political and ideological unity was weak and transient.

Obviously this type of growth was short-lived, partially because it was centered on infrastructure development and there are limitations to what we can utilize within our infrastructure at any given moment. This led to a kind of bottle-necking that stalled the rapidity of our growth.

We now have a very efficient recruitment and membership office under the leadership of the Secretary General, that has an unprecedented level of competency in its recruitment and membership maintenance capacity. The Office of the Secretary General will give even better definition to recruitment and membership. The Secretary General's Office contains within it the ability to tailor recruitment, membership and assignment of our forces according to the strategic direction and requirements of the Party at any given time.

The work of the Secretary General must now be directed at the Party's dual power strategy which, among other things, will boost the Party's recruitment exponentially. We must create the regional economic-political hubs, initially radiating out from our West Coast, Midwest, Southern and Northern Regions. The Secretary General must plan to concentrate the necessary cadres where they are needed to consolidate our regional capacity whence all the work to build and lead the Party in every state is centered.

The entire Party must be armed to participate in the process of recruitment. This means that we must put more emphasis on training rank-and-file members as revolutionary African Internationalist evangelists. They must become active recruiters. Much of our new member sponsorship must be assigned to Party members by local Party organizations that the Secretary General will assist in creating.

Working closely with the President of the International People's Democratic Uhuru Movement and the Office of the Deputy Chair, the Secretary General must prepare to train our local organizations to procure and operate our local Party offices, keeping in mind that they will also serve as distribution arms of our economic products.

The growing manifestation of the Advanced Detachment of our colonized African nation will increasingly be found in the day-to-day work being done by the rank-and-file heroes and heroines of our Party and Movement.

The job description and much of the responsibility of the Secretary General can be found in our Constitution and Party Organizational Manual. Nevertheless, the work of the Secretary General is being developed daily and must reflect the strategic direction of the Party at any given time.

The Office of the Secretary General is being enthusiastically assumed by Comrade Gazi. He had already added an element of professionalism to the National Office of Recruitment and Membership (NORM) before its inclusion into the Office of the Secretary General. We expect Comrade Gazi to successfully build the Office. His fundamental stumbling block at the moment is petty bourgeois subjectivism, and because of the scope of this office in the Party, unchecked subjectivism can destroy the progress we make in every area of work.

Cadres are the best sons and daughters of Africa

Throughout the history of our Party, we have always put emphasis on the significance of cadre development. The success of the Party will always be determined by the quality of our cadres, those members of the Party who are the most dedicated to the African nation and working class.

Our cadres represent the best of our Party. They are most committed to the Revolution and fight hardest to live up to the principles of African Internationalism.

The work of the African People's Socialist Party following our Seventh Congress will rely on our cadres more than ever. We will be calling on you to multiply your presence more than a hundred-fold, more than a thousand-fold, so that our strategy of building strong power bases in the heart of the African working class colony throughout the U.S., Africa, Europe and the world can be realized.

In the recent period, the Party has concentrated much of our efforts on the task of building much-needed infrastructure. We have focused on locating and placing leadership for our many institutions, strategic committees and departments.

Obviously, we still have shortcomings in all of our departments, including Agit-Prop, the Secretary General's Office, even the Offices of the Chairman and Deputy Chair. The rapid growth of the Party, with so many recruits that are new to political life, guaranteed there would be a period of difficulties. Nevertheless, we are stronger and more competent than we have been in a long time.

The kind of growth we require now will rely more on the contact of our cadres with the African working class. The rank-and-file members of the African People's Socialist Party must become ubiquitous throughout our colonized working-class communities through our regional strategy.

We cannot overemphasize the need to redouble our work to sell our Party's journal, *The Burning Spear*. Again, the political work of every rank-and-file Party member should be winning more African workers to reading, writing for and distributing *The Spear.*

Our Fifth Party Congress declared our intent to transform contacts to members, members to cadres, and cadres to leaders and we must carry this out with enthusiasm and efficiency. This is ultimately what allows us to characterize ourselves as the Advanced Detachment. We firmly declare that the success of our Party will rest on every rank-and-file member assuming responsibility for that success.

A firm commitment to selling *The Burning Spear* within the most oppressed sectors of our colonized community makes all Party members immediately accessible to the African working class. We are there to provide political education around the pressing issues of the day, in our local communities and throughout the world.

We have a newspaper that speaks directly to the African working class, explaining their conditions in their own words whenever possible, and providing leadership wherever necessary. In the period ahead, *The Burning Spear* will become more of an organizing tool. Every Party member is transformed into a community leader through intensified massive distribution of *The Burning Spear* within our colonized communities.

Spear distribution is not a new task. It is something all Party members should already be involved in all the time.

The emphasis now placed on the importance of Party members religiously distributing *The Burning Spear* throughout the African colony, especially among the African working class, is a measure of the great importance placed on the role and responsibility of every individual member to fight to build the Party and provide direct leadership for our people everywhere.

Party cadres must also be the most dedicated members of our mass organizations, to the extent that much of the Party's work will occur from within the ranks of these formations. Party members within the mass organizations will ensure their stability and guarantee that they have real capability beyond what the new recruits will be able to contribute without further testing and development.

Mass organizations usually experience rapid turnover because, by nature, their work is most often initially built around symptoms of our colonized existence rather than by African Internationalist ideological conviction. In fact, it is usually through their participation in our mass work that recruits gain the political education to begin to discover the universal anti-colonial contradiction located in the particular struggle that has brought them into political life.

Party leadership within our mass organizations is another way the Party maintains firm links with the masses of our people, without which the Revolution is impossible. This will serve to remind both Party members *and* the African working class of our leading role as the Advanced Detachment and general staff of the African Revolution.

Today our primary work going forward is in the immediate locales of our individual members. New recruits must be assigned to organize in the cities and communities where they are located, building the presence of our Party directly or indirectly, in the form of one of our mass organizations, especially, but not exclusively, the International People's Democratic Uhuru Movement.

We will continue to target recruits for specific areas of need within our Party's growing infrastructure. However, Party members will be mandated to build the Party wherever they are.

This should maximize the growth of InPDUM. The Party members assigned to the organization will not only function as leaders and members of InPDUM; they will be tasked to build InPDUM through recruiting hundreds and thousands of non-Party members into the organization. This will thereby grow a massive reserve force for the Revolution and provide a deep connection with the masses who are being organized to fight against colonialism.

New Party recruits must be trained to work in and provide leadership for InPDUM and all our mass organizations. We do not want a Party that allows its members to hide in the organization without having to take direct, personal responsibility for our work.

Our participation in organized political education, rallies, programs and events are extremely important, but it must not be considered a substitute for *individual* Party members selling *The Spear* and building our organizational presence throughout the African colony, in the communities.

Office of Deputy Chair builds the independent African economy

The Party's Office of the Deputy Chair (ODC), led by Ona Zené Yeshitela, is involved in some of the most consequential work of the Party. It is moving in a solid Garveyesque manner to demonstrate the unity of economic and political work.

Comrades, all our political work is designed to overturn our relationship to colonialism, to become totally free, independent and prosperous based on applying our labor and wit to production for ourselves. Our struggle is to liberate the productive forces of the African nation, something that is impossible under foreign domination.

We have employed the anti-colonial strategy of creating dual power, a power of the people under the leadership of our Party, as part of the process of pushing the power of the colonial capitalists into irrelevancy. The greater the independent power of African people, the less is the power of the colonizer. Indeed, this is what democracy looks like for the colonized; this is the path to self-determination, the highest expression of democracy.

Evidence of the Party's dual power projects can be seen throughout the U.S. and increasingly they will be obvious throughout the African world. We don't have to elaborate on the success of our projects, especially since Comrade Deputy Chairwoman Ona Zené has assumed the helm of the office responsible for all our economic work.

However, in addition to all the expansive economic work that is already emanating from the ODC, there are other really exciting programs being developed by the Deputy Chair.

The first of these projects is a collective lending program that will allow Party organizations to contribute a meaningful amount of money to a microloan system that will enable these same Party organizations, programs, campaigns, to borrow money needed for projects, campaigns, equipment, etc.

This will not be a giveaway program. A loan committee will be established to weigh the viability of every loan request made in accordance with the rules of the loan program. The borrowed money will have to be repaid with a small interest necessary to pay for program administration, training, etc. In many ways, this program will be an incipient bank providing the necessary capital for self-reliant projects within our

Movement that will ultimately have the capacity to include other sectors of our colonized community as well.

The success of this program is simply another practical application of our strategy for dual power. Eventually it will sit side by side with an array of economic institutions of our Party and Movement that can supplant whatever influence the colonial-capitalist economic institutions enjoy within our community at this time.

As we know, the African working class does not have easy access to the economic institutions of the ruling class. Huge blocs of our people do not even have bank accounts. This leaves them vulnerable to vultures allowed to function in colonized communities by our colonizers worldwide charging exorbitant fees for financial services that deepen our dependency and contribute to the crisis of our colonized existence.

Our Party is responsible for many economic projects that need capital at any given time, sometimes for special projects that can expand our economic capacity and sometimes to meet shortfalls that a one-time loan can overcome.

Many capitalist businesses conduct their affairs with a relationship to financial institutions that forward them necessary capital from payday to payday or between business cycles. Most African businesses do not have that kind of relationship with bourgeois economic institutions. Certainly our Party organizations and economic projects do not either. With the implementation of the microloan project coming out of the Office of the Deputy Chair, we will no longer be dependent on colonial bank loans that dig us into a deeper hole of colonial dependency.

The Office of the Deputy Chair must create avenues for individual African businesses to work for collective, independent, anti-colonial economic development for the African nation as African businesses generally do not do this.

Often African businesses are influenced by the capitalist system within which they function.

Capitalism came into existence at the expense of any kind of independent economic activity by Africans and most other colonized peoples of the world. Profit is the primary motive in all capitalist economic activity. No matter how nice the owner of any economic venture may be, that owner is motivated to make profit, all of which comes as a consequence of exploitation of workers, either directly or indirectly.

Our economic activity must contend with the power and very existence of colonial capitalism by destroying its underpinning, the colonial domination and value extraction from African people at the expense of African self-reliance. The Party's anti-colonial programs will ultimately give us full access to African productive forces, the ability to create life for Africa and Africans.

Build the African National Independent Business Association

The struggle for dual power cannot be confined to the activities of our Party and Movement. It must incorporate the economic interests and activity of masses of our people whether they are part of our Party or Movement or not. Unfortunately, most of the barely-existing economic activity of our colonized community is driven by individual interests that are often informed by inefficiency, economic desperation and inadequate training.

Over the years of Party economic activity within our own independent institutions, we have accumulated a wealth of know-how. In the past, leaders of our economic institutions have paid to participate in trainings by experts in the retail industry. Now, *we* have become experts ourselves, not only in retail, but also in running commercial kitchens, bakery-cafes, rental spaces and innumerable Uhuru Movement related operations, commercial and otherwise.

Deputy Chairwoman Ona Zené Yeshitela has correctly concluded that we have acquired the skills and knowledge that can be transferred to Africans engaged in or wanting to engage in economic enterprises. Moreover, we can do so in a manner designed to win unity with participating in anti-colonial economic activity. This can satisfy the objective requirements of African businesses to fight for national emancipation from foreign capitalist white power.

This will not automatically make the businesses anti-capitalist, but it can make them anti-colonialist, placing them in objective unity with the struggle for national liberation that must be led by the African working class under the leadership of its Advanced Detachment. Indeed, it is the general staff of the African working class, the African People's Socialist Party, that is leading this charge to unite the national interests of all African people with the class interests of the African working class to defeat our national oppressors and build a new, liberated and united Africa and African people globally.

The Office of the Deputy Chair must move to organize as many independent African businesses as possible into an association that can offer training for business creation and development. The African National Independent Business Association will provide for Africans what the white colonial associations that sponsored the retail training we received over the years provided for us.

With this association we will not only contend with the capitalists that occupy the economic spaces in our communities all over the world, from Brixton in London, Accra in West Africa to the Southside of St. Petersburg, Florida, U.S. We will also be contending with the African petty bourgeois businesses that function as willing arms of white power, make no contributions to advance our oppressed communities and sometimes even imitate the hostile economic enterprises in their treatment of Africans who patronize them.

The independent African business association, organized under the leadership of the ODC, will compete with the "Buy Black" slogan of the African petty bourgeoisie with the anti-colonial slogan, "Buy Black Power!" This slogan was advanced by AAPDEP leader Aisha Fields through the Zenzele Consignment store and is already being advanced in all our economic institutions.

The African National Independent Business Association will offer annual week-long trainings to African entrepreneurs in business and those desiring to establish businesses. We will be able to provide these trainings for less than what we have paid for trainings over the years. Hosted in different cities, these trainings will provide access to information and visits to different African businesses for direct contacts that exemplify the possibilities of an independent African economy.

This business association will create an entirely new dynamic within the African colony. Currently all the economic leadership within the colonized African community is foreign and contributes to the ongoing dependency of African people. This is true whether the businesses are owned by Europeans, Chinese, Lebanese or Palestinians. The outcome is the same: Africans are dependent on others for our lives and livelihood. This is a direct result of colonialism. In fact, our colonized communities globally have often provided the stepping stones to success for economic outcasts of the capitalist system.

The Buy Black Power project will provide an important anti-colonial fightback, allowing African businesses to lower their prices to our community by buying together and reducing their cost. It can collectivize training for existing business owners and teach others how to go into business to serve our community. This work can help with the development of anti-colonial economic activity within the colonized African community that is not automatically or wholly connected to or dependent on foreign capitalism.

Most importantly, the African National Independent Business Association will become a conscious arm of the anti-colonial movement. The African businesses within our communities have an *objective* interest in the preservation and development of our colonized communities if only to protect their African market. The role of the Party of the African working class will be to provide anti-colonial ideological and political leadership for the businesses through the association.

The Office of the Deputy Chair must also investigate the possibility of organizing the many African contractors that are struggling independently to compete with colonial contractors in our own communities. The Black Power Blueprint project brought us into contact with many of these Africans who, for the most part are simply skilled workers who have had to create their own jobs by becoming contractors.

These previously unorganized contractors can be brought together and their skills organized in a way to contribute to their own betterment while uplifting our community. Separately, they find themselves having to compete for the same contracts. Sometimes these contracts are awarded by local or federal governments, who offer jobs that compromise our community's security or require them to take on work that functions to harm other people.

In St. Louis where we are concentrating on the Black Power Blueprint, the federal government has accumulated more than 100 acres of land upon which they intend to build a $1.75 billion super-spy agency. Although the agency intends to bring their own workers to build the project, African contractors are still expected to compete for the ability to participate in this death-wielding enterprise.

The participation of the African contractors in the St. Louis Black Power Blueprint project provided them with the practical evidence of the power of independent anti-colonial activity. At "The Big Reveal," that publicly unveiled the Uhuru House in St. Louis, there was an ongoing expression of appreciation by the African contractors for the presence and anti-colonial work of the Deputy Chair, her office and our Movement.

The contractors themselves actually donated to the project at "The Big Reveal," after many had already donated through price reduction for the magnificent work they had done and are doing with the Black Power Blueprint. Organized together as an anti-colonial African contractors' association they can even purchase some of the properties being captured by colonial interlopers who are pushing our people out of our communities in the process of "gentrification" or what is really African removal.

When the state of the Party is measured by the progress made within our infrastructure, the departments and committees responsible for the operation of our organization, it is clear that our Party has made incredible progress and stands today at the doorway of the future of African liberation and unification.

Nothing of this sort has occurred for our struggle since the magnificent Universal Negro Improvement Association and African Communities League of Marcus Garvey a hundred years ago. This is what the Advanced Detachment looks like. This is Garveyism of the 21st century.

VIII. The state of the Party, part 2

InPDUM: The mass fight for self-determination

The explosive growth of the African People's Socialist Party since our last Congress is evidenced by the development of our constituent mass organizations, the primary means by which the Party maintains firm links with the colonized African working class, as the Advanced Detachment of the African Revolution.

One of the most important organizations of the Party is the International People's Democratic Uhuru Movement (InPDUM).

Although the date given for the formal founding of InPDUM is April 1991, its predecessor was organized in Oakland, California in the mid-1980s as the People's Democratic Uhuru Movement (PDUM). The Party built PDUM as our mass organizational response to the brutal counterinsurgency that continued to impact the lives of African workers throughout the U.S.

By the time of PDUM's founding, our Party had built a powerful movement in Oakland. We were organizing on the streets every day fighting for the rights of the African working class, which had been demoralized by the U.S. military defeat of the Black Revolution of the Sixties.

During the Party's historic Oakland years, we had organized a massive land reform campaign following on the heels of a powerful struggle against the forced mass homelessness of African people. We got 30,000 signatures putting Measure O, the Community Control of Housing initiative on the Oakland ballot, winning more than 20,000 votes in 1984.

In the face of the growing mass incarceration of African people we had built the African National Prison Organization (ANPO) and helped to resurrect remnants of the U.S. Front of the African

Liberation Movement with the brilliant international campaign to "Free Dessie Woods, Smash Colonial Violence!"

We had succeeded in our goal of making reparations a household word when we created the African National Reparations Organization (ANRO) following the First International Tribunal on Reparations to African People in Brooklyn, New York in 1982.

Nevertheless conditions did not support the effort to take a revolutionary program directly to the masses. The U.S. counterinsurgency had so enfeebled the African Liberation Movement that the Party was nearly alone in our efforts to advance the Revolution. Moreover, the masses of our people suffered serious demoralization from the assassinations, jailings and the imposition of a drug economy within our community as neocolonial politicians were elevated to office.

We intended to use PDUM as an organizational front that would be engaged in ongoing struggle to win Africans to political action around the critical issues confronting us on a daily basis. These issues included the symptoms of colonialism such as police brutality, mass imprisonment, homelessness, mistreatment of our children in the schools, among others.

With this strategy the Party was soon able to bring more Africans in Oakland into a dynamic anti-colonial political movement. We resurrected former Black Panther Party leader Huey P. Newton back into temporary political life.

As we stated in the Political Report to our 2016 Plenary, it was with PDUM that we also created a free healthcare movement based in the mobile Bobby Hutton Freedom Clinic which won general support among the colonized African community and the people at large. We did this and more while creating an intensely activist, street-based, mass anti-colonialist, anti-capitalist movement that smashed the class peace in Oakland and allowed the masses to regain confidence in their own independent, revolutionary organization.

As it was initially conceived, PDUM also recruited North Americans through the involvement of our solidarity movement that took our campaigns and issues into the white colonizer nation community. This was a strategy to prevent isolation of our people and Party by winning support for our campaigns and raising much-needed material solidarity.

By 1991 it was clear to us that PDUM's work had to be taken beyond the Oakland Bay Area and everywhere throughout the U.S. where African workers were facing the same conditions. This was the basis of our decision to build the *National* People's Democratic Uhuru Movement (NPDUM) with a founding convention in Chicago on April 6, 1991.

My Political Report to the founding convention of NPDUM was clear on our need to complete the Black Revolution of the Sixties. We were explicit that NPDUM was founded and led by the African People's Socialist Party, the Advanced Detachment of the African working class, the Vanguard of the African Revolution. As we declared in the Political Report to the representatives from 25 cities and 24 states at the first NPDUM convention:

> *Some of you who are present today may very well see your presence as accidental. Perhaps you accidentally came upon a copy of* The Burning Spear *newspaper, or a brochure announcing the founding of the National People's Democratic Uhuru Movement today. Perhaps you saw Akua Njeri [Fred Hampton's widow and herself a survivor of the December 4, 1969 pre-dawn massacre] on television and heard her announce today's convention. Perhaps you heard a solidarity worker*

on the radio or bumped into an Uhuru organizer on your campus or in your community.

Whatever the case, we want to say right now that your presence here is no accident. It is a consequence of hard work that is consistent with a major strategic aim to complete the Black Revolution of the Sixties....

For 19 years we have worked to build and consolidate the African People's Socialist Party as the advanced detachment of the most slandered, feared and despised African working class that continues even today to experience the brunt of the counterinsurgency....

Nor are these empty boastful statements. The reality of my words is to be seen in the essentially working class composition of the African participants in this meeting and the fact that everyone who is here is here essentially through the independent efforts of these African workers and their revolutionary Party.

All the comrades who are here—from California and Florida, from Indiana, Kansas, Maryland, Oklahoma and other places—are here through their own efforts to facilitate our own agenda without the contamination of white liberal [trade] unionism, any front of the Democratic party or white nationalist leftists or connections with the liberal African petty bourgeoisie. We are here through our own efforts and that is a turning point in our movement, an indication that the counterinsurgency is being overcome and the masses of African people are re-entering political life on our own terms.[1]

The founding convention recognized that "to defeat U.S. parasitic white capitalism we must struggle for real democracy." Our convention made it clear that we mean something different by "democracy" than the liberals of the oppressor and oppressed nations:

> *...[E]ven as we struggle to defend the national democratic rights won by our people in the past, rights which are constantly being abrogated by the U.S. government in the name of fighting a war against drugs, the National People's Democratic Uhuru Movement will struggle to extend the question of democracy beyond the definition of the liberal African petty bourgeoisie.*[2]

We explained that for colonized people the highest expression of democracy is self-determination. This became the guiding line of NPDUM. It was our understanding that because democracy is simply a form of the state, in the struggle for liberation and socialism we must overturn bourgeois democracy itself. In fact, for colonized people the struggle for democracy can only be won by eliminating the authority of the colonial state over our lives.

NPDUM soon grew internationally into the *International* People's Democratic Uhuru Movement (*In*PDUM) with the establishment of branches in Europe and Africa.

Over the years, InPDUM has waged intense struggles against virtually every manifestation of anti-democratic

1 *Report by Omali Yeshitela to the National People's Democratic Uhuru Movement Founding Convention*, April 6, 1991, https://archive.org/details/NationalPeoplesDemocraticUhuruMovement

2 Ibid.

activity by the colonial state in various places around the world. This includes London, Sierra Leone, Toronto, Canada and cities throughout the U.S.

Before the people of the world had ever heard of Mike Brown and Ferguson, Missouri, InPDUM had been leading a mass fightback for decades against police terror on the streets of Philadelphia, Chicago and London.

It was InPDUM that confronted the neocolonial government in Sierra Leone in West Africa. It was InPDUM that withstood and defended ourselves against a military assault on our St. Petersburg, Florida headquarters by more than 300 colonial police personnel with light airplanes, helicopters and the city's entire reserve of tear gas against our organization and leaders.

Political conditions and the dearth of Party cadres at the time prevented us from immediately achieving the full potential of InPDUM. Nevertheless the organization tremendously impacted the ability of our colonized people to fight back from the terror-induced stupor experienced by Africans everywhere, still recovering from the setbacks to our struggle against foreign and alien domination.

With imperialism in crisis InPDUM leadership takes the offensive

That era of InPDUM as a *defensive* response to the counterinsurgency is surely over. Today's world is characterized by a determined, if not-yet-consolidated, shift in the global balance of power. This is a period of frenzied despair by colonial powers, caused by the growing confidence of colonially oppressed peoples everywhere. What is true of the world in general is also true within the borders of the U.S., where the government is using all of its compromised political power to push back the incipient organizational expression of mass African anti-colonial re-entry into political life.

InPDUM has gone through a number of leaders since its founding. Each was a reflection of the period and the political and ideological development within the Party and the African Liberation Movement of the time.

While each leader was a person of conviction, none of them constituted revolutionary cadre in the truest sense of the term. We have lost leaders because of their unwillingness to recognize that InPDUM is an instrument of the African People's Socialist Party's strategy to mobilize and organize the masses of African people into a determined revolutionary anti-colonial process.

We have had at least one leader of InPDUM whose primary role at a critical moment was to provide stability and continuity to the organization.

Subjectivism and other expressions of individualism and liberalism also played roles in the contradictions of past leaders. Another leader was characterized by cadre-like tendencies—boldness, creativity and a willingness to initiate, engage with and participate in mass struggle—but whose activities were directed more toward self-promotion than building InPDUM.

Today, things have been turned around and each day the future looks brighter for InPDUM. The leadership provided by Comrade Sister Kalambayi Andenet, fresh to political life and new to the Party and the Uhuru Movement, is a major factor in rectifying some past errors.

In August 2014 our Party encountered Sister Kalambayi in a demonstration in Ferguson, Missouri protesting the police murder of Mike Brown. That murder was the straw that broke the camel's back, kicking off a new era of struggle that helps to shape the mission of InPDUM at this time. In this short period of time Kalambayi has become a member of our Party and has come to exemplify the power and will of the conscious African proletariat.

Since her September 2015 appointment as InPDUM President, this young mother of two daughters has brought a new energy to the mass organization of the Party and to all who have been touched by her presence and leadership in the struggles characterizing the period. Kalambayi has moved swiftly with the daunting task of consolidating InPDUM's leading body and breathing life into the too-often neglected organizational structures.

Clearly Kalambayi Andenet is the right leader for InPDUM at the right time. Now InPDUM must prepare to effectively move to the offensive after its beginning as a defensive response to the military defeat of our Movement.

This is the Party's most important connection to the masses of our people. It is the Party's instrument for intervening in the struggles of our people with revolutionary science.

InPDUM is the method through which African Internationalist cadres can root ourselves among the people and provide leadership for the thousands of Africans who, for any number of reasons, are not members of our Party.

Currently the general response to the U.S. colonial police murders of Africans is not led by our Party or any anti-colonial organization of the African working class for that matter. Every hustler and charlatan quickly descends to the scene of the latest colonial crime and positions himself at the front of mass demonstrations brandishing reformist banners and slogans.

African students, many with bourgeois political aspirations of their own or misdirected by assumptions of colonially-defined education, sometimes militantly rush to the forefront of the mass movements blithely regurgitating political conclusions from colonial civic lessons.

This range of forces, combined with the conscious opportunists, is determined to smother the ability to advance long-term revolutionary conclusions that answer the question: "To what end?"

This gives greater urgency than ever to the role of InPDUM.

Our Party encountered all these forces upon our arrival in Ferguson. None of these forces are new to us. The truth is that Africans suffer *colonial* oppression, oppression that affects the entire African nation. It is logical that non-proletarian forces will move to take the leadership of the response to colonial brutality. All of them have more resources and meet the standards of bourgeois media compared to the African working class.

The contradiction InPDUM was formed to overcome is the absence of the organized leadership of the proletariat. InPDUM, as an organization of our Party, has to be present to directly contend with non-proletarian forces for the leadership of our people.

The presence of opportunist, petty bourgeois forces in mass struggle should not be used as an excuse for our lack of participation. Such a failure to intervene would be the basis for self-criticism, for relinquishing the field of combat to non-revolutionary social forces.

The mass resistance of the past few years is a sign of the growing African national consciousness. The expansion of our Party's influence and the enthusiasm for the Black Power Blueprint in St. Louis are evidence that we have entered a new period of anti-colonial African resistance within current borders of the U.S. InPDUM must build for the long term to contend with the pending whirlwind of struggle.

We reiterate that every member of the Party must join InPDUM even if our primary work prohibits us from the fullest participation. Our membership dues and presence in local meetings give the organization greater capacity on many levels.

InPDUM must be the most zealous distributor of the Party's press, especially *The Burning Spear* for which it must also supply articles that will facilitate its organizing efforts.

Our Party leaders must also be cognizant of the role of InPDUM as a major producer of a deep pool of potential Party recruits, a reserve force for the Revolution, where Africans learn organization and how to be organized.

InPDUM must become the method with which we actually contend with non-proletarian forces for political, ideological and territorial influence and power.

Community political education classes and integration of InPDUM members into other campaigns and institutions of the Party will become weapons in the struggle to win this battle against colonialism.

As we discuss thoroughly in Chapter VI, the strategic direction following our Seventh Congress will require InPDUM to open offices in the various working class communities throughout the African colony. This is how we move toward real organizing of the African working class with a strategy that places us in the midst of the colonized communities with our people, sharing their circumstances and building our own solutions.

Chapter VI lays out a detailed plan for how local InPDUM offices in the heart of the African working class communities will become outlets for Party economic development products, from African and Movement clothing to Uhuru Foods & Pies. Under the determined leadership of our cadres, they will be the place where community food gardens and other ventures will be organized by the people and among the people. This is the most important strategic direction for InPDUM moving from our Seventh Congress, the strategic direction that truly requires members of our Party to assume the responsibility of the Advanced Detachment.

InPDUM has moved to repair its recruitment and membership process to make it consistently reliable with a growth in numbers that reflects its influence and the obvious desire of the thousands of African workers to join our Movement.

InPDUM must construct an internal apparatus for initiating and overseeing an effective, scientifically-based branch building campaign. Membership and branches, while always important, are even more critical today with our plans for dual power advances led by individual members of InPDUM from local offices wherever we are.

The fact that InPDUM's international office is currently located at the Uhuru House in St. Louis is recognition of the role of that city in the re-energized consciousness of the colonized Africans throughout the U.S.

St. Louis is the front line of the struggle at this moment. Additionally, the rich history of African culture and resistance in St. Louis also plays a major role in the organizing efforts of the Advanced Detachment in a city where the African working class clearly desires an ability to fight in its own selfish interests.

Our designation as the Advanced Detachment can be seen in the ongoing work being done by President Kalambayi to overcome contradictions and build InPDUM into a massive organization. Its growth will meet the task imposed on us by history at this moment of imperialist crisis where the bloated underbelly of white power is being daily exposed for revolutionary assault.

InPDUM President Kalambayi comes directly from the African working class. As an African mother of two children she brings an important connection to the 50 percent of the colonized African population that is too often left out of all the political discussions and struggles we are making to capture political power and change the world. To the dismay of some, perhaps many, Comrade Kalambayi's presidency contributes to the obvious inclusion of many African women in the struggle for our liberation and unification of Africa and Africans worldwide.

The intense struggle within InPDUM to transform the organization into the best possible mass vehicle for waging the struggle against colonialism contributes to our ability to loudly declare that we are winning, that the ranks of the Advanced Detachment are growing daily and becoming more competent in the process of doing so.

Now, we must build InPDUM, this incredibly important arm of the Party and our Revolution, into an organization of tens of thousands. We must do this quickly and efficiently, using all the protocols and manuals for building and recruiting.

InPDUM is in a position to operate in the various working class communities of our dispersed colonized nation that have been abandoned by the African petty bourgeois opportunists. These are communities that are always under the cruel boot of colonial oppression. These are our communities, the communities of the Advanced Detachment, the Vanguard.

AAPDEP leaps forward with Zenzele and Project Black Ankh

Another critical weapon in the arsenal of our Party is the All African People's Development and Empowerment Project (AAPDEP), formed to collectivize the vast skills of Africans around the world in order to establish community based development projects that improve the quality of life for African people everywhere while promoting self-reliance and self-determination as key to genuine, sustainable development.

The work of AAPDEP made major leaps this year despite the previous uncertainties and ups and downs of this work headquartered in Huntsville, Alabama. A significant turning point of AAPDEP work was the creation of Zenzele

Consignment, AAPDEP's economic development institution in August 2016.

Zenzele marks an important contribution to our Party's fight for anti-colonial economic self-reliance, but it is more than that. Zenzele provides AAPDEP with a permanent physical presence, a place where Africans in Huntsville can come to participate in the work and the various events that we initiate from this location.

Zenzele provides AAPDEP with an office and a recruitment station as well as African clothing and accessories that complement our cultural outreach.

The consignment store also opens the door for participation in the Party's work by volunteers who sympathize with the causes promoted by AAPDEP. Party and Movement meetings are conducted there. Already the store has magnified the Party's presence many times over. It enhances the Party's work by helping the working class to recognize us as more than some fly-by-night operation of militants who only talk a good game. We are made real in the minds of many by the presence of Zenzele.

An outstanding example of cadre was seen in the work by Comrade Aisha Fields to build AAPDEP's November 2017 national convention in Huntsville. Attended by Africans from throughout the U.S., including new members and leaders, the convention was especially important for what it promised through its work to build the Project Black Ankh, our response to the imperialist Red Cross. Project Black Ankh established a presence and reputation during the Ebola crisis in Sierra Leone in 2014.

The AAPDEP convention also unveiled a program related to the Black Ankh that teaches disaster preparation to our colonized communities. This will make Africans less dependent on the imperialists for aid. AAPDEP is contributing to the self-determination of African people with this and other programs that empower the people and can be easily implemented in virtually every African community in the world.

Much of AAPDEP's work will be showcased at our Seventh Congress. It is consistent with our approach to our struggle to end our colonial subjugation and reliance on our colonial oppressors. AAPDEP's work exemplifies the unity of practice and theory that we find so important. It is the work that keeps us out of the category of simple dispensers of information and people with great ideas that, for whatever reason, cannot be implemented in the real world. This is what makes us the Advanced Detachment of the African Revolution and the Vanguard of the African working class.

ANWO: African women key to African national liberation

The African National Women's Organization (ANWO) is another example of genuine cadre work that embodies the theme of our Seventh Congress.

ANWO's 2018 convention, the first since its founding, clearly opened the door for women to come fully and enthusiastically into revolutionary political life. It proved for everyone that the struggle of African women does not have to be bogged down in the swamps of petty bourgeois feminism. African women want revolution and they want the removal of any obstacle that stands between them and revolution.

The convention revealed that African women want to struggle around all the issues affecting them and not just the issues affecting upper class women.

ANWO recognizes that the contradictions between colonized African men and African women are non-antagonistic. ANWO helps everyone to see that while there are contradictions in everything, we can only win our liberation by being able to identify the *main* contradiction, the one around which all the others revolve, the one which provides the conditions for the existence of the others. That main contradiction is colonialism, the foreign and alien domination of our whole people: men, women and children.

While the main contradiction afflicting us all is colonialism, ANWO recognizes that there are contradictions between African men and women and that the struggle to resolve these non-antagonistic contradictions must be ruthlessly fought in the process of destroying the system of colonial capitalism.

ANWO's March 2018 convention offers profound evidence of the general state of our Party approaching our Seventh Congress. Comrade Yejide Orunmila, President of ANWO and the head of the Party's Women's Commission is truly stepping up to provide leadership for ANWO and the struggle against the hostile, petty bourgeois, feminist ideological invasion of our colonized community.

The convention reported on the programs and campaigns of ANWO including the Uhuru Kijiji Childcare Collective, a dual power do-for-self institution that takes the childcare and education of our children out of the hands of the state that colonizes, oppresses and kills them and empowers the parents and our community to re-assume responsibility over the lives of African children.

Black is Back Coalition unites around self-determination

The Black is Back Coalition for Social Justice, Peace and Reparations (BIBC) is one of the most important areas of mass work our Party has been involved in for the last nine years.

The Coalition has allowed the Party to participate in developing and implementing a revolutionary national democratic program designed to unite the U.S. domestically colonized African population in an anti-colonial trajectory. The Coalition has also been important for winning different political tendencies within the basic anti-imperialist sector of our community in a common organization. Previously they were just individuals or organizations working in isolation from each other without any general, united-upon program.

The Black is Back Coalition is another accomplishment that permits us to recognize our Party as the Advanced Detachment of the African Revolution and the Vanguard of the African working class. The more than forty years of consistent Party work prepared our Party for the task of organizing the Coalition. We organized this much-needed, united, anti-colonial formation because we were the only organization with the capacity to do so. Unlike the African petty bourgeoisie that is always blinded by its own narrow selfish class interests, the Party is the only social force capable of uniting the fight for the liberation of our whole people.

The existence of the Coalition defied the petty bourgeois cynical assumptions of the inability to win the unity of different class and ideological expressions of self-determination into a single, unified organization.

It has taken the skill and determination of the African People's Socialist Party to hold the Coalition together for nine years as a critical force for advancing our struggle against colonial capitalism. This happened despite the obvious differences in class and ideological outlooks in the Coalition from its very inception. We were able to do this because the Party has always embraced the struggle for national liberation as an instrument for winning the liberation and unification of Africa and African people worldwide under the leadership of the African working class.

The participation of the Party in the Coalition has contributed to a new definition of the antiwar or peace movement. We have challenged the notion of imperialist peace championed by the antiwar movement, a peace that does not call for the victory of the oppressed.

Through our work in the Coalition we have defined and organized against the war of colonial terror imposed on Africans and others in the U.S. and around the world that is usually ignored by the white antiwar movement. This includes the relentless aggression against the Indigenous people in the concentration camps and the barrios of the U.S.

The struggles of the people of the Philippines and throughout the Americas were seldom if ever raised by the peace movement before the intervention by the Coalition. Our Party played no small part in helping to force these issues onto the anti-imperialist peace agenda.

The Coalition organized a National Conference Against the Other Wars in Washington, DC in 2011. Before the advent of the Coalition the antiwar movement saw no interest in opposing imperialist aggression against our people and the peoples of the world when there was no direct or indirect potential for North Americans or white people being harmed by existing or pending war.

Over the years the Coalition has continued to grow and win greater recognition within the anti-imperialist and anti-colonial movement in the U.S. The Coalition has provided important mass political education through its annual mobilizations and conferences attracting hundreds of people and opening up political discussions that had been muted by the defeat of our Revolution of the '60s.

After the 2008 election of Barack Hussein Obama, the Black is Back Coalition began a serious discussion around the electoral process and the role of Obama as president. This allowed the Party to participate in defining the role of bourgeois elections before extremely receptive audiences. The Coalition also organized schools to challenge the hegemony of the reactionary African petty bourgeoisie over the electoral process, a process that we recognize in our Party as a major method used by the white ruling class to implement neocolonial domination of our people.

The participation of our people in these schools was the best possible evidence of the effectiveness of the Coalition and the role of our Party in this mass work. The Black is Back Coalition electoral schools also provided the unambiguous basis for legitimate anti-colonial intervention in the electoral process, an issue that has been controversial within the U.S.-based African Liberation Movement since universal suffrage for Africans in the U.S. was legalized in 1965.

The years of uninterrupted revolutionary work of our Party also made it possible to provide a variety of resources to the Coalition, human and material. We had the capacity within the African People's Socialist Party to put organizers on the ground to bring many of the Coalition projects to fruition. The years of development and leadership of our Party made it possible for our institutions to often provide meeting spaces for Coalition conferences and events. The independent capacity of our Party allowed us to confer an independent capacity to our Movement.

Within the Coalition there are Africans who are actively engaged in work to win black community control of the police, reparations, release of and relief for political prisoners and black community control of education, the National Black Political Agenda for Self-determination and a process for determining the legitimacy of black elected officials and anyone campaigning for the African vote. All found in a single organization!

This is not to say that the Coalition is a revolutionary organization. It is not. So far it appears that the Party is the only participating organization that even claims revolution as its objective. In fact, there are some within the Coalition who still unite with traditional liberal white Left antiwar assumptions that call for the end of war and U.S. "militarization" including slogans like “Money for Jobs, Healthcare, and Education, Not for War.”

This, of course, is a total misunderstanding of colonialism and imperialism in general. The colonial-capitalist system is a colonial-capitalist system and it does not make resources available for the colonially oppressed during recognized periods of war *or* periods of “peace.”

However, the nature of the Black is Back Coalition allows for the coexistence of different worldviews. We are a revolutionary organization with the seizure of power on our agenda. This is not true of any other Coalition organization. Our participation in the Coalition revolves around a broad anti-imperialist national agenda that forwards the struggle for national liberation without necessarily addressing the issue of class, tactics and strategy and the kind of social system being pursued.

Unlike some Coalition partners, our Party does not depend on an epiphany from the Congressional Black Caucus or any other variation of the “congressional strategy” traditionally embraced by the Communist Party USA as a substitute for fighting for the independent power of a working class. The record of the Congressional Black Caucus is clear. It is deeply attached to imperialism and does not even have the capacity for any kind of anti-colonial activity or statement. We see dependence on the Congressional Black Caucus or some liberal wing of the Democratic party as conceding our leadership of the African working class struggle to the white ruling class.

Unlike some other activists in the Coalition, our Party is free to pursue an anti-colonial peace, as opposed to an imperialist peace. Because we are an independent Party with a real capacity we are not in the position of having to curry favor with the liberal white Left, representatives of the colonizer population, to win support for a real anti-imperialist agenda. While our Party is a revolutionary anti-colonial-capitalist Party of the African working class, most of the antiwar or peace movement is led by specific liberal Left party-type formations, such as the Workers World Party or its splinter group, the Party for Socialism and Liberation.

The Coalition is an organization of organizations and institutions. There are also individual members of the Coalition who are advised to join one of the various working groups. The very nature of the Coalition means that it is comprised of different ideological, political and even class expressions, a fact that seriously challenges the permanent unity of the organization. However, because ours is a Party of the working class, we have always recognized the importance of anti-colonial unity to advance the revolutionary interests of the African nation under the leadership of the African working class.

APSC builds "unity through reparations!"

There is no way to speak of the state of the Party without acknowledging one of our most significant organizations, the African People's Solidarity Committee (APSC). APSC was organized by the Party in 1976 in St. Petersburg, Florida. Its creation was one of the most important occurrences in the history of our revolutionary struggle for the total liberation and unification of Africa and African people worldwide.

We must also recognize the role in the development of APSC that was played by its Chairwoman, Comrade Penny Hess. Comrade Penny has been the most important factor in the development of the African People's Solidarity Committee and the solidarity movement as a whole. After years of struggle with the North American comrades to move beyond white liberalism to a genuine stance of anti-colonial solidarity, it was Comrade Hess who finally broke from the pack, united with the Party's line and realized our efforts to build a movement of principled white solidarity with African liberation.

It was Comrade Hess' intervention that resulted, for the first time after an initial eight years of struggle waged by the Party with the solidarity forces, in a political stance and theoretical unity by APSC that reflected our African Internationalist worldview and practice. It was through Comrade Hess that the Party was first able to experience our political line, theory and practice coming back to us from the APSC.

The initial formation of APSC was met with hostility and suspicion from the colonizer communist organizations and other liberal white Leftists. A recurring criticism by the white Left revolved around the idea of whites working under the leadership of African people.

One colonizer nation communist party went so far as to say that APSC would fail because whites "would not work against their own interests," a most revealing statement suggesting that working under African working class leadership was not in the interests of whites. This was an especially instructive criticism as it was uttered by an organization that otherwise extolled the leadership of the working class.

Some African race nationalists were also opposed to the founding of APSC. Some stated opposition despite the fact that many had secret, which is to say, unprincipled relationships with white Left liberals that their race nationalist politics could not justify. Some, including those with secret relationships, opposed the founding of APSC because "white people cannot be trusted."

Today APSC and the solidarity movement directly under its leadership number hundreds of members who are constantly and actively involved in fighting for black power within the colonizer community. This means even within their families these North Americans are fighting to win African Internationalist, anti-colonial unity with our struggle. This requires more than simply having forums and participating in debates and the like with white Left organizations.

APSC, its mass formation Uhuru Solidarity Movement (USM) and other sectors of the solidarity movement under its leadership, fight for *material* solidarity. Through APSC our Party has been able to extend the struggle for reparations to African people to the colonizer nation population.

The founding of APSC has permitted the Party to do what has never been done before: we are actually collecting reparations from thousands of white people who want to rectify their relationship to African people and have been educated to understand the relationship between white affluence and the destitution of the rest of the world. They understand the difference between reparations as an anti-colonial struggle and charity which benefits the colonial donor.

APSC and USM are growing exponentially. The work under the leadership of APSC represents the most dynamic, fastest growing anti-imperialist movement within the North American community. Daily, mostly young people from the colonizer nation are being brought into the embrace of our Party through the work of APSC. At the time of this writing the Uhuru Solidarity Movement has members in at least 30 states within current U.S. borders. All signs indicate that the number will continue to grow.

The Party's 2017 political campaign in St. Petersburg, Florida was highly effective in popularizing the movement for reparations to African people inside of the white community. The Party ran a member of the African People's Solidarity Committee, Jesse Nevel, the National Chair of USM, for mayor of St. Petersburg, Florida, along with Party leader Akilé Anai for District 6 city council.

Although we lost the election, we were able to initiate an unending campaign that saw hundreds of white people marching through the streets chanting "unity through reparations" and "solidarity with the black working class." This is the kind of work the Party has been able to do through APSC that will have lasting political implications throughout the world.

APSC and USM have also played critical roles in the Black Power Blueprint campaign in St. Louis. They have been able to win reparations in the amount of thousands of dollars from other white people who are consciously uniting with the African working class Party to overturn colonialism. Many white people express their gratitude for this opportunity to take a principled, non-opportunist stand in the struggle against colonial capitalism.

If they are not joining the solidarity movement they are certainly being influenced by our Party. There are literally thousands of white people who patronize the economic institutions of Black Star Industries and the African People's Education and Defense Fund (APEDF) that are currently managed by members of the African People's Solidarity Committee under the leadership of Deputy Chair Ona Zené Yeshitela. All of them receive basic information that informs them that the solidarity presence in our institutions—our furniture stores, our food booths, the One Africa! One Nation! Marketplace—is voluntary, informed participation in the struggle for black power under the leadership of our Party.

The work of the solidarity movement continues to introduce and win support from whites for reparations to African people. We are certain that many Africans who organize around reparations among the colonized African population are unaware that their reparations work is being made easier by the existence of APSC inside the colonizer nation population.

Party's St. Pete electoral campaign spawns C.U.R.E.D.

One of the most impressive mass campaigns of our Party, one that speaks eloquently to our growing capacity and strategic clarity, was the 2017 electoral campaign in St. Petersburg, Florida, where the Party fielded two candidates, one for city council and the other for mayor. The Party's candidate for the District 6 city council seat was Akilé Anai. Our mayoral candidate was Jesse Nevel from the African People's Solidarity Committee.

In a six-month campaign that lasted from March through August our candidates forced the issue of reparations to African people onto the electoral ballot and the consciousness of the city's population. Millions of people throughout the U.S. are unfamiliar with the reparations demand. Within six months we made it a popular issue precisely because it was on the electoral ballot, the primary means by which political ideas achieve legitimacy for most people within the U.S. prison of nations.

Despite the fact that the African population of St. Petersburg comprises only 23 percent of the total population, our candidates electrified all the electoral debates. On one occasion they led hundreds of white people in a march through downtown St. Petersburg chanting, "Unity through Reparations!" and expressing solidarity with black power under the leadership of the African working class!

This has never happened in the history of the colonial domination of our people in the U.S. or in the world for that matter.

Local elections in St. Petersburg are officially nonpartisan, but almost everyone understands that the candidates are representatives of their respective ruling class political parties. Our campaign split the local Democratic party whose secretary and treasurer joined with our Uhuru candidates and actually became precinct leaders. On the other hand the chair of the Pinellas County Democratic party joined with the head of the Police Benevolent (sic) Association and declared our Movement a domestic terrorist organization. This led to a reprimand by an African leader of the Democratic party in another county.

For the first time in the city's history one of the candidates for mayor—ours—was denied access to the only televised mayoral debate. The ruling class debate sponsors even denied the people of St. Petersburg free access to the "debate" venue because of fear of attendance by the enthusiastic base of the Uhuru Movement. Eventually they decided on an "invitation only" policy for attendance.

A summation of the groundwork done for the campaign was printed in the November 2017 issue of *The Burning Spear*. It is impressive and speaks volumes to the state of our Party. Here is what it says:

> *During the 6-month campaign the committee:*
>
> - *Submitted 1,800 signed petitions to get Jesse Nevel's name on the ballot.*
> - *Held 15 press conferences.*
> - *Held 15 of our own actions and events.*
> - *Knocked on or dropped literature at 25,000 doors.*
> - *Made 10,000 calls to voters and our base.*
> - *Distributed 700 yard signs.*
> - *Had one 6,000 piece mass mailing.*
> - *Made one TV commercial that ran on 15 cable stations.*
> - *InPDUM held 24 Sunday Rallies to meet the candidates.*
> - *Participated, spoke or intervened at 20 community events, debates and churches.*
> - *Had a social media reach in the tens of thousands.*

- *Raised $14,500 for Jesse Nevel's campaign and $11,700 for Akilé's.*[3]

The Burning Spear article ended with this declaration:

> *Although we did not win the election, we built a powerful movement based in the African working class of St. Petersburg. We created the foundation for winning numerous reparations elections in the future by forming the vibrant precinct-based organization Communities United for Reparations and Economic Development (C.U.R.E.D.) led by Akilé Anai and Jesse Nevel.*[4]

C.U.R.E.D. joins the long list of mass fronts through which the Party continues to express its profound influence and revolutionary leadership in this upcoming period. The growth of our mass organizations represents practical evidence that we are the Advanced Detachment of the African Revolution. We have always moved with the conviction that our deep relationship with the masses of our people, who are the real makers and shapers of history, will ensure the inevitable victory in our struggle for national liberation. Our strategy is working.

Comrades, we are winning! If we carry out the mandates laid out here and implement the regional strategy unveiled in Chapter VI, by the time of our next Congress in 2023, we will have put organizational roots down in the heart of colonial capitalism throughout the African world, with the capability of choking the life out of our colonial oppressors. With this strategy the Advanced Detachment of the African working class will make revolution the main trend in the world

3 "Uhuru campaign committee waged powerful ground war in St. Pete election," *The Burning Spear* newspaper, November 2017.

4 Ibid.

again and unite with oppressed peoples everywhere to wipe imperialist white power off the face of the Earth.

IX. The theory of African Internationalism

The chapter "The theory of African Internationalism" from Chairman Omali Yeshitela's Political Report to the Sixth Congress held in 2013 and published in the book, An Uneasy Equilibrium: African Internationalism versus Parasitic Capitalism *has been included in the Political Report to the Seventh Congress.*

The depth of the Chairman's explanation of African Internationalism with its profound political and historical documentation makes this chapter a must-read for all members and supporters of the African People's Socialist Party. This piece on African Internationalism is considered by the Party's Department of Agit-Prop to be definitive and is a necessary tool empowering everyone to successfully defend the Party's African working class political theory of African Internationalism against all challenges.

The science of African Internationalism enabled our Party to avoid the ideological pitfalls that validate the assumption of the superiority of white people. Thus, we have never been diverted from our mission of capturing power and uniting Africa and our nation under the leadership of the African working class.

Our Party brought science to our defeated African Liberation Movement at a time when it was generally bogged down in racial and cultural nationalism that indulged in candlelit ceremonies, religious obscurantism and nostalgia for an often-imaginary African past. Through African Internationalism we were able to discover the material basis for the exploitation and oppression of Africans and others in this world.

With African Internationalism we can understand the material forces at work in the movement of history. We can clearly see the current shift in the balance of power between the oppressor and the oppressed, between Europe and the rest of us, between the "white man" and the "black man."

We determined long ago that characterizing our Movement as a struggle against racism was a self-defeating waste of time. What is called racism is simply the ideological foundation of capitalist imperialism. Racism is a concept that denies Africans our national identity and dignity, rather than defining the system of our oppression. It relegates us to the Sisyphean task of winning acceptance from, and often of becoming one with, our oppressors.

With African Internationalism we have proven that race is simply a colonial invention originating from the enslavement and colonization of Africans and Africa that gave birth to capitalism and, simultaneously, the European nation. Our struggle has always been for power, not against racism. To the extent that we win power, the "racism" of others becomes irrelevant. Power is the great equalizer, the fundamental "aphrodisiac" that is capable of turning a racist of today into a fawning sycophant of tomorrow.

The struggle against "racism" is the struggle of the petty bourgeoisie fighting to integrate into the white capitalist world, to board the sinking ship of white power. It is a diversionary struggle reliant on failed philosophical assumptions that must be cast aside as a precondition for moving forward.

This is not an innocent issue of semantics. The way this is understood informs our practice. The struggle against "racism" presupposes one approach and the struggle against imperialist colonialism another.

Africans are not a race but a nation of people, forcibly dispersed across the globe. We have been pushed out of history by our imperialist oppressors, partially through the concept of "race." Our national homeland has been occupied in various ways for millennia. Our people have been captured and shipped around the world as capitalist commodities. Our labor and land have been violently extracted to build the European nation and the international capitalist system. This is what determines our reality and the contours of the struggle in which we have been engaged for more than 500 years.

The fight against AFRICOM[1] cannot be characterized as a struggle against "racism" any more than the liberation of our people in Haiti from France in 1804 or the necessary unification of Africa to stop the rape of our Motherland and the theft of its resources.

The material conditions Africans suffer worldwide have their origin in the attack on Africa that led to the capture of our national homeland and our people. Our poverty and susceptibility to ignorance, violence and material want throughout the world—including in the U.S., UK and the rest of Europe—result from the material conditions of existence in Africa since its capture and partition!

Are the Iraqis and Afghans fighting against racism? What about all the people of South America and the Caribbean? Certainly, the bourgeois ideology of "racism" serves to unite the vast majority of whites and even some Africans in support of the imperialist agenda.

Increasingly though, this ideology is running up against the material reality of a global power shift, where the oppressed are clearly the locomotive of history. More and more whites are themselves running from their own "racial" designation.

Patrick Buchanan, whose worldview is informed by assumptions of white superiority that we recognize as racism, is himself alarmed by the growing evidence that shifting power relations are chasing whites away from solidarity with their "racial" identity. Apparently this phenomenon has achieved such significance that Buchanan has conceptualized it as

1 The United States Africa Command with U.S. military involvement in at least 49 African countries.

"ethnomasochism." In his book *Suicide of a Superpower*, Buchanan laments:

> *Questions about the future arise. If the end of white America is a cultural and demographic inevitability, what will the new mainstream of America look like—and what ideas or values might it rally around? What will it mean to be white after "whiteness" no longer defines the mainstream? Will anyone mourn the end of white America? Will anyone try to preserve it?*
>
> *One reaction professor Hsu reports is that, among cultural elites, some are shedding their white identity. "[I]f white America is 'losing control,' and the future will belong to people who can successfully navigate a post-white, multicultural landscape—then it's no surprise that many white Americans are eager to divest themselves of their whiteness entirely...."*
>
> *The day after Obama's inaugural, television host Larry King blurted out to an uneasy Bob Woodward a secret desire of his son. "My younger son Cannon...is eight. And he now says that he would like to be black. I'm not kidding. He said there's a lot of advantages. Black is in. Is this a turning of the tide?"*

Indeed, black *is* in. The tide has turned; black is the future—not because of some defeat of "racism" but because Africans are a part of the dispossessed, the Wretched of the Earth that are overturning a world social system whose ideological foundation is racism. This system is no longer able to withstand the tide of history sweeping all forms of capitalist parasitism into the proverbial dustbin of history.

The anti-racists would have us fight for a place in the dying system by fighting against its ideology instead of the system itself. In this way they would have us objectively uniting with our oppressors. Anti-racists would transform us into "house Negroes," fighting to save the master's burning mansion, to paraphrase Malcolm X.

Parasitism is the essential question

Up to now, since the successful rise of imperialism some 500 years ago, Europe and white people have been the subjects and Africans and others have been the objects of imperialist history.

We have been voiceless and reduced to invisibility in stature and significance. Karl Marx characterized the slavery, rape, pillage and genocide associated with the emergence of white power and our current status as "primitive accumulation." In another instance, he referred to slavery as "an economic category of the greatest importance."

In the book *One People! One Party! One Destiny!*, the Political Report to our Fifth Congress, we commented on what that meant:

> *Here the relationship between peoples and countries is...obscured and mystified. Marx attributes European "development" solely to the "genius" and productive forces inside of Europe. He is thereby covering over or liquidating the fact that this so-called development for Europe requires the parasitic impairment of the capacity for independent development in Africa and other places victimized by Europe.*
>
> *In another place in the Political Report this rhetorical question was raised:*

> *Would capitalism and the resultant European wealth and African impoverishment have occurred without the European attack on Africa, its division, African slavery and dispersal, colonialism and neocolonialism?*

The answer is obvious to anyone with even a smattering of historical knowledge: No! No! No! and a thousand times no!

But Marx didn't get it. Most of our Movement still doesn't get it. Revolutionaries around the world have missed this crucial understanding of the foundation of imperialist existence.

The most erudite practitioners of the superstition called capitalist economics don't get it. This is one of the reasons nothing they say about the extant economic crisis of the imperialist world makes any sense.

Our summation of this imperialist dilemma is reflected in this quote from *One People! One Party! One Destiny!*:

> *The North Americans, like most Europeans, assume they have some idea of the basis of the contradictions because of the fantasies passed on to them historically about the source of their comparative wealth and "good fortune."...*
>
> *Nevertheless, those are resources stolen from others that have become increasingly difficult for them to afford in their malls and supermarkets. It is somebody else's oil, wrenched from the earth with bloody consequences, for which they now have to pay more.*
>
> *The bauxite, coltan, gold and diamonds along with the cocoa beans, cotton and cheaply produced clothing have cost the rest of us dearly and our combined struggles to seize control of our lives*

> *and resources are affecting the ability of North Americans and other Europeans to enjoy a parasitic economy that requires global misery for an oasis of white happiness.*

In reality the essential feature of capitalism is parasitism. The inconsistent materialism of Patrick Buchanan as well as Zbigniew Brzezinski, cited in Chapter I [of *An Uneasy Equilibrium*], allows them to recognize some relationship between the decline of imperialism and the rise of formerly subject peoples.

Yet their overarching philosophical idealism, a worldview stemming from white assumptions of superiority, blinds them to the dialectic between Western or "white" success and African impoverishment. They cannot accept that the changing relations of power are exposing the real dependency—the dependency of the colonizer upon the colonized and of whites on Africans.

This is as true for the capitalism of Adam Smith, the 18th century free market proponent, as it is of the capitalism of Karl Marx, the 19th century scientific socialist. Wage labor, commodity production, private ownership and control of the means of production are features of capitalism that function on the foundation of parasitism, the "primitive accumulation," that Marx correctly identified as the equivalent of "original sin." This is the starting point of capitalist accumulation and production, of the capitalist system itself.

This is not to say that everything that Marx said was wrong, but it is to say that everything he said must be re-evaluated based on a materialist appreciation of the centrality of capitalist parasitism, what he called the primitive accumulation of capital. Otherwise we will continue to be duped by those who verbally claim to oppose capitalism, but who cannot oppose *parasitic* capitalism—the reality that capitalism rests on the backs of African, Indigenous and oppressed peoples everywhere.

We are not Marxists. We are historical materialists. We have used the historical materialism of Marx, the science of investigating and analyzing society, to investigate and analyze our reality as Africans. Our findings prove that we are a part of the "primitive accumulation" mentioned by Marx in his works.

Malcolm X, a materialist of sorts in his own right, has been quoted as saying that a person watching someone sitting on a hot stove would describe the experience differently from the person actually sitting on the stove. This is true. The spectator is not required to have a full understanding of the experience. The victim of the hot stove is provoked by his reality; it becomes a historical necessity to understand the question.

Using the collective experience of African people as a starting place, we were able to use the science of dialectical and historical materialism, cleansing it of its Marxist metaphysics and idealism, to investigate and analyze our relationship to the world.

For us, the rise of capitalism in the world is not based on some purely abstract Marxist theory about the development of human society. It is not a theoretical question. *"Primitive accumulation" is not a theory.* The rape of Africa, the enslavement of our Continent and our people, the forcible dispersal of Africans throughout the world as a means of rescuing Europe from disease and poverty—the process that gave rise to capitalism—is a matter of historical record.

Marx, the spectator, did not have to understand this. The person sitting on the hot stove—the living, breathing, thinking "primitive accumulation"—would either understand this question or perish. We chose to understand. More than that, we chose to develop a worldview stemming from this understanding. This is the origin of African Internationalism. African Internationalism is simply the worldview stemming from a historical materialist investigation and analysis of the world with its starting point being the experience and role of Africans and Africa in the advent of capitalist-imperialism as the rise of white power.

Parasitic capitalism is the real issue. It is this reality that ultimately distinguishes African Internationalist socialism from the struggle for "white rights" that usually characterizes most movements of Europeans worldwide. It is the difference in socialism resulting from overturning the pedestal upon which all capitalist activity occurs and some variation of the national socialism achieved by the infamous Nazis of Germany.

In the past few years the crisis of imperialism has thrust a number of North Americans and Europeans into motion, from Tea Partiers and Wall Street Occupiers in the U.S. to thousands of militants in Greece, Spain, Brazil and other crisis-ridden countries.

White people have been mobilized by the inability of capitalism to live up to their expectations. They are demanding to be restored to their "rightful" place atop the pedestal of capitalist prosperity, sharing in the stolen loot of colonial plunder.

The problem is that this can only happen at the *expense* of the well-being of the historical victims of capitalist prosperity—the subject and colonial peoples of the world, whose exploited labor and resources create the pedestal upon which all white people sit. Europe's economic uncertainty has been brought about by oppressed peoples who are currently fomenting the crisis with our struggle for the recapture of our resources, our sovereignty, dignity and our history.

It is an error to assume that "primitive accumulation" is dead history, something that happened a long time ago with no implications for today. The truth is that today's capitalist-imperialist structures, the ones being challenged in a thousand different ways, are structures that originated in the very genesis of capitalism as it emerged through the assault on Africa and the majority of humanity from the primordial sludge of backward and disease-ridden Europe.

These understandings of African Internationalism *require* action. They are not for consumers of information. Our Party's theory is the only body of political understanding that can make sense of what is happening in the world today.

Our African Internationalist theoretical contributions serve to break the shackles historically imposed on revolutionary theory as perceived through the lens of oppressor nation intellectuals whose worldview was determined by their existence on the pedestal of our oppression.

African Internationalism for the first time allows for Africans and the oppressed of the world to become the subjects of history, defining our own destiny, something not possible with the theory of Marx or his contemporaries and followers.

Today the conditions of the real world manifested by the crisis of imperialism are beginning to confirm what African Internationalism has so long predicted.

The reality of primitive accumulation of capital and the fact that capitalism was born at the expense of the suffering of African and Indigenous peoples and is therefore parasitic; the reality of Africans as one people dispersed around the world who are colonized wherever we may be located; the understanding that African people live under a policy of U.S. counterinsurgency in the U.S.—these are some African Internationalist understandings whose significance is becoming recognized by the world.

Seeing the world as it is, not as we wish it were

African people, like all of humanity have always been motivated by the struggle to understand our place and destiny in the world. We, like others, have through our collective life experiences been compelled to find answers to the fundamental philosophical questions revolving around the primacy of the spiritual versus the material world.

What is the basis of our oppression? Can the answer be found in religious scripture? Are we oppressed because we have offended the gods or perhaps sought solace from the wrong gods? Are the white colonial oppressors and some of the African petty bourgeoisie correct when they say we are experiencing the consequence of insufficient civilization or inadequate education or that we are morally depraved?

Those who see the spiritual as primary are philosophical idealists. For them the idea of reality is greater than reality itself. For idealists, the real, material world is dependent on the spiritual. Philosophical idealists do not look for answers about the nature of the world by examining the world itself. They see the world as the creation of an external force that is incapable of standing up to scientific investigation.

This is a ruling class worldview that is funneled into the consciousness of the working masses through the African petty bourgeoisie as well as other petty bourgeois and bourgeois mediums. Philosophical idealism assumes that there are things that humans are unable to comprehend. It claims that the hand of the mysterious is somehow responsible for what we perceive as reality.

During the historical period when our Party was founded, philosophical idealism was central to the worldview of the Black Liberation Movement which relied mainly on religious, moral and colonial explanations to understand and analyze our situation.

African philosophical idealists of that period sought explanations for our conditions of existence and our future in the articulations of great leaders or simply in the consciousness of the Black Liberation Movement itself.

In other words, the idealists accepted the Movement's and its leaders' own self-definition as primary, rather than fundamentally examining the actual material conditions that *gave rise* to the Movement and its leaders.

Other philosophical idealists with whom our Movement had to contend were the various white liberals including those who defined themselves as "leftists."

Many of the white leftists relied on religious and moral explanations for their analysis, attributing our oppression to the flawed character of our oppressors. According to these idealists our oppressors were people who had strayed from the American or European moral ideal. In this way the white liberals were not that different from the petty bourgeois leaders of the Black Liberation Movement.

White leftist ideological intervention usually represents itself in the paternalistic, condescending tendency to approach the issue of the oppression of African people from a predetermined assumption of the universality of the white experience. This Eurocentric viewpoint shows that the leftists have pretty much the same viewpoint as all other whites.

Often influenced by Karl Marx, many "leftists" deny being philosophical idealists. Their idealism, nevertheless, is reflected in their demand that Africans, the Indigenous of the Americas and the majority of the world's peoples understand our struggle as objects of European-defined and experienced history.

From their perspective, Africans and others are relegated to the position of auxiliary forces whose ultimate unhappy destiny, independent of our will, history and experience, is to facilitate the emergence of the industrial or white working class as the new ruling class in a utopian post-capitalist world.

The African People's Socialist Party sprang from the very bowels of the remorseless reality and struggles of our people. As we developed, we were increasingly forced to shed all reliance on religion, other forms of superstition and the good will or moral epiphany of our oppressors.

Our struggles to understand our reality, while occasionally encumbered and influenced by the worldview of the educated and upper classes, were rooted in attempts to solve the real problems of the concrete contradictions in which our people are embroiled.

We were forced to learn that our preconceived notions gleaned through colonial civics books, preachers and liberal white friends only helped to obscure the real contradictions with which our people are confronted. We came to recognize that we must understand the world just as it is, not as we would wish it to be.

We were forced to become philosophical materialists.

Materialism teaches us that the world is tangible, knowable and can be experienced through the senses. It teaches us that all existing phenomena result from material causes that come into being, develop and pass away according to the laws of the motion of matter. Materialism informs us that the material world is primary. It is objective reality that exists independently of the mind and will of individuals. It does not require the permission of gods or important persons for its existence.

The development of the African People's Socialist Party during our historical 41-year trajectory in the midst of intense struggle compelled us to understand that the savage and genocidal brutality inflicted upon our people and the world by Europeans or whites has a material basis. It is not due to the will of the gods or simply some moral deficiency on the part of whites.

While the humanity of Europeans was clearly open to suspicion (the original Nation of Islam, for example, declared the white man to be the "devil"), the answer to the avaricious motivation of white people is not to be found in an examination of morality, religion or genetics.

Our Party and Movement were forced to conclude that all humans, including Europeans, are trapped by an absolute necessity to secure and develop the means of subsistence. In other words, the primary motivating factor in human society is the production and reproduction of life. Without life, all other questions—religion, culture, genetics, etc.—are moot, meaningless. Indeed, culture is a byproduct of the process of producing and reproducing life.

However, the process of Africans producing and reproducing life was drastically disrupted and altered by the European attack that resulted in the capture and colonial enslavement of Africa and Africans. This attack by Europeans on Africa also resulted in the imposition of artificial borders that separate the dispersed African nation from our human and material resources and from a meaningful relationship among ourselves and with the peoples of the world.

The material *and* human resources of Africa have gone to satisfy the requirements of life for Europeans at the expense of Africa and Africans. The process of Africans producing and reproducing life has not been primarily for Africa and Africans—it has been primarily for Europe and the white world at our expense.

This progenitor of world capitalism—the attack on Africa and Africans, along with the European assault on Asia and the Americas—rescued Europe and Europeans from an oppressive, thousand-year-long, disease-ridden, impoverished existence known as feudalism. This was the genesis of the capitalist system as a world economy, created on a base of the enslavement of Africans and others.

A scientific analysis of human society requires that we take a dialectical approach. We cannot see the world as static and ready-made. Society has to be analyzed as a process that is in a constant state of motion, change and development. There is always something new arising to replace the old and all social motion occurs in relationship to this process of coming into existence and dying away.

Europe's attack on Africa was effectively an assault on Africa's ability to produce life for itself. This assault has had the effect of pushing Africa and Africans out of history—history being the summation of the ongoing struggle to produce and reproduce life.

Slavery, genocide and colonialism are the stuff of which capitalism was born. African enslavement was the *first capital* in the development of capitalism. The prevailing legal system, culture, religion and general philosophical outlook or worldview constitute the superstructure of capitalism thus conceived. This superstructure is a natural product and reflection of this economic base of colonial slavery.

Slavery and colonialism gave rise not only to capitalism but also to the capitalist and working classes alike of Europe and North America. The workers and the bourgeoisie, the two primary capitalism-defining classes, have occasionally fought great battles with each other since their inception as contending social forces.

Nevertheless both were born and developed on a platform of slavery and colonialism. Consequently, what is often called "class struggle" inside the U.S. and Europe is actually contention among the workers and the ruling class for control of the parasitic capitalist pedestal and its stolen resources.

The parasitic foundation of world capitalism continues to exist up to now as the true economic base upon which the entire superstructure of the capitalist-defined, capitalist-dominated world rests.

The total existence of "white" people and their ability to produce and reproduce life is dependent on this parasitic relationship that came into being with the attack by feudal Europe on Africa and the world.

Instead of separate, more or less self-contained worlds existing in casual relationship to each other, *there is one capitalist world system united by a parasitic economic relationship imposed by Europe upon the rest of us.*

There is, therefore, no European reality separate from that of Africa and the rest of the world. The entire world is now locked into a single dialectical process, a unity of opposites, whereupon the gruesome extraction of life and resources from Africa and the rest of the world is a condition for the life and "development" of what we now know as Europe, "white people" and the capitalist system to which we have been forcibly affixed.

The legal system, culture, white sense of sameness and political institutions are reflections of this parasitic economic base. Every white aspiration and dream, every expectation for happiness and a good life—from a successful marriage to a secure future for their children—requires drone strikes in Pakistan, police murders and mass imprisonment in the African colonies and barrios of the U.S., and starvation and forced displacement of the oppressed throughout the world.

Our theory, practical struggle prepared Party to lead

While not fully appreciative of the parasitic foundation of the entire capitalist system resting on the brutal oppression of Africans and others, Karl Marx nevertheless recognized the relationship between the economic foundation of society and the resultant institutions and ideas.

In his preface to *A Contribution to the Critique of Political Economy*, published in 1859, Marx expounds on this relationship between the economic base and superstructure that defines society:

> *In the social production of their existence, men inevitably enter into definite relations, which are independent of their will, namely [the] relations of production appropriate to a given stage in the development of their material forces of production. The totality of these relations of production constitutes the economic structure of society, the real foundation, on which arises a legal and political superstructure, and to which correspond definite forms of consciousness. The mode of production of material life conditions the general process of social, political and intellectual life. It is not the consciousness of men that determines their existence, but their social existence that determines their consciousness.... The changes in the economic foundation lead, sooner or later, to the transformation of the whole, immense superstructure. In studying such transformations, it is always necessary to distinguish between the material transformation of the economic conditions of production, which can be determined with the precision of natural science, and the legal, political, religious, artistic, or philosophic—in short, ideological forms in which men become conscious of this conflict and fight it out. Just as one does not judge an individual by what he thinks about himself, so one cannot judge such a period of transformation by its consciousness, but, on the contrary, this consciousness must be explained from the contradictions of material life,*

> *from the conflict existing between the social forces of production and the relations of production.*

The era of struggle and resistance within which our Party was born was an era of ebb and flow in the challenge to this parasitic relationship. The survival and longevity of the African People's Socialist Party, our persistent involvement in and learning from the practical struggles of the African working class and the fighting and oppressed peoples of the world, are among the things that prepared us more than any other political formation for the tasks that confront Africa, Africans and the world today.

The birth of capitalism did not simply involve the replacement of the old feudal economic system in Europe with a new system. The death of European feudalism threw the entire European world into turmoil. All the institutions and ideas that held feudal society together were challenged and sometimes cast aside, leaving Europeans with the frightening experience of ideological drift, foundering without a stable belief system.

This is because capitalism required a different set of values and beliefs than feudal society. In feudal society the Church had been a powerful presence in the life of Europeans for a thousand years. The Divine Right of Kings functioned as a key belief of feudal society that tied the peasant serfs to the land and to service to the lords and nobility, fettering every aspect of their lives.

In addition to the social chaos that befell Europe with the arrival of capitalism, the existing philosophical coherence was also a casualty. It was the end of one world and with it the end of the effectiveness of a worldview.

Karl Marx was one of the many who vigorously sought to explain the world and Europe's destiny in that world, although generally the Europeans saw the destiny of Europe and the world as being the same thing—and still do.

Marx's *Capital* and other works were products of this effort to explain the world and Europe's destiny. Moreover, Marx sought to distinguish himself and his works not simply as attempts to explain the world, but as agents for changing the world.

Today the people of the world find ourselves very much in the same situation as the Europeans of dying feudal society. We are watching and experiencing the world changing beneath our very feet.

The old world is gone. The white ruling class is busily, frantically, attempting to explain the world and humanity's destiny in it while refusing to recognize that the social system is irreversibly broken. It cannot be fixed. No explanation based on an assumption of the continued domination of white power, whether by socialist workers or the capitalist bourgeoisie, will suffice.

This is the significance of African Internationalism at this historical moment. African Internationalists understand that what is required is the ideological leadership to show the way forward. Only we are able to explain the crisis of the old, dying capitalist system.

Only we can predict the unfolding future shaped by the oppressed masses of the people, whose resistance deprives the capitalist parasite of access to the resources, life and blood of the colonized, subject and dominated peoples whose conditions of existence represent the foundation of capitalist white power and imperialism as we know it today.

Unlike Marxism and the bourgeois philosophers that have been blinded by their relationship with the world, African Internationalism gives Africans and the oppressed our own voices and our own brains, capable of investigating the world from our reality and making an analysis stemming from that investigation.

Africans are "primitive accumulation"

We recognize that capitalism has always rested and depended on a parasitic foundation. As a part of the "primitive accumulation" that Marx spoke of as a function of capitalist development, we are *key to capitalism's destruction.* Indeed, the historical basis for the advent of socialism lies in the struggles of the colonized and dominated oppressed of the world coming to power under the revolutionary leadership of our own workers and laboring masses in all countries.

Marx was unable to fully understand the importance of this question. Marx was able to declare that this "primitive accumulation" is the historic equivalent of "original sin" in theology. He was able to characterize the earth-shaking events that resulted in the theft, sale, forced labor and enslavement of hundreds of millions of African human beings. Nevertheless, Marx's position on the pedestal of our oppression prevented him from seeing the centrality of African and oppressed peoples in the struggle to overturn capitalism.

What Marx termed primitive accumulation was in fact the deadly European assault on Africa, North and South America and Australia, and the extinction and the near decimation of whole peoples. It was the brutal rape of much of Asia and the Middle East, and the numerous internecine wars between European states battling for control of the slave trade and the colonies. It was the resultant growth in wealth that overturned European feudalism and ushered forth capitalism and the European nation.

A real understanding of "primitive accumulation" would have required Marx to center most of his work on an examination stemming from this reality and to look to

Africa, Asia and the Americas for the leading forces against capitalism.

But, objectively Marx was himself a beneficiary of "primitive accumulation." Like others, his consciousness was shaped by this material relationship to imperialism during his lifetime. The libraries and universities he used for his research were filled with books and philosophy that were informed by this parasitic relationship. Historical necessity did not require Marx to understand and center his work on this reality.

However, the African working class is required by history to understand this parasitic historical process that has from the beginning linked Europe, capitalism and the rest of us in the embrace of death from which we are now disengaging.

This is why Buchanan and Brzezinski are crying copious intellectual tears! Understanding the reality of parasitic capitalism and drawing the correct conclusions from this understanding is the task that our Party willingly undertook. To the dismay of the Buchanans, Brzezinskis and all the defenders of the imperialist status quo, our success in this area constitutes a fundamental component of the existential crisis of imperialism.

For centuries, the advent of capitalism has been shrouded in mystery and superstition. Every explanation, whether by capitalists or anti-capitalists, has overlooked the source of capitalism's emergence as the dominant world economy and its implications for the present. This has happened despite the fact that the truth has been hidden in plain sight.

The problem is that the arrival of capitalism marks the emergence of Europe and white people as the driving economic and political force in the world. It marks a signal moment, a turning point, in the fortunes of white people and the world. It is the beginning of an era from which the progressive material development of the white world would henceforth be measured.

This is an issue that is increasingly being forced into the public domain. In 2012, *The New York Times* carried an article by Harvard professor Walter Johnson entitled, "King Cotton's Long Shadow."

The premise of the article, excerpted here, is that African enslavement was crucial to the development of global capitalism.

Johnson wrote:

> *It is not simply that the labor of enslaved people underwrote 19th century capitalism. Enslaved people were the capital: four million people worth at least $3 billion in 1860, which was more than all the capital invested in railroads and factories in the United States combined. Seen in this light, the conventional distinction between slavery and capitalism fades into meaninglessness.*

Capitalism born of imperialism—not other way around

Certainly slavery was the main contributor to the emergence of capitalism, not only in the U.S., but in the world. However, while slavery was the main contributor to capitalism it was not the only contributing factor.

In the early 20th century, Vladimir Lenin, a Russian revolutionary of profound significance, struggled with other socialists of the era to come up with a definition of imperialism at a critical time in the anti-capitalist struggle in Europe.

Lenin defined imperialism as capitalism developed to its highest stage. Imperialism, Lenin liked to say, is capitalism that has become "rotten ripe."

The term "imperialism" comes from the word "empire," which can be defined as the complete domination of territories and peoples by foreign state power. During the era of the First Imperialist World War that was fought to divide the world among several European bandits, the term "imperialism" was used to define political and economic features of capitalist-dominated European social behavior and reality.

Lenin's definition of imperialism was one of several at the time, but it has come to dominate the understanding of politically active European and other anti-imperialists to this day.

According to Lenin's *Imperialism, the Highest Stage of Capitalism*:

> *Imperialism is capitalism at that stage of development at which the dominance of monopolies and finance capital is established; in which the export of capital has acquired pronounced importance; in which the division of the world among the international trusts has begun, in which the division of all territories of the globe among the biggest capitalist powers has been completed.*

In *Imperialism and the Split in Socialism*, Lenin declares,

> *We have to begin with as precise and full a definition of imperialism as possible. Imperialism is a specific historical stage of capitalism. Its specific character is threefold: imperialism is (1) monopoly capitalism; (2) parasitic, or decaying capitalism; (3) moribund capitalism.*

Indeed, it is certainly true that Lenin has described certain features of capitalism. However, Lenin is wrong about imperialism being the highest stage of capitalism.

The discussion of imperialism in Europe was a response to contradictions being experienced primarily by Europeans in Europe itself. The foray into an inclusion of the partitioning of the world and the intensification of colonization was to contribute to the definition of European reality. It was not a discussion of the reality of Africans and the colonized.

Lenin characterized himself as a Marxist, a revolutionary whose worldview was fashioned by his acceptance of revolutionary theory and conclusions advanced by Karl Marx. We African Internationalists have found particular interest in a critical insight of Marx that was clearly not understood as such by Marx's followers or by Marx himself.

Again we return to the brilliant insight of this quote that we often cite from *Capital*—the quote that Marx himself did not recognize the significance of:

> *The discovery of gold and silver in America, the extirpation, enslavement and entombment in mines of the aboriginal population, the beginning of the conquest and looting of the East Indies, the turning of Africa into a warren for the commercial hunting of black skins, signalized the rosy dawn of the era of capitalist production. These idyllic proceedings are the chief momenta of primitive accumulation.*

In the same work Marx also explains, though not intentionally, the obvious contradiction impacting the relationship between white people, including "workers," and Africans and other oppressed peoples. This is the contradiction that is responsible for a commonality of cross-class or national interests within European society, and one of Marx's most important statements:

> *Whilst the cotton industry introduced child slavery in England, it gave in the United States a stimulus to transformation of the earlier, more or less patriarchal slavery, into a system of commercial exploitation. In fact the veiled slavery of the wage*

> *workers in Europe needed, for its pedestal, slavery pure and simple in the new world.*

There is no little irony attached to the fact that Karl Marx wrote much of *Capital* while being supported financially by his friend and collaborator, Friedrich Engels. Engels received his income from his father, a bourgeois factory owner whose wealth was derived from cotton and textile mills supplied by plantations in the Caribbean.

Stated simply, Marx's work on the plight of the working class that promised the future to the white workers of the world was financed by the labor of enslaved Africans who constituted what Marx would refer to as the primitive accumulation of capital, the beginning of the process, equivalent in political economy to "original sin" in theology.

African Internationalists are historical materialists whose investigation and analysis of the world has its starting point in an examination of the capitalist-dominated world from the objective reality and experiences of Africans and the vast majority of the peoples on the planet, including "white" or European people.

It is clear to us that imperialism is not a product of capitalism; it is not capitalism developed to its highest stage. Instead, capitalism is a product of imperialism.

If anything, capitalism is imperialism developed to its highest stage, not the other way around.

The imperialism defined by Lenin has as its foundation the "primitive accumulation" spoken of by Marx. Finance capital, the export of capital, monopoly, etc., are all articulations of a political economy rooted in parasitism and based on the historically savage subjugation of most of humanity.

Road to socialism is painted black

Unlike Marx and Lenin, we African Internationalists deny that there has ever been anything progressive about capitalism.

Capitalism was born in disrepute, of the rapes, massacres, occupations, genocides, colonialism and every despicable act humans are capable of inflicting.

Capitalism was *not* responsible for some great, otherwise unimaginable leap in production, which "despite its contradictions" resulted in human progress and enlightenment.

What capitalism did was to rip the vast majority of humanity out of the productive process—in Africa, Asia, the Middle East, Australia and what has come to be known as the Americas.

The hundreds of millions dead due to the slave trade and slavery itself; the millions exterminated everywhere Europeans ventured—these are people whose hands were forever removed from a relationship with nature that would result in "production."

Europeans achieved their national identity by way of this bloody process. This is not something that only happened a long time ago. The world's peoples are suffering the consequences of capitalism's emergence right now.

Locked in colonies and the indirect rule of neocolonialism; restricted to lives characterized by brutality, ignorance and violence in the barrios of the Americas; in other internal colonies characterized as Indian reservations and black ghettos; kept under the paranoiac, nuclear-backed, armed-to-the-teeth watch of military forces born of a state power that has its origins in protecting the relationship between capitalism and its imperial pedestal, capitalism has been the absolute factor in restricting our production and development. It has concentrated productive capacity in the hands of the world's minority European population that sits atop the pedestal of our oppressive reality.

Capitalism was not the good, "progressive" force that is the precursor to something better for "humanity." Capitalism was a disaster that rescued Europe from a diseased, feudal existence at the expense of the Africans and the rest of the world. In the 17th century, Galileo, an Italian scientist, ran afoul of the Catholic church with his claim that the Earth circumnavigated the sun, as opposed to the prevailing view in feudal Europe, supported by the church, that the Earth was the center of the universe.

The white Left has always been locked into a worldview that places the location of Europeans at the center of the universe.

If this were not the case, Marx would have been forced to declare that the road to socialism is painted black. The destruction of the "pedestal" upon which all capitalist activity occurs, not some maturation of contradictions within European capitalist society resting upon the pedestal, is the key to overturning imperialist capitalism.

In an earlier work entitled *The Poverty of Philosophy*, Marx made this startling admission:

> *Direct slavery is just as much the pivot of bourgeois industry as machinery, credits, etc. Without slavery you have no cotton; without cotton you have no modern industry. It is slavery that gave the colonies their value; it is the colonies that created world trade, and it is world trade that is the pre-condition of large-scale industry....*
>
> *Without slavery, North America, the most progressive of countries, would be transformed into a patriarchal country. Wipe North America off the map of the world, and you will have anarchy—*

> *the complete decay of modern commerce and civilization. Cause slavery to disappear, and you will have wiped America off the map of nations.*

What an excellent formula for the overthrow of capitalism! The "slavery" of today is comprised of the colonial, subject and oppressed peoples of the world. The existence of our Party and the convening of our Sixth Congress are part of the trajectory to cause slavery to disappear and, objectively, to achieve the consequence predicted by Marx.

African Internationalism is the way forward

African Internationalism has brought us to a different understanding than that held by Marx and Lenin regarding the way forward in the struggle against capitalism. It is rooted in our recognition, supported by the quotes from Marx above, that it was imperialism that gave birth to capitalism and not the other way around.

Lenin stated that imperialism is capitalism that is characterized in part by parasitism. But from what we have already seen from the pen of Marx, and what we know from our own experiences and historical investigation, capitalism was born parasitic. That is the meaning of the enslavement, colonization and annexation of other countries and peoples by Europe.

A direct line of connection, a unity of opposites, a dialectical relationship exists between the vast majority of the planet and Europe and Europeans. There is no other explanation for the vast differences in the conditions of existence of Europeans and the rest of us.

The original peoples of the Americas, Australia, Canada, the Caribbean, much of Asia, the Middle East and everywhere the U.S. and Europe are currently engaged in bloody wars and intrigues, represent what Marx has objectified with the term "primitive accumulation."

Indeed, the current irreversible crisis of imperialism is the result of the imperialist "pedestal," the very foundation of capitalism, freeing itself from its supporting role of the capitalist edifice.

Objectively, this is the meaning of Afghanistan, Iraq, Palestine, Venezuela, Bolivia and other countries where the people are attempting to liberate themselves from the yoke of empire. It is in self-defense that the U.S. and its partners are engaged in every effort, no matter how brutal or duplicitous, to protect the capitalist status quo.

This is the meaning of AFRICOM, the U.S. military project created to ensnare the entire African continent in the permanent embrace of U.S. imperial domination to the exclusion of other avaricious imperialist contenders and African people ourselves.

The future of capitalism also rests on the continued subjugation of Mexicans and Indigenous people within current U.S. borders, and especially of internally colonized Africans whose conditions of existence demand a permanent state of often spontaneous and unorganized but ever-present resistance.

The enduring impact of Marx's theory is the fact that it was a response to a desperately needed explanation of the world and the way forward during a time when the thousand-year reign of European feudalism was colliding with the emergence of capitalism, a time when the existing European superstructure was incapable of representing the transforming economic base of society. The established political, legal and cultural institutions and philosophy were incapable of representing the emerging capitalist social system that was ruthlessly uprooting feudalism.

The similarity to today's world is obvious to African Internationalists. Confusion abounds in every arena. Prior explanations fail to satisfy the test of reality. The U.S. popular culture is replete with examples of decadence and philosophical inadequacy. The most oft-viewed movies and TV shows in the U.S. include those of white super heroes, mostly from a past era of imperialist strength and ghoulish vampires and zombies of today.

In other words, one is offered a thrill of nostalgic, vicarious super strength reflecting the imperialist past or the "walking dead," representative of the imperialist socio-political purgatory of today. A superstructure resting on the shaky foundation of a terminally ill imperialism is incapable of seeing the future.

Nor are Buchanan and Brzezinski the only ones confused by how imperialist crisis expresses itself today. The special 90th anniversary issue of *Foreign Affairs,* the political journal of the Council on Foreign Relations, a bourgeois entity historically associated with the Trilateral Commission and the Rockefellers, is dedicated to scrambling for an ideological grasp of this era of imperialism in crisis.

The January/February 2012 anniversary issue is entitled, "The Clash of Ideas, the Ideological Battles that Made the Modern World–And Will Shape the Future."

Among the submissions to this journal is one by Francis Fukuyama. With the implosion of the Soviet Union and the capitulation of China to the capitalist model, Fukuyama popularized the term "End of History" to suggest the U.S. Western imperialist model represents the extent to which human society would develop.

Today Fukuyama is one of the many who have had to reconsider outdated notions of imperialist permanency. In his submission to *Foreign Affairs*, "The Future of History," Fukuyama is now advancing a modified outdated defense of imperialism, in which he asks the question in the subtitle, "Can liberal democracy survive the decline of the middle class?"

Interestingly, Fukuyama addresses what is for him, one of the "most puzzling features of the world in the aftermath of the financial crisis," the fact "that so far, populism has taken primarily a right-wing form, not a left-wing one..."

Fukuyama continues:

> *The main trends in left-wing thought in the last two generations have been, frankly, disastrous as either conceptual frameworks or tools for mobilization. Marxism died many years ago, and the few old believers still around are ready for nursing homes. The academic Left replaced it with postmodernism, multiculturalism, feminism, critical theory, and a host of other fragmented intellectual trends that are more cultural than economic in focus.*

The 41-year history of the African People's Socialist Party is clear evidence that history did not end. In anticipation of Fukuyama's current intellectual dilemma, the Main Resolution of our First Congress, held in Oakland, California, all the way back in 1981, laid out direction and leadership for our struggle. Its revealing title is, *A New Beginning: The Road to Black Freedom and Socialism.* Indeed, Fukuyama's end *is* our beginning!

This Sixth Party Congress and the theory of African Internationalism represent the "future of history" that Fukuyama is searching for.

The emphasis on African Internationalist theory in this Political Report to the Congress is a refutation of Fukuyama's outdated assumptions. The slave, previously brutalized into silence, has found a voice, and we do understand the world and the future. Our Sixth Party Congress is living testimony to that reality.

We are not the "Left" that Fukuyama speaks of. We are not some radical, loyal opposition. We are African Internationalists, committed to the overthrow of the entire system of empire that has feasted off the blood and resources of Africans and others around the world. We are the African People's Socialist Party that survived the war without terms unleashed against our revolution of the sixties.

Indeed, what is reflected in the popular culture of vampires and geriatric superheroes is the end of history that Fukuyama presumed to see with the failure of the Soviet Union. Were it not for the seriousness of the occasion of our Sixth Congress, we would be tempted here to say to Fukuyama, not without some element of smug satisfaction, "Be careful what you ask for!"

Class question found in the colonial contradiction

It is the liberty of the oppressed, the colonized and enslaved laboring masses of the world currently involved in a massive attempted jailbreak, that will destroy capitalism, the prevailing dominant social system that has the world in lockdown.

Therefore the crisis of capitalism does not cause us anxiety. We know that this is the crisis of the parasite that has, since its historical emergence, required the lives and resources of Africans and others for its success and survival.

While this is not a new position of our Party, confusion on this question has led to profound errors within the African liberation and socialist movements. *Izwe Lethu i Afrika*, the 1990 Political Report to the Third Congress of our Party, attempted to bring clarity and leadership to this crucial issue. In that report we stated:

> *We have always said that those who saw the fundamental struggle in the world as existing between the minority white workers and bosses of the world were mistaken. We have always said that the essential class struggle in the world does not exist between the white workers and the white ruling class but is actually concentrated in the struggle against colonialism and economic dependency. Indeed whether he knew it or not, Marx inferred as much himself when in Part VIII of Capital he wrote [in a quote that we find so important that we use it for the third time in this current report]:*
>
> *"In fact, the veiled slavery of the wage workers in Europe needed for its pedestal slavery pure and simple in the new world."*
>
> *This statement by Marx is simply another way of saying that capitalism, the entire basis and superstructure of white power as it exists, has its origin in and rests upon a pedestal of African oppression.*

This point is further elaborated in *Izwe Lethu i Afrika*:

> *The significance of this research is its usefulness in exposing that the fundamental contradiction, the resolution of which would result in the historically based advent of socialism, has never existed between the industrial (white) working class and ruling class. The real locus of the class contradiction in the real world exists in the contest between capitalism born as a world system, and the "pedestal" upon which it rests.*

> *Hence the 1917 revolution in Russia was not a true socialist revolution since the real historical basis of socialism, which is the destruction of the pedestal upon which capitalism rests and which is required for its existence, had not occurred. What happened in Russia in 1917 was the emergence of conditions that constituted the political basis for socialists to seize power.*
>
> *However, this seizure of state power by socialists did not change the reality that the world economy, even the world economy within which Russia existed, was and continues to be, a capitalist world economy. It is the same world economy created by the slave trade and augmented by other facets of parasitic or "primitive accumulation" that transformed the vast majority of the peoples and countries of the world into great reservoirs of human and material resources largely for European and North American exploitation.*

This is why the presence of our Party is so important. We are the living custodians of the history of struggle and the political, ideological and organizational bridge from the last era of struggle up to now. We are the organization whose every action is guided by our political theory and whose political theory always has been tested and deepened by our action.

Some stuck in last period of struggle

Many of the African liberation organizations of the past period no longer exist, and most that do have lost all semblance of revolutionary content. Though some forces act as if the Black Panther Party (BPP) still exists, there has been no functioning BPP in the U.S. for nearly 40 years. The race nationalist hybrid that calls itself the "New Black Panther

Party" has absolutely nothing in common with the Black Panther Party of the 1960s except for appropriating the name and the fact that its members wear berets.

The New Black Panther Party is a caricature of the original Black Panther Party, whose founding was tied to the historical process in which the questions of class struggle and nonviolence were being hotly debated throughout the African Liberation Movement in the U.S. and by diverse liberation movements in contests with colonialism and their own petty bourgeoisie around the world.

Unlike the New Black Panther Party the original Black Panther Party was not a race nationalist organization that perceived a race-based society locked in a Manichean battle between evil whites and good blacks. And, while for much of its short, effective existence, the Black Panther Party was ideologically eclectic, it was, unlike the New Black Panther Party, never religiously based and almost always consistently socialist.

Today, some forces formerly associated with the original Black Panther Party consider themselves a kind of post-revolutionary alumni functioning primarily as guardians and beneficiaries of the legacy of the long dead entity. For them the struggle is over. Through their actions they have either declared victory or conceded defeat.

The original Nation of Islam, through which the world came to know Malcolm X, does not exist. The original organization was, in fact, slipping into *revolutionary* irrelevance, despite the best efforts of Malcolm X when he split with the organization prior to his assassination.

Philosophical idealism, which prohibited the organization from actively engaging in political life during the heat of the African Liberation Movement of the 1960s, was one of the factors leading to Malcolm X's departure from the Nation of Islam.

Malcolm's continuous move into secular politics, embracing some of the civil rights activists and offering scientific, revolutionary analysis for the most important events of his times, endeared him to Africans and oppressed peoples throughout the world. At the same time it created friction between him and leaders of the Nation of Islam who thought Malcolm was straying too far from the religious idealism around which much of the Nation of Islam was defined.

Even so, the leader of the existing Nation of Islam rides the coattails of Malcolm X's legacy. It was Malcolm X who, to his personal detriment, raised the Nation of Islam from relative obscurity as a religious organization to the most influential black nationalist political organization of that era. It was Malcolm X who gave revolutionary legitimacy to the Nation of Islam in a period when the oppressed of the world sought revolutionary direction for ending the colonial domination of Africans and the world's oppressed.

The Provisional Government of the Republic of New Afrika (RNA) was an organization that from its inception in 1968 considered itself the political heir to Malcolm X. The RNA was a militant organization that held up the principle of self-determination that included a real struggle to capture five geographically contiguous states of the southern U.S. as a national homeland for Africans whom the RNA called "New Afrikans."

The RNA experienced years of U.S. government repression. This included military assaults on their meetings and headquarters and jailings of their members and leaders. While the organization continues to exist, it appears to be merely a shell of its earlier self, despite the ongoing political activism of some militants that continue to identify with the organization's aims.

Of the Civil Rights organizations of the era, only the NAACP continues more or less unchanged. It continues to be a shameless expression of African petty bourgeois opportunism. It is essentially a wing of the bourgeois Democratic party and functions mainly as a pipeline through which the liberal white ruling class imposes informal, indirect, neocolonial authority over the colonized African community of the U.S.

The situation is no better on the continent of Africa. The African National Congress (ANC) is probably the best known of the liberation organizations of the sixties. This is mainly because the struggle against the South African apartheid regime succeeded in winning support from much of the world, and its leader, Nelson Mandela, became the world's most recognized political prisoner.

The ANC was initially recognized due to the former Soviet Union's designation of the organization as one of its "Authentic Six" revolutionary groups on the Continent during that period. The politically influential Soviet Union did much to win support for the ANC throughout the world.

Later, in 1994, when apartheid was no longer viable because of mass resistance, and the Soviet Union no longer existed, Mandela was released from prison through pressure from the liberal bourgeoisie of the world. Because a black face was necessary to represent white imperialist interests in South Africa, the U.S. took the lead in world sponsorship of the ANC.

In the 1960s the African National Congress was recognized along with the Pan Africanist Congress of Azania (PAC) as one of the two legitimate liberation organizations in South Africa. The ANC was for all practical purposes the mass organization of the South African Communist Party, a mainly white political formation that could not fight for control of a black African movement and government with its own white face.

Today it is clear to most of the world that the ANC is not fundamentally different from the white nationalist regime it replaced. At the time, however, our Party was the only force that was clear and outspoken on this question as documented in articles from *The Burning Spear* from the 1970s and '80s. As we predicted, the only thing that has transpired since ANC's rise to power is that a sector of the African petty bourgeoisie or middle class has been recruited to administer the white capitalist state after direct white rule became untenable.

Now in South Africa there is *settler* neocolonialism. Now it is the "black" government that protects the interests of international capital and the white minority that still owns more than 80 percent of the land, an area four times larger than England and Northern Ireland combined. Today the ANC government orders police murders of protesting African miners.

The ANC presides over a regime under which more than 40 percent of African workers are unemployed in steadily deteriorating conditions, while the conditions of the whites have improved considerably.

APSP represents interests, aspirations of African working class

In Zimbabwe, Algeria, Egypt, Angola, Kenya, Guinea Bissau, Mozambique, Democratic Republic of Congo and other places where armed organizations led struggles against the prevailing forms of colonial white domination, there is no forward motion. In most instances there has only been a replacement of white oppression by imperialist-backed black oppression of the masses of our people.

However, we are here—the African Socialist International, the global expression of the African People's Socialist Party. We are here, forged and prepared over the last 41 years for the tasks confronting Africa, Africans and the toiling masses of the world.

We represent historical continuity, the ongoing development of a revolutionary process guided by our ever-developing revolutionary theory, despite the shortcomings and failures of various expressions of our Revolution at particular moments in history.

Our Party has become the custodian of the interests and aspirations of the oppressed and dispersed African nation. It is our existence that represents the dynamic future of Africa and the African Revolution, despite the setbacks experienced by the limitations and/or abandonment of particular African personalities or organizations of the past period.

Political parties are always organizations that represent the interests of particular classes, although efforts are often made to disguise this fact. In so-called democratic capitalist societies, political parties often obscure their class character. This is especially true in the United States, where the main ruling class parties are the Democrats and Republicans.

These two parties most often share political power in a number of ways, including elected offices, as well as appointments to posts within the administrations of either or both parties in government.

Regardless of the capitalist political party in power, each party looks out for the interests of capitalism in general, even as it pursues the specific interests of the specific sector of the bourgeoisie that is responsible for its elevation to power.

The African People's Socialist Party is also the Party of a class, the African working class. Our work is responsive to the interests of our class, interests that distinguish it from other social forces, whether those of the oppressor nation capitalists or the oppressed nation, neocolonial-aspiring African petty bourgeoisie.

Our objective is to provide the political leadership for the African working class in its pursuit of political power, the power to govern, the power to become the new ruling class of a liberated, united Africa and African population whose conditions of existence worldwide are a reflection of the rape and colonization of Africa.

African Internationalism is our scientifically based, ideological guide that informs our actions and keeps us on the right track. It keeps us away from the lures of race nationalism, superstition and other toxins that attempt to divert the masses and us from our historical mission of African liberation, unification and socialism.

What we are currently experiencing, sometimes in the name of revolution, is the consequence of revolutionary defeat. This is what has contributed to the stupefication of the masses of our people and the peoples of the world. This is why our Party and African Internationalism are so important. Our Party represents the clearest evidence of revolutionary continuum in the world. And it is revolution that continues to be necessary; not prayer to the "right" god while turned in the correct direction. It is not that we need cultural enrichment, nor is social media militancy—audacity in front of a computer screen—the missing element.

It was revolution that won the hearts of masses of Africans and other oppressed peoples around the world. It was revolution that was defeated and counterrevolution that succeeded almost absolutely, except for the presence and work of the African People's Socialist Party.

Material basis of white terror

One of the issues that has served to befuddle sectors of the African Liberation Movement in the U.S. and elsewhere is the definition of "white people," their role in history and their place, if any, in the struggle to end oppression and exploitation.

This is an issue that has been complicated by the fact that for centuries, race-based biological definitions have been used by European oppressors as justification for the horrors they have inflicted on most of the world and especially on Africans.

To justify the colonial enslavement and brutal oppression of Africans, Europeans concocted pseudo-scientific biological "evidence" purporting the inherent inferiority and bestiality of the colonized. Africans and other oppressed peoples were the primary victims of the violent oppression that accompanied the ruthless exploitation used to create the capitalist system and the sense of sameness necessary for the consolidation of the European nation.

Capitalism entered the historical scene as a world system stemming from slavery and colonialism, and its power to define reality was nearly absolute. What is known as "racism" is a consequence of the power of capital built on the backs of Africans and Indigenous peoples. In fact, racism, as we discussed earlier in this chapter, is the ideological foundation of the global capitalist social system. Racism is a component of the superstructure spawned by the process of capitalism's conception. Therefore it is nearly impossible to exaggerate the extent of its intellectual influence in the U.S., Europe and the world.

What is called racism is a biological analysis. It is reinforced by the creation of such things as the discipline of anthropology, used for the express purpose of proving the superiority of whites or Europeans over Africans and all others. This analysis had an understandable influence over how Africans would begin to explain "white people" as oppressors in the struggle to recapture our humanity, resources and freedom.

Victimized by this pseudo-scientific approach Africans adopted a competing biological analysis to explain the evil nature of the white man.

One result of this has been a hodgepodge of theories that spanned the genetic gamut. This included assertions that the white man is a mutation; the white man's depravities are expressions of melanin deficits; and finally, from the Nation of Islam, the white man was created by an evil black genius named Yakub through a selective breeding process.

Contributing to the complexity of the issue has been the perennial willingness of the white majority to suffer voluntary isolation from the majority of humanity in exchange for the material benefits of imperialist colonialism, as well as the extraordinary, irrationally based spiritual or ideological rewards of "whiteness."

As long ago as 1858, in a letter to Karl Marx, his comrade and collaborator, Friedrich Engels, offered this materialist observation about the ability of the whites to unite with their ruling class in the exploitation of the colonial world: "For a nation which exploits the whole world this is of course to a certain extent justifiable."

Later, in 1882, in a letter on the same subject, Engels would comment to Karl Kautsky: "You ask me what the English workers think about colonial policy. Well, exactly the same as they think about politics in general...the workers gaily share the feast of England's monopoly of the world market and the colonies."

What Engels has begun to do here is attempt a scientific, materialist-based explanation for white behavior. We have spoken to this issue earlier in our description of the economic foundation of capitalism and the resultant superstructure. However, our Party has much more to say on this issue that has provided such a Gordian knot until cut asunder by the incisive blade of African Internationalism.

Writing in *A History of Africa*, a book we have often quoted, Hosea Jaffe makes another important contribution to a materialist explanation for the emergence and behavior of Europe or the "white man," declaring:

> *Europe was born out of colonialism, as the exploiting, oppressing, negating pole that tried always to destroy and assimilate its opposite pole: the rest of the world....*
>
> *It was out of this process that the very idea of a European man arose, an idea that did not exist even in etymology before the 17th century. Before the slave trade in Africa there was neither a Europe nor a European. Finally, with the European arose the myth of European superiority and separate existence as a special species or "race"; there arose indeed the myth of race in general, unknown to mankind before—even the word did not exist before the lingua franca of the Crusades—the particular myth that there was a creature called a European, which implied, from the beginning a "white man." Colonialism, especially in Africa, created the concept and ideology of race. Before capitalist-colonialism there were no races; but now, suddenly and increasingly, there were races: once born, the myth grew into a reality.*

Clearly this and other African Internationalist philosophical materialist analyses offer a correct explanation for the "creation," power and influence of the "white man."

This is the same explanation provided by our book *A New Beginning:*

> *Living in a country built and sustained off slavery, colonialism, and neocolonialism, the impact of victorious revolutionary struggles reaches down into the gas tanks, shopping centers and tax brackets of the North American population. There is an objective relationship between world slavery and*

> *U.S. affluence, and up to now the North American population, opportunistically and demagogically led by their stomachs, pocketbooks and corrupt leadership, have chosen the continued enslavement of the world.*
>
> *In the U.S., imperialism was constructed off the enslavement of African people and the near-decimation of the Native population. This system has been the cornerstone of world capitalism since the Second Imperialist War, which means among other things, that the resources, the wealth, the near-slave labor of the vast majority of the peoples of the world have been the basis for the development, not only of the wealth of the ruling class, but of the entire North American society.*

African Internationalism helps us to understand that white people are just that, people. And, like all people their actions can be explained by material causes. African Internationalism teaches us that key to the actions of white people is the fact that they have lived on the pedestal of the oppression of most of the world since the advent of capitalism as a social system.

White people: join humanity; commit national suicide!

This is not to state that white people are not beset with various contradictions with their own ruling class within the capitalist system. Certainly they are. However, these contradictions require for their existence the primary contradiction—the parasitic extraction of value from Africans and others that constitute the foundation of the entire capitalist social system that has been generally beneficial to Europe and white people at our expense.

For white people to overturn the contradictions with the white ruling class they find themselves contending with from time to time they must end their voluntary exile from the rest of the toiling masses of the world and their parasitic relationship to us. They cannot simply claim to be a part of the "99 percent," as the Occupy Movement proclaimed, when it suits them to suddenly identify with the oppressive circumstances of the rest of us. They are not a part of the 99 percent and it is dishonest for them to make such a statement.

However, this is not simply a complaint about the capacity of white people for truth and veracity. The problem is that the claim by whites to be part of the rest of us is an attempt to use the energy of Africans and the oppressed of the world, whose exploitation facilitates the extraction of value that feeds the white population, as a means of remedying white people's problems on the pedestal. The problems of white people are the direct result of the struggles of the oppressed to take back our resources and our future.

In other words, the contradictions faced by many white people today are the result of the crisis of imperialism brought about by the resistance of oppressed peoples who are struggling against the imperialist theft of their oil, minerals, land and resources.

It is insane for Europeans or whites to assume that the 80 percent of the world that attempts to survive on $10 or less a day would be a willing part of a struggle defined and designed for reinstatement of white student loans or retirement guarantees for the white elderly.

The real, legitimate struggle for white people is to commit national suicide by joining in the struggle for black power and against the white power that is representative of the oppressor nation relationship with the rest of us. The various contradictions plaguing the world are contradictions born of the ascent of white power.

Like Africans, Mexicans, Arabs, Iranians, Roma, South Americans, etc., white women, white homosexuals and white workers are all victims of capitalism that was born as white power at the expense of everybody else in the world. Yet, white people have always attempted to solve their contradictions with capitalism at our expense rather than in solidarity with us.

Progressive, forward-looking whites who are committed to the creation of a new world without war and exploitation have to join in this struggle by the world's majority against white power instead of using inane slogans and opportunistic subterfuge to attempt to win world participation in solving their perceived problems at our expense.

We have already discussed the opportunism of the Euro-North American Left. It is real, historical and universal. In *Izwe Lethu i Afrika* we quoted from the 1907 congress of the Second Communist International, held in Stuttgart, Germany and attended by more than 800 delegates. This piece was cited in *Lenin's Struggle for a Revolutionary International*, edited by John Riddell.

The crux of the quote revolves around a majority resolution at that congress that, "Under a socialist regime, colonization could be a force for civilization." While today most opportunists attempt to disguise the self-serving basis for their opportunism, the "99 percenters" at this congress were refreshingly and unreservedly open in their intent to preserve white power on the backs of the rest of us.

Let us listen in to the debate on the question. This statement by Hendrick van Kol of the Netherlands is in support of the majority socialist colonization resolution:

> *The minority resolution also denies that the productive forces of the colonies can be developed through the capitalist policy. I do not understand at all how a thinking person can say that. Simply consider the colonization of the United States of*

> *North America. Without it the native peoples there would today still be living in the most backward social conditions.*
>
> *Does Ledebour want to take away the raw materials, indispensable for modern society, which the colonies can offer? Does he want to give up the vast resources of the colonies even if only for the present? Do those German, French, and Polish delegates who signed the minority resolution want to accept responsibility for simply abolishing the present colonial system? ...Surely there are few Socialists who think that colonies will be unnecessary in the future social order. Although we do not need to discuss this question today, I still ask Ledebour: does he have the courage now, under capitalism, to give up the colonies?*
>
> *Perhaps he can also tell us what he would do about the overpopulation of Europe. Where would the people who must migrate go, if not to the colonies? What does Ledebour want to do with the growing production of European industry if he does not want to create new export markets in the colonies? And does he as a Social Democrat want to shirk his duty to work continually for the education and further advancement of the backward peoples?*

We are tempted to quote more extensively from this discussion as we have in past documents. However, the point is made perfectly clear here: there is a solid, clearly understood material basis for white opportunism that is not limited to the U.S. or to the "backward," "duped" white working class. It includes its most advanced sector, communists who claim to be organized to struggle for the power to lead the world to a new day of society free of oppression and economic exploitation.

African Internationalism is not simply an empty discussion dealing with purely abstract questions. It is a theory that has profound implications for how we understand the world and our approach to changing it, as we must.

This is why this Political Report has become a tome of sorts to dig deeply into the theoretical issues confounding much of the world. As an organization of propagandists the Party is the tool of the Advanced Detachment of the African working class used to spread the gospel of African Internationalism among the oppressed African workers and all the toilers of the Earth.

X. The question of the nation

The chapter "The question of the nation" from Chairman Omali Yeshitela's Political Report to the Sixth Congress held in 2013 and published in the book, An Uneasy Equilibrium: African Internationalism versus Parasitic Capitalism *has been included in the Political Report to the Seventh Congress. The "question of the nation" is also a definitive explanation of the meaning of the African nation.*

In this chapter Chairman Omali Yeshitela soundly defeats every other contending political line and irrefutably proves that Africans are one people all over the world. He shows that we are not a "race" but a nation of people forcibly dispersed around the world by the kidnapping and enslavement of African people. Chairman Omali shows that we are colonized everywhere we are located and that our struggle is for the total unification and liberation of Africa and African people everywhere.

Imperialist political oracle and Obama adviser, Zbigniew Brzezinski, is a ruling class observer of the crisis of imperialism. In his book *Second Chance: Three Presidents and the Crisis of a Superpower*, Brzezinski makes this observation about the significance of the question of identity today when imperialism is being challenged to its parasitic foundation by the political intervention of the peoples upon whose oppression this system was founded.

> *Global systemic instability...is likely to be prompted in many parts of the world by challenges to existing state frontiers. In Asia and Africa especially, state borders are often imperial legacies and do not reflect ethnic or*

> *linguistic boundaries. These borders are vulnerable to increased pressure as heightened political consciousness leads to more assertive territorial aspirations....*
>
> *The largely anti-Western character of populist activism has less to do with ideological or religious bias and more with historical experience. Western (or European) domination is part of the living memory of hundreds of millions of Asians and Africans, and some Latin Americans (though in this case its sharp edge is pointed at the United States)...In the vast majority of states, national identity and national emancipation are associated with the end of foreign imperial domination...This is true in such large and self-confident states as India or China as it is in Congo or Haiti.*

In addition to Brzezinski's consideration of the question, there is a bevy of other publications attempting to address the same issues of the nation and identity. They include David Cannadine's 2013 book, *The Undivided Past: Humanity Beyond Our Differences*, and the 2004 Samuel Huntington book entitled, *Who Are We? The Challenges to America's National Identity.*

Patrick Buchanan's *Suicide of a Superpower: Will America Survive to 2025?* is another of the intellectual forays into the arena of the nation and its future from the vantage point of various representatives of U.S. and/or European imperialism. These farseeing thinking representatives of the white ruling class are being forced to contend with the earth-shattering consequences of a European civilization resting on the historical fault line of economic parasitism.

The shifting center of gravity in the world, the omnipresent upsurge of the "wretched of the earth" to realize our dreams of happiness and security come at the expense of imperialist stability. The resistance of the oppressed unhinges the previous definitions of social reality that required imperialist-imposed tranquility for its foundation and raises the question of the nation and identity to center stage.

In his 2007 book, *Day of Reckoning: How Hubris, Ideology, and Greed Are Tearing America Apart*, Patrick Buchanan probes the question of the nation:

> *Yugoslavia and Czechoslovakia, it is said, were artificial nations created by the treaties of Versailles and St. Germain in 1919. And the Soviet Union was but the Russian Empire reconstituted by the Red Army, the KGB, the Communist Party, and Leninist ideology, not a nation at all....*
>
> *The sudden disintegration of these three nations into twenty-six seemed to substantiate Strobe Talbott's prediction in his 1992* Time *essay, "The Birth of the Global Nation":*
>
> *"All countries are basically social arrangements, accommodations to changing circumstances. No matter how permanent and even sacred they may seem at any one time, in fact they are all artificial and temporary....*
>
> *"[W]ithin the next hundred years...nationhood as we know it will be obsolete; all states will recognize a single, global authority. A phrase briefly fashionable in the mid-20th century—'citizen of the world'—will have assumed real meaning by the end of the 21st century."*
>
> *Is the time of nations over? Is the nation-state passing away? Are the bonds that hold them together so flimsy? Since Talbot's essay, events have not contradicted him.*

Buchanan's summation is representative of the anxiety of the international white ruling class, whose concerns about defending their world hegemony are reflected in the drone bombings, assassinations, unrelenting war and threats of war. The current policies of the imperialists designed to crush the will of the peoples' resistance in Afghanistan and the Middle East, all of Africa, Asia, the Americas and the world, are attempts to maintain the shaky empire and its ideological reflections that define identity and the nation according to its interests and will.

Our entry into this discussion of the nation is mandated by the seriousness of the times. It is mandated by the requirement of Africans and the oppressed to provide a summation of reality that reflects our interests and our aspirations. Our summation is based on science and objective analysis grounded in material reality that predicts the defeat of imperialism and the emancipation of the toiling masses of Africa and the world.

Our discussion of the nation is informed by our inevitable elevation as workers to the role of the ruling class in the transition to a world shorn of classes, borders, nations and states. To win our liberation we must know who we are and who our enemies are.

Let us begin.

Most often the question of African nationality is handled in careless, offhanded and vague ways, making no pretense of ascribing to any particular scientific approach or definition.

The common practice among Pan-Africanists of referring to the international African community as African "peoples" is an example. More commonly, there is the practice of characterizing Africans forcibly dispersed from the Continent as African "descendants" with the intent of differentiating the national identity of such Africans from those who suffered imperial white domination on the Continent itself.

Africans are not unusual in the ambiguous manner in which the question of the nation is handled. In the past few centuries there has been much debate concerning this issue among some of Europe's most erudite intellectuals. Their approach is equivalent to the quote: "I don't know anything about art, but I know what I like."

Similarly, it is difficult to get a uniform definition of the nation from different scholars or intellectuals. Some claim outright that there is not an a priori definition of the nation. "I can't tell you what it is," they might say, "but I know it when I see it."

What is probably the most influential definition of the nation is one offered by Joseph Stalin. This is because as leader of the Soviet Union and the international communist movement from 1924 to 1953 Stalin took the question out of the classrooms and into the fray of political movements throughout the world. Stalin applied his interpretation to the real conditions impacting and tormenting millions of people struggling to define their places in the world.

Written at the end of 1912 or early in 1913, Stalin's position, later published in pamphlet form, defined the nation's key elements, which, according to Stalin, included a "historically constituted, stable community of people, formed on the basis of a common language, territory, economic life, and psychological make-up manifested in a common culture." Obviously the situation for Africans does not satisfy Stalin's definition of the nation, whether applied to the artificially created African "countries" carved out at the imperialist Berlin Conference in 1884-85 or to African people forcibly dispersed around the world.

While Stalin's definition of the nation is one of many, it contains within it elements being offered by others at the time and even today. In fact, Stalin's definition was a struggle against contending definitions forwarded by European socialists at a time when nationalist sentiments were roiling in Europe. These ideas would soon facilitate the European bourgeois war to redivide the world, the First Imperialist World War or World War I.

In his book *The Undivided Past*, referred to above, author David Cannadine challenges many of the prevalent ideas around which the definition of the nation revolves. Here he deals with the requirement that makes language a prerequisite. While not addressing Stalin specifically, Cannadine had this to say about the self-defined European "nations" involved in the First Imperialist World War:

> *To begin with, the idea that the belligerents of 1914 were unified, homogeneous nations does not survive detailed examination. Consider, for example, the matter of common language, often regarded as essential to any shared sense of national identity. It certainly did not exist in the nation created by the Risorgimento. "We have made Italy," Massimo d'Azeglio observed at the time, "now we have to make Italians." With less than five percent of the population using Italian for everyday purposes, they had a long way to go. In France, almost half the school children engaged with French as a foreign language, speaking another tongue at home: dialect and patois were widespread, and in departments bordering other nations, it was often Flemish, Catalan, or German that was spoken. A similar picture could be found in Germany, where in the east many spoke Polish as their first language, whereas in Alsace and Lorraine many spoke French; and in Russia, educated people conversed in French, while workers and peasants used a wide variety of Slavic languages and dialects. In*

> *Austria-Hungary the array of different tongues was even more varied, including German, Czech, Italian, Hungarian, Polish, Croatian, and Greek, and many of the Hapsburg emperor's subjects were multilingual, speaking one language at school or at work and another at home. Insofar as a common tongue could be considered an essential criterion, none of the major powers that went to war in 1914 qualified as a "nation."*

Cannadine challenges other ideas generally used to determine the nation, some of which also dispute Stalin's influential definition. We know many of the limitations of Stalin's work from our own observations. However, this does not relieve us of the need to enter into this discussion.

It is true that nations exist if only because the nation is a commonly held idea along the lines of Marx's maxim that theory, when grasped by the masses becomes a material force. Indeed, the idea of the nation is something that *has* been grasped by the masses to the extent that people actually kill and die in the name of furthering its perceived interests.

Slavery, colonialism basis of the European nation

One of the least discussed questions concerning the nation is the basis for its advent in history. How is it that the world is perceived as a place where for thousands of years there was no such thing as the nation only to have it suddenly emerge in Europe, dominating the 19th century, often referred to as the era of "nation building"?

One attempt at an explanation for the advent of the European nation is provided by Modibo M. Kadalie, Ph.D. in his book published in 2000, entitled *Internationalism, Pan-Africanism and the Struggle of Social Classes*. This rather lengthy and vacuous quote illustrates the general lack of clarity that surrounds this issue:

> *After thousands of years of change, transformation, setbacks, rapid advances, monstrous defeats, unevenness in human conflicts with nature and with other human beings, which was constantly changing in its character; the colossal units of production and exchange that have come to be known as the modern nation-state came into being ruled and fashioned by a class of people who resulted from this long and arduous path of dialectical development. The modern nation-state was the creation of the modern bourgeoisie and serves as the political form or funnel through which this class continues to perpetuate itself in its quest for historical immortality.*
>
> *The most highly developed political formations of this type took place in Europe and later in North America. It is for those reasons that the brutality that has come to be a part of this class slashing its way across the planet has come to be associated with Europeans generally. Rightfully so. Capitalism and the European predatory nation state became to Europe and the rest of the world what feudalism, in its most advanced forms, was to Asia, and communal and intricate pre-feudal modes along with a variety of early forms of social production were to the continent of Africa....*
>
> *The European bourgeoisies could become international precisely because they were national. After carving out and consolidating their sway within a certain geographical area which defined its boundaries, a given national state could*

> *continue its expansion. This occurs because of the organic and predatory nature of the capitalist mode of production. With this expansion bourgeois rule spreads. It, therefore, became a highly developed system for international conquest with its ruling class at the helm guiding, in a deliberate and calculating way, its own realization and affirmation through continuous conquest.*

What Kadalie has done here is to detail the obvious: indeed, "The modern nation-state was the creation of the modern bourgeoisie," and indeed, it is predatory. However, after all is said and done, we still do not know its origin nor the historical basis for its emergence in Europe. In addition, we are misinformed by Kadalie who claims: "The European bourgeoisies could become international precisely because they were national." In fact, the bourgeoisie and the bourgeois nation were products of imperialism, the "international" activities of slavery and colonialism.

This is the point made by Hosea Jaffe in his book *A History of Africa*:

> *The 15th century, then, saw the multiplication of the primary accumulation of European capitalism; and Africa played the most important part in the process as the principal arena of European colonialism, the very genesis and foundation of the capitalist system. From the turn of the 16th century the Americas and Asia were added to this foundation, and out of this totality arose capitalism and modern Europe itself. Before capitalist colonialism there was no Europe, only a collection of feudal, mercantile and tribal towns, farms, villages, discrete states and kingdoms vying and*

> *warring with each other, just as in Africa, but on a different property basis—that of private property in the land. Europe then was neither a concept nor a reality, at most a vague idea that Arabs—but not "Europeans"—had long ago of some place northwest of Greece. As long as Europe remained isolated from the world, there was no Europe. When it became connected with, and dependent on, first Africa, then the Americas and finally Asia, it began to become a reality and an idea. Only when Portuguese, Spanish, French, Italian, Dutch, English, German, Danish and Swedish confronted and clashed with Africa, America and Asia did the need arise for them to consider themselves as a set, a whole, different from, hostile to and, eventually, superior to Africans, Americans and Asians. Colonialism gave them a common interest.*

This "common interest," the sense of sameness, common history and psychological make-up manifested in a common culture—elements contained in most definitions of the nation—was forged through slavery and colonialism. This was the nation-building process; the sense of sameness and common culture of violence are features of the subjective factors identifying the European nation.

Contrary to white leftists and modern-day Marxists, both the white ruling class *and* the white working class owe their existence to this process. They are historical twins, containing the same DNA and spawned by a history of genocide and enslavement of other peoples that is repugnant in its entirety. The parasitic capitalist economy is the objective factor, the material basis upon which the subjective relies; it is the bonding element of the nation that holds this collective community together.

The European nation, and we do mean "European," with its multiplicity of languages, classes and internal borders, was born as a bourgeois nation, a white, Christian nation, spawned through the blood and gore of slavery and colonialism and resting on a foundation of capitalism benefiting Europe at the expense of Africans and the rest of the world.

Aspects of the European nation's subjective content, its self-perception, were forged through the assault on Islam during the Christian Crusades in the feudal era for control of much of the same territory in North Africa and the "Middle East" that imperialism is contending for today. However, the most essential component of Europe's subjective identification grew out of its history of genocidal aggression against Africa that included colonial slavery.

Herein lies the process that bonded Europe into a single nation, though differentiated by sometimes competing capitalist centers designated as countries and incorrectly identified as nations. This, like the anti-Islamic national component, is residual from the pre-colonial European feudal era where contending European powers defined themselves primarily in relationship to each other, except for the united looting expeditions through the Middle East that occurred under the religious banner of Christianity.

Thus the European nation was born white and Christian. Moreover, it was born as a bourgeois nation, as the center of capitalist production stemming from parasitic accumulation of "capital" flowing from colonial slavery. Even the European working class was born on the pedestal of colonialism and slavery, therefore ultimately realizing the benefits of an oppressor nation and identifying with its own bourgeoisie.

Marx was wrong!

Feudalism preceded capitalism in Europe. Feudal society was defined primarily by the relationship between the nobility, impoverished peasants and serfs, agricultural workers who were tied to the estates of the feudal lords who expropriated most of what the serfs produced.

While serfs could not be individually bought and sold as was the case with Africans, the serfs had little or no rights that were not granted by the lords. The role of the feudal state was to protect this relationship that required permanent attachment of the serfs to the landed estates.

As we know, in describing the transformation of feudalism to capitalism, Karl Marx authored the term "primitive accumulation," naming the European enslavement, genocide, wars and occupations of oppressed peoples around the world as the source of the vast wealth extraction out of which the entire capitalist system was born.

But Marx erroneously includes in his definition of primitive accumulation the internal process of European peasants and serfs being driven from the land through England's Enclosure Acts beginning in the early 1600s that privatized lands that had been collectively farmed by peasants for centuries.

According to Marx from Part VIII, Volume I of *Capital*:

> *The economic structure of capitalist society has grown out of the economic structure of feudal society. The dissolution of the latter set free the elements of the former.*
>
> *The immediate producer, the laborer, could only dispose of his own person after he had ceased to be attached to the soil and ceased to be the slave, serf, or bondsman of another. To become a free seller of labor power, who carries his commodity wherever he finds a market, he must further have escaped from the regime of the guilds, their rules for apprentices and journeymen, and the impediments of their labor regulations. Hence, the historical*

> *movement which changes the producers into wage-workers appears, on the one hand, as their emancipation from serfdom and from the fetters of the guilds, and this side alone exists for our bourgeois historians. But, on the other hand, these new freedmen became sellers of themselves only after they had been robbed of all their own means of production, and of all the guarantees of existence afforded by the old feudal arrangements. And the history of this, their expropriation, is written in the annals of mankind in letters of blood and fire.*

Marx was wrong. Though this process involves the creation of the social mobility and capitalist labor force previously prohibited by feudalism, it is not primitive accumulation.

European capitalist society may have very well "grown out of the economic structure of feudal society" but it was *conceived* by way of:

> *The discovery of gold and silver in America, the extirpation, enslavement and entombment in mines of the aboriginal population, the beginning of the conquest and looting of the East Indies, the turning of Africa into a warren for the commercial hunting of black skins....*

Notably, in *Capital*, Marx devotes far more pages to the conditions of peasants and serfs in the transformation from feudalism to capitalism than he does to the enslavement and genocide that created immense wealth for Europe but destroyed the lives and means of production for millions and millions of African and oppressed peoples for centuries to come.

Equating the removal of the European peasants from their land with the fact that Europe transformed Africa into a "warren for the commercial hunting of black skins" is a historical lie. It relegates African people to mere footnotes of history.

The expulsion of the peasants from the land is a *result* of the process of primitive accumulation of capital, not a part of it. Ultimately, the former serfs became European workers who now also sit on the pedestal of our oppression and benefit from it enormously.

This Eurocentric error by Marx subordinates the historical basis of the existence of Africans and others to the requirements for European development. It objectifies the history and civilization of African people, rendering us invisible and leading to wrong conclusions that disguise the bloody reality of parasitism, making it seem that African people exist merely for the needs of Europeans.

This Political Report is replete with examples that challenge Marx's confusion on this issue. When it comes to objectively describing the historical process that gave rise to capitalism, and its impact on Europe and the development of capitalism, Hosea Jaffe, quoted earlier in this chapter, and the African People's Socialist Party do a better job.

Marx's lack of clarity obviously stems from his own social location on the pedestal of African slavery, a location that provided the superstructure for the European capitalist society within which Marx's consciousness was forged and that his life's work relentlessly criticized.

In *One People! One Party! One Destiny!*, the Political Report to our Party's Fifth Congress, we commented on the tendency by Marx to muddle this issue. Here is a selection:

> *We have to note here as well that Marx's description of slavery as an "economic category," and his concept of primitive accumulation provide*

outstanding examples of historic objectification of African people by Europeans.

The entire historical process that resulted in the total disruption of the political economy of Africa, the imposition of colonial borders and the capture and dispersal of millions of Africans whose forced labor was responsible for the development of Europe and European society is characterized as an "economic category"!

Marx reduced the process of European pillage and plunder of the world and the ensuing genocide and enslavement to "primitive accumulation" of capital, a footnote whose function in history is to explain the "development" of Europe.

In other works Marx developed the concept of the "fetish of the commodity" to explain how commodity production, production for the market, obscures and mystifies the relationship between people, allowing it to be confused with a relationship between things. A similar thing happened with the concept of "primitive accumulation." Here the relationship between peoples and countries is also obscured and mystified. Marx attributes European "development" solely to the "genius" and productive forces inside of Europe. He is thereby covering over or liquidating the origin of such "development" in the parasitic impairment of the capacity of independent development in Africa and other places victimized by Europe.

European nation is white and Christian

The European nation became the means of securing the loyalty of the emancipated laborers to the emergent capitalist state and, by association, ruling class. Now, it is not the feudal state or sheriff of Nottingham that forces the toilers to fight the wars of the ruling class or put the interests of the state above their own.

It is the flag, the national anthem, the pledge of allegiance along with the collective identification with a common history that transcends individual European countries or territories: this is what facilitates the new relations of production[1] necessary for capitalist production, relations of production resting on a parasitic economic foundation whose genesis is colonial slavery.

In summation, the European nation derives from relations of production contained within capitalism that was spawned by slavery and colonialism. It was born as a parasitic capitalist or bourgeois nation that encompasses all classes within it.

The European sense of sameness, self-perception and subjective expression, necessary for binding the emergent working class to its newly forged bourgeoisie, is white and Christian. The material base of the European nation is the parasitic capitalist system that bore it in Europe. The capitalist system feeds the entire European nation through its cannibalistic, parasitic relationship to Africa and most of the world.

We have belabored this discussion and description of the European nation because its arrival on the world historical scene with the advent of capitalism has determined, through the barrel of a gun, how other national expressions would be defined by other peoples in various parts of the world.

It is no accident that Europe would describe the nation in a manner that would not be applicable to Africans, the Indigenous of the Americas and many others whose

1 Relations of production is a Marxist term for the material and human relationships involved in how a society comes together to produce the necessities of life. Relations of production could be capitalist, socialist, feudal, etc.

enslavement was a condition for the emergence of the European or "white" nation in the first place.

European scholars have demanded a common definition of the nation. It is a declaration of European universalism that requires every nation to contain the same elements apparent in the European nation.

It is an extraordinary example of philosophical metaphysics to suggest that we should determine the quality of any social phenomenon without first examining the specifics and history of the phenomenon being defined. It is an extraordinary example of imperialist national narcissism to define the validity of all social phenomena based on proximity to one's own reality.

The function of the European nation was to serve the development of Europe alone; the rise of the European nation is an attack on the development and survival of much of the world.

Historical basis of the African nation state

Our discussion of the African nation and its definition, resting on a real, material basis, must serve African development. The research and writings of Cheikh Anta Diop demonstrate quite scientifically the cultural unity of Africa going back through millennia. Diop authored the book, *The Cultural Unity of Black Africa: The Domains of Patriarchy & of Matriarchy in Classical Antiquity*, that today remains the standard for investigation of ancient Africa by any serious historian.

Below we examine a quote extracted from Diop's otherwise deeply scientific work. Here he not only explores the spiritual aspect of African identity, but he also compares it to that of Europe. This is because the discussion of characteristics specific to national identity always distinguishes one people or nation from an "other."

The nation cannot be defined by measuring itself against itself. If there is no "other," there is no logic for the "nation." The "white man" needed the existence of the "black man" to achieve his identity. So it is with nations.

Of course, the problem for the European nation is that it resulted from a false, self-serving European definition of the African. Since this false definition was the basis upon which the sense of white sameness, necessary for the definition of the European nation is anchored, the ability of the African to successfully achieve self-definition marks the beginning of the end of a crucial subjective factor necessary for European national coherence.

Diop's works place significance in what he characterized as the Southern or Meridional cradle of human development versus the Northern cradle, and how the differences in material conditions peculiar to each of them contributed to shaping the worldview and character of their respective inhabitants. This is Diop's summation that contributes to defining the national character of African people as compared to Europeans:

> *In conclusion, the Meridional cradle, confined to the African continent in particular, is characterized by the matriarchal family, the creation of the territorial state, in contrast to the Aryan city-state, the emancipation of woman in domestic life, xenophilia, cosmopolitanism, a sort of social collectivism having as a corollary a tranquility going as far as unconcern for tomorrow, a material solidarity of right for each individual, which makes moral or material misery unknown to the present day; there are people living in poverty, but no one feels alone and no one is in distress. In the moral domain, it shows an ideal of peace, of justice, of goodness and an optimism*

> *which eliminates all notion of guilt or original sin in religious and metaphysical institutions....*
>
> *The Northern cradle, confined to Greece and Rome, is characterized by patriarchal family, by the city-state...; it is easily seen that it is on contact with the Southern world that the Northerners broadened their conception of the state, elevating themselves to the idea of a territorial state and of an empire. The particular character of these city-states, outside of which a man was an outlaw, developed an internal patriotism, as well as xenophobia. Individualism, moral and material solitude, a disgust for existence, all the subject matter of modern literature, which even in its philosophic aspects is none other than the expression of the tragedy of a way of life going back to the Aryans' ancestors, are all attributes of this cradle. An ideal of war, violence, crime and conquests inherited from nomadic life, with as a consequence, a feeling of guilt and of original sin, which causes pessimistic religious or metaphysical systems to be built, is the special attribute of this cradle.*

However, notwithstanding the usefulness of the works of Diop and similar scholars, all of which had to battle against hundreds of years of European prejudice disguised as scholarship to reach the light of day, our discussion of the African nation will revolve around the same time period to which the birth of the European nation belongs. It is clear from what has already been revealed in this Political Report that there is a direct causal relationship between the existence of the European nation and the aspirations of Africans to consolidate the African nation.

Like the European nation, the emergent African nation is a response to necessity. We are facing the historical requirements for advancing and developing Africa and African people, whose generally oppressive conditions of existence derive from the stuff resulting in the emergence of the European or "white" bourgeois or capitalist nation.

One People! One Party! One Destiny! addressed this necessity. It raises the issue of the consolidation of the African nation as a practical political problem that we must solve to forward the national liberation of our people from imperialist domination worldwide. African Internationalism is a theory of practice, as exemplified by this passage:

> *An African Internationalist investigation...leads us to conclude, among other things, that key to the liberation of African people is the defeat of the parasitic stranglehold that has been imposed on us by imperialism.*
>
> *Moreover, as African Internationalists we recognize that Africa has been under some kind of attack for millennia, but that our struggle today is contextualized by the fact that the world economy that gives life to our oppression is a capitalist economy.*
>
> *Our struggle is not fueled by a subjective need for vengeance against every group that has historically attacked Africa. This means that the struggle must be waged against the capitalist social system that is the basis of our exploitation and wretched conditions of existence today. Our struggle for the unification and emancipation of Our Africa and our people is also a struggle against capitalism.*
>
> *Hence, our struggle, if it is to be fought to its successful conclusion, must be led by the African*

working class. It must result in the establishment of a united, socialist Africa responsive to the needs of African people worldwide.

African Internationalism teaches us that slavery, colonialism and neocolonialism, along with African disunification and dispersal, provided the material basis for the European bourgeois national consolidation, the sense of white sameness resting on the pedestal of the oppression of African and colonized peoples.

Hence, we understand that a key function of the revolutionary struggle for the permanent defeat of imperialism and to liberate Africa and her scattered children is the reunification of African people worldwide into a revolutionary, proletarian nation.

"It is slavery that gave the colonies their value; it is the colonies that created world trade, and it is world trade that is the pre-condition of large scale industry." These words by Marx recognize the role of the plunder of Africa in the establishment of capitalism and carry within them the suggestion of what it will take to destroy the capitalist world economy. The African who gave value to the "colonies" is now the oppressed and exploited inhabitant of the colonies that are sometimes incorrectly referred to as nations.

Our conditions of existence in the "colonies," and elsewhere in this world of imperialist-created borders are centered in and derive from the conditions of existence in Africa that are the consequence of the primitive accumulation of capital, the "original sin."

Our revolutionary struggle for liberation, unification and socialism in Africa, throughout the "colonies" and other areas of the world to which we have been forcibly dispersed in the construction of capitalism, will prove to be as significant in the defeat of the capitalist social system as the slave trade was in its advent.

The socialist liberation and unification of Africa and African people under the leadership of the African working class will be the central factor in the defeat of world capitalism and will provide the material basis for the advent for world socialism.

African Internationalism, which demands the total revolutionary liberation and unification of Africa and African people worldwide under the leadership of the African working class, is informed by this scientifically sound dialectic.

Hence, the African Internationalist struggle for the liberation and unification of Africa and African people is at the same time the key factor in the achievement of socialism as a world economy. It is the way forward for those Marxists and other socialists who are confronted with the false conundrum surrounding the question of "socialism in one country."

As capitalism was born as a world economy with its basis in the enslavement and dispersal of African people, leading to [as Marx wrote] "considerable masses of capital and labor power in the hands of producers," so, too, will socialism be born as a world economy in the process of reversing the verdict of imperialism.

Hence, socialism will not be born in one country, but in many countries that are tied to the defining economy of a liberated and united Africa and people under the revolutionary leadership of the African working class.

This is why a fundamental task of the African revolutionary is the consolidation of the proletarian African nation.

African petty bourgeoisie attacks Garvey, nation

This was not the extent of our discussion of the nation in the Political Report to our Fifth Congress. Then, as now, we were engaging in serious struggle with the ossified notions that have hampered and misdirected our struggle since the political defeat of the Universal Negro Improvement Association (UNIA) led by Marcus Garvey in the 1920s.

At that time the struggle for African national consolidation, though seriously debated, was essentially being advanced by the program of the UNIA with its membership of 11 million Africans around the world and its slogan of "Africa for the Africans, those at home and those abroad."

Since its founding in 1919, the Communist Party USA had joined with an assortment of African liberals and the U.S. government in hounding Garvey because of the UNIA's position on the African nation. In 1928 a resolution of the Sixth Communist International held in Moscow admitted that Africans constituted a separate nation inside the U.S., just as the now deported Marcus Garvey had explicitly stated all along. The Communist Party USA was forced to reluctantly comply with this position.

This came after the CPUSA, NAACP and others had eagerly promoted and united with the U.S. government's attack, imprisonment and deportation of Garvey to Jamaica, the island of his birth. The Comintern's position on the "Negro Question" suggested that Africans were a nation within a contrived national homeland of the "Black Belt South" in the U.S.

This manufactured nation of sorts, as described in the "Negro Question," was designed to take advantage of the obvious national consciousness among the African population of the U.S., influenced by the successful Garvey Movement that the CPUSA helped to destroy. The CPUSA attempted to infiltrate the UNIA with undercover communist organizers.

As we stated in "African Internationalism versus Pan-Africanism," presented at the Conference to Build the African Socialist International held in London in 2005, and printed in my book *One Africa! One Nation!*, the Communist Party "... did not address the fact that our homeland had been taken away from us and we from it, which is what Africans were responding to by joining the Garvey Movement."

The CPUSA "Black Belt South" position, moreover, completely obscures the fact that the land of what is now called North and South America—including the "Black Belt South"—was stolen by Europeans from the Indigenous people in the same genocidal process that brought about the birth of parasitic capitalism and the consolidation of the white nation. The Indigenous people continue to suffer the consequences of this assault even today. This land belongs to the Indigenous people.

The CPUSA's position nevertheless implicitly recognizes the commonality of national interests linking Africans worldwide. This passage is one example of that:

> *The Negro race everywhere is an oppressed race. Whether it is a minority (U.S.A., etc.) majority (South Africa) or inhabits a so-called independent state (Liberia, etc.), the Negroes are oppressed by imperialism. Thus, a common tie of interest is established for the revolutionary struggle of race*

and national liberation from imperialist domination of the Negroes in various parts of the world.

The 1928 Communist International Resolution on the Negro Question became the template for succeeding positions on the question by various Marxist communists and an assortment of black nationalists, some of whom were not communists and sometimes even anti-communist in their outlook.

One of the most influential advocates of this position before his defection from the Communist International to the ranks of Pan-African anti-communism was George Padmore. Padmore was a well-known Trinidad-born activist who penned an authoritative book entitled *The Life and Struggles of Negro Toilers* that was published by a section of the Communist International in 1931.

Like the entire worldwide Marxist movement that made up the Communist International, Padmore was a rabid, visceral anti-Garveyite.

The introduction to Padmore's 1931 work, written during the Great Depression, could have easily been written today considering the current economic crisis. Whether intentional or not, Padmore's book exposes his own opportunism and that of the Communist International he represented. Padmore uses all the evidence that supports Garvey's efforts to organize the liberation of the African nation as the basis for joining and celebrating the attacks on Garvey. It was attacks such as these that helped to destroy Garvey's extraordinary anti-imperialist movement for the happiness and material well-being of African people.

Padmore's introduction inadvertently supports our Party's position concerning the commonality of African conditions and interests internationally, our common national identity, its class character and the African national territory that helps to define us as the nation, though dispersed.

Here's Padmore:

> *It has been estimated that there are about 250 million Negroes in the world. The vast majority of these peoples are workers and peasants. They are scattered throughout various geographical territories. The bulk of them, however, still live on the continent of Africa—the original home of the black race. There are, nevertheless, large populations of Negroes in the New World. For instance, there are about 15 millions in the United States, 10 millions in Brazil, 10 millions in the West Indies and 5 to 7 millions in various Latin-American countries, such as Colombia, Honduras, Venezuela, Nicaragua, etc., etc.*
>
> *The oppression of Negroes assumes two distinct forms: on the one hand they are oppressed as a class, and on the other as a nation. This national (race) oppression has its basis in the social-economic relation of the Negro under capitalism. National (race) oppression assumes its most pronounced forms in the United States of America, especially in the Black Belt of the Southern States, where lynching, peonage, Jim-Crowism, political disfranchisement and social ostracism is widespread; and in the Union of South Africa, where the blacks, who form the majority of the entire population, have been robbed of their lands and are segregated on Reserves, enslaved in Compounds and subjected to the vilest forms of anti-labor and racial laws (Poll, Hut, Pass, taxes) and color bar system in industry. The general conditions under which Negroes live,*

either as a national (racial) group or as a class, form one of the most degrading spectacles of bourgeois civilization.

Since the present crisis of world capitalism began, the economic, political and social status of the Negro toilers are becoming ever worse and worse. The reason for this is obvious: the imperialists, whether American, English, French, Belgian, etc., etc., are frantically trying to find a way out of their difficulties. In order to do so, they are not only intensifying the exploitation of the white workers in the various imperialist countries by launching an offensive through means of rationalization, wage cuts, abolition of social insurance, unemployment, etc., but they are turning their attention more and more towards Africa and other black semi-colonies (Haiti, Liberia), which represent the last stronghold of world imperialism. In this way the bourgeoisie hope to unload the major burden of the crisis on the black colonial and semi-colonial masses.

Padmore's introduction continues to assert:

It is also necessary for the workers in the capitalist countries to understand that it is only through the exploiting of the colonial workers, from whose sweat and blood super-profits are extorted, that the imperialists are able to bribe the reformist and social-fascist trade union bureaucrats and thereby enable them to betray the struggles of the workers.

There are a number of erroneous assumptions found in Padmore's words. It is clear that he does not recognize that capitalism was born as parasitic white power that liberated the European bourgeoisie *and* working class from the fetters of the feudal social system. He does not understand that this occurred at the expense of Africans and the oppressed of the world that are overturning that historical relationship at the very moment of this, our Party's Sixth Congress. Capitalism represented progress only for European development, for the workers, the bourgeoisie and society in general.

Padmore does not explain why the imperialists would try "to find their way out of their difficulties" by "turning their attention more and more towards Africa and other black semi-colonies." Of course, for African Internationalists, 21st century Garveyites, the answer is simple: it is the raw, terror-laden exploitation of Africa upon which the entire imperialist edifice rests.

What Padmore warns the white workers about, the super-profits coming from the colonies, is normal capitalist functioning. There is nothing "super" about these profits. The thing that may make the profits appear to be super is simply the fact that white workers, as part of the white nation, share in the imperialist exploitation of the rest of us.

The concept of "super" profits muddles the fact that the vast majority of Africans and other colonized workers constitute the true base of capitalist exploitation and always have. The fact is that the level of profit extraction from this relationship is normal! White workers achieve a greater return for the value of their labor power because they exist as part of a parasitic nation that originates from parasitic capitalism stemming from slavery and colonialism.

"Super" profits infer an exceptional level of exploitation. However it is the white or European oppressor nation worker that experiences the exceptional relationship with capitalism. Ours is not an exceptional relationship. It is the norm. It is the European oppressor nation worker that experiences a "super" relationship with capitalism that is revealed in the different conditions of existence experienced by European workers and the rest of us.

Padmore's concern about the "reformers" and "social-fascist trade union bureaucrats" is also misdirected. While reformism certainly is a problem, when it comes to the issues within the European/white nation, the real question is opportunism, the tendency to sacrifice the long term interests of the struggle against imperialism rooted in the colonial question for the short term interests of white workers, which can only be served at the expense of the rest of us, something the white working class as a social force has never hesitated to do.

Perhaps the root of Padmore's opposition to Garvey and true African national liberation can be found in his characterization of "social ostracism" as one of the oppressive consequences defining the conditions of existence of Africans colonized within the U.S. The question is: social ostracism from whom? The issue of social ostracism only concerns those whose interest is in integrating, assimilating into the social domain of the white oppressor nation, not those who recognize their interests in liberation of the African nation.

This struggle for black or African national independence is usually called black separatism, a subjective response by whites who never speak of the Declaration of Independence proclaiming the establishment of the U.S. bourgeois state on stolen Indigenous land as a "Declaration of Separation."

However, it is in the section of his book entitled "Revolutionary Perspectives" that Padmore unleashes the full force of his venom on Garvey and the struggle for African national emancipation. According to Padmore:

> *The struggle against Garveyism represents one of the major tasks of the Negro toilers in America and the African and West Indian colonies.*

> *Why must we struggle against Garveyism? As the "Programme of the Communist International" correctly states: "Garveyism is a dangerous ideology which bears not a single democratic trait, and which toys with the aristocratic attributes of a non-existent 'Negro kingdom'! It must be strongly resisted, for it is not a help but a hindrance to the mass Negro struggle for liberation against American imperialism."*
>
> *Garvey is more than a dishonest demagogue who, taking advantage of the revolutionary wave of protest of the Negro toilers against imperialist oppression and exploitation, was able to crystallize a mass movement in America in the years immediately after the war. His dishonesty and fraudulent business schemes, such as the Black Star Line, through which he extorted millions and millions of dollars out of the sweat of the Negro working class, soon led to his imprisonment. After his release Garvey was deported back to Jamaica, his native country. Isolated from the main body of the organization, Garvey has been unable to maintain his former autocratic control over the movement, as a result of which there has been a complete disintegration of the organization, which is now under the control of a number of warring factional leaders.*

Padmore continues:

> *Despite the bankruptcy of the Garvey movement, the ideology of Garveyism, which is the most reactionary expression in Negro bourgeois nationalism, still continues to exert some influence*

> *among certain sections of the Negro masses. The black landlords and capitalists who support Garveyism are merely trying to mobilize the Negro workers and peasants to support them in establishing a Negro Republic in Africa, where they would be able to set themselves up as the rulers in order to continue the exploitation of the toilers of their race, free from white imperialist competition. In its class content Garveyism is alien to the interests of the Negro toilers. Like Zionism and Gandhism, it is merely out to utilize the racial and national consciousness for the purpose of promoting the class interests of the black bourgeoisie and landlords. In order to further their own aims, the leaders of Garveyism have attempted to utilize the same demagogic methods of appeal used by the leaders of Zionism. For example, the promise of "Back to Africa," behind which slogan Garvey attempts to conceal the truly imperialist aims of the Negro bourgeoisie.*

We have been generous in the space given Padmore because he is one of the best representatives of this backwards view on the struggle for African national liberation that poses as progressive. It is clear that without intending to do so Padmore validates Garvey's position when he says "the oppression of Negroes assumes two distinct forms: on the one hand they are oppressed as a class, and on the other as a nation."

However, echoing many of the written attacks on Garvey by W.E.B. Du Bois, Padmore goes on to manufacture conclusions about Garvey's intentions that cannot be substantiated by science and rely solely on clearly prejudiced, subjective rantings.

It is instructive that Padmore's great fear is the "imperialist aims" of the Garvey Movement at a time when there were only two nominally independent countries on the continent of Africa and the entire African world was locked in the stranglehold of white colonial slavery.

It borders on insanity that Padmore's fears would be directed at an alleged intent of Garvey to create a black imperialism in Africa that would, in fact, overturn a real, existing white imperialism! The movement to stop Garvey, of which Padmore was an illustrious participant, was in reality a movement to protect white imperialist domination of Africa from African people ourselves.

It is clear how Padmore's position against Garvey mirrors that of the white ruling class, blaming Garvey for the imperialist attacks that were responsible for Garvey's imprisonment and deportation as well as the destruction of the UNIA, events that Padmore gleefully describes.

His barely concealed joy at the downfall of Garvey and the UNIA reveals a commonality of interests among the imperialist white ruling class, Padmore and the Communist International on one side, and Garvey, along with the millions of Africans who supported him and the UNIA vision of national liberation on the other.

Three years after the publication of his book, Padmore left the Communist International, perhaps after discovering it was the headquarters of "reformers and social-fascists" from whom he wanted to protect the white workers. He would eventually end up a Pan-Africanist in the company of

W.E.B. Du Bois, whom he had characterized in this same book as a petty bourgeois reformist. He was now a virulent anti-communist and author of the book, *Pan-Africanism or Communism*, for which he is probably best known and revered by petty bourgeois Pan-Africanists.

As we stated in "African Internationalism versus Pan-Africanism," quoted above:

> *People ask, "Can there be revolutionary Pan-Africanists? I think that's an oxymoron, a contradiction in terms. Pan-Africanism does not have the ability to recognize the class question, therefore whoever wants to be a Pan-Africanist can be. [Kwame] Nkrumah was a communist, but I've been in London with people who call themselves Pan-Africanists who are anti-communist. A Pan-Africanist is whatever somebody who calls himself a Pan-Africanist wants to be."*

Pan-Africanism liquidates the class contradiction that's killing us all over the world. To win the total liberation and unification of Africa and consolidate our nation we have to be absolutely clear. African Internationalism informs us that the African working class aligned with poor peasants must unequivocally lead this struggle for African liberation. Every other class force wavers in its loyalty to imperialist white power that affords them the promise of material or other benefits at the expense of the suffering African working class and the subjugated African nation.

The success of the Garvey Movement and its program is the best concrete evidence of the sense of sameness experienced by Africans worldwide. The UNIA was an organization of several million members and supporters throughout the world, including Australia.

Its influence continues to be experienced by Africans even today, a century after its founding. The Garvey Movement's 1920 Convention of the Negro Peoples of the World, held in Manhattan at Madison Square Garden attracted between 25,000 and 50,000 people from throughout the African world. This was an amazing accomplishment at a time when communications and transportation were considerably more difficult than they are today and our national oppression placed formidable constraints on our mobility, both within the U.S. and in the colonial territories in Africa and elsewhere. The historic Garvey Movement convention was the only place in the world that afforded Africans a democratic opportunity to vote their political preferences. Marcus Garvey was elected the Provisional President of Africa by convention attendees and the Red, Black and Green flag was adopted as the national colors for African people.

It was also at this convention that the delegates enthusiastically adopted the Declaration of the Rights of the Negro Peoples of the World as their program giving political definition to the collective, national interests of the struggle of Africans worldwide. The 1920 Garvey Movement convention addressed the common issues of oppression and resistance. It cemented a united, world African consciousness and expression of power that sent the Communist Party scurrying to the U.S. government to collaborate in the attack that would imprison and deport Garvey and destroy the Garvey Movement.

The crushing of the Garvey Movement took the combined endeavors of the U.S. and other imperialist governments of the time, along with a motley assortment of enemies of various hues and ideological leanings, who were all opposed to the notion of our national liberation as Africans. With the destruction of the Garvey Movement went the dreams of African people who aspired to consolidate our African nation—an aspiration left to our Party to accomplish.

The African nation and commonality of culture

The African nation is real. It is distinguished by a number of elements, both objective and subjective. Clearly there is a sense of sameness, something that European and Negro scholars often pretend does not exist, but which nevertheless exposes itself to public view every time Africans come to harm from or achieve victory over imperialist white power.

Few quibble that black people in Africa itself are some variation of African, although sub-identities of ethnicity or "tribe" and/or religion often challenge the significance of the fact that they are African.

The colonial, dividing borders imposed on Africa by Europeans are part of the parasitic process of achieving European national identity through destroying the African collective identity and facilitating the colonial theft of African resources. One function of the borders has been to prevent the consolidation of a single, continental-wide national economy that would be the primary, material foundation of national unification, including one African language.

The commonality of African culture and language would consolidate, develop and flourish under the influence of African self-serving economic forces unleashed from the distorting, limiting imposition of borders that divert all things of value to the service of external forces. Historically our resources and labor have benefited Europe and Europeans primarily, but today this increasingly involves China, India, Turkey and every imperialist-aspiring predator capable of entering the feeding frenzy on Africa's soil.

In the U.S. it is generally agreed that Africans constitute a distinct community, with a distinct history and culture. No scholarly studies are needed to make this point. There is disagreement, of course, on the question of whether these distinct features contribute to the definition of Africans as a distinct nation.

Some of the problems surrounding this question in North America revolve around two issues. One is the fact that Europeans themselves are new to this continent, having wrenched it from the custody of the Indigenous people through brutish, horrendous, genocidal aggression that contributed to the culture of violence that defines the European nation. To admit that Africans constitute a nation is to thrust to the surface an underlying question that the white nation cannot tolerate. Namely: "If they are Africans, then who are we?"

Secondly, there is the question of the size and viability of the African population inside the U.S. Of course, there are more African people in North America than white people in some European countries that pose as nations. Nevertheless, Africans are held to a different standard on this issue.

This takes us back to Garvey and the UNIA. This takes us back to the African People's Socialist Party and the African Socialist International. This takes us to the recognition that the African nation is *not* confined to the borders imposed on us by Europe, whether in Africa or the various places to which we have been forcibly dispersed.

As African Internationalists we recognize that the basis of our struggle is the European attack on Africa, the forced dispersal and colonization of untold millions of its inhabitants and the creation of artificial borders used to facilitate the alienation of Africans from each other, from our resources and from our national identity.

Our position here does not ignore the fact that false national consciousness has been imposed on Africans worldwide through the violence of the imperialist state and imperialist-imposed ignorance.

In West Africa there is a territory known as Cameroon, named for the Portuguese word for shrimp after the Portuguese colonizers discovered an abundance of shrimp in its waters. The fact that there are thousands of Africans there that refer to themselves as shrimp does not make them shrimp any more than an African in England is a "Black Brit" or an African in the U.S. a "Negro" or "African-American."

Africans throughout the world continue to exist under some form of colonial domination. In this era, that takes the form of indirect or neocolonial rule by the European imperialist state in disguise. The capitalist-imperialist state, unlike its feudal predecessor, was born as an "international" state through imperialist colonial slavery, the foundation of capitalism and the European nation.

The bourgeois state manifests itself in Europe as relatively benign in relation to white people. In Nigeria, Sudan and all of Africa, as well as in Ireland, India, the Middle East, Asia and in all the colonized territories of this planet, including inside the U.S., the North American-European imperialist state has been highly armed and unremittingly violent.

Hence, the British state that was vicious in its colonies, bragged about police not carrying guns in England. That is until their colonial subjects emigrated to England in enough numbers to create *domestic* colonies like the ones found in the U.S. since its bloody advent through genocide and colonial slavery.

The United Nations, the North Atlantic Treaty Organization (NATO), a host of international institutions along with the U.S. Africa Command (AFRICOM) and the various U.S. and European military function as arms of a combined European capitalist state with the purpose of violently barring us from seizing control of our African nation. This is also the case for the neocolonial African governments that for the most part rely on charity handouts from imperialist states or institutions for funding, training and leadership.

Nevertheless, we can say without hesitation that the African nation does exist. We are one nation in need of consolidation, a nation definable by objective and subjective characteristics, with features arising specifically in response to historical necessity—just like the European nation. While the objective, material foundation of the African nation is fundamental, this does not limit or undermine the subjective element, the sense of sameness experienced by Africans everywhere.

The most important defining, material or objective element of the African nation is its derivation from Africa, the national homeland of African people. This is the critical component of African identity from which most of the subjective factors derive. The African nation is also defined in part by physiognomy. We are black people of and from Africa, the equatorial continent.

This common connection to Africa carries with it deep and profound cultural connections going back thousands of years, as previously shown in the quote by Cheikh Anta Diop. In 1962 Joseph Ki-Zerbo made similar assertions about the African nation. Included in a 1975 anthology entitled *Readings in African Political Thought*, Ki-Zerbo discusses in, "African Personality and the New African Society":

> *Contrary to the colonial image, which presents pre-colonial Africa as a collection of tiny groups torn by internal strife and tribal warfare, sociologically frozen at the stage of a protozoan or an amoeba, African society was highly organized. Its principal features, in my opinion, were the following: first, the authority of the old people...[I]n Africa the hierarchy of power, of consideration, and of prestige, was in direct rapport with the hierarchy of age.... The council of elders in traditional Africa was the supreme political master of the city or the tribe. It was often this autocracy of the old that evolved into a veritable cult of ancestor worship....*
>
> *Another important characteristic of the traditional society is solidarity, and this point is too obvious to require any lengthy examination. I would, however, like to say that this solidarity*

is not just a phenomenon of the superstructure, a trembling of the spirit, or a tenderness of heart towards others. This solidarity is imprinted on the very basic structure of African culture, and especially in its economic organization. You know that in the traditional African society the notion of property was defined in terms of the family, community or the village and not in terms of the individual. The concept of personal property in terms of the individual is generally alien to African social concepts. Fields are often common property and work is most often collective. Another social manifestation of this solidarity is hospitality, which, it is true, is obviously not an African monopoly but which nevertheless is particularly strong there; and here I am pleased to associate North Africa with the rest of the continent....

Another important feature is the equalitarian character of African society. Naturally, I do not intend in any way to idealize or present traditional Africa as the best of all possible or imaginary worlds. Africa has had its tyrants, as have other nations throughout history. But it must be stressed also that the traditional African society often included classes based solely on functional differentiation. There was, for instance the mason class, the blacksmith class, the warrior class. But the fact that in Africa property was common, the fact that there was no class that accumulated the capital property and reduced others to the state of mere tenancy—mere peasants or farmers whose toil was used to amass profit—well, that fact proves that the exploitation of man by man never achieved the status of a system in the traditional society of Africa. And, moreover,

> *by reason of the unlimited solidarity of which I have just spoken, the true principle of such a society was "To each according to his needs," to the extent of the complete utilization of common revenues.*

Who is an African?

We can see our commonality in Africa, but as we pointed out earlier, no nation is defined solely in relationship to itself. To say that the nation is one thing is to say that it is not another. Dark skin is a product of equatorial Africa, the land of "black" people. "Black" people among ourselves would be incapable of defining ourselves as such. It is through our relationship with "white" people and the dialectic of the oppressor nation and the oppressed nation that Africans became "black."

We can say, therefore, that the African nation is one born of its historical ties to its African national homeland, with a core sense of sameness that includes a common culture, history and physiognomy.

Still, to arrive at a full definition of the African nation we must say more than this. The African nation is informed by historical necessity, determined by our conditions of existence at this very moment, hundreds of years subsequent to our defining conflict with the European predator nation. Europe's parasitic attachment to Africa and Africans shapes and determines both its successful existence and our national incoherence.

A critical feature of our conditions of existence as a people is the imperialist near-total control of the economic life of Africa and African people wherever we are located in the world. Neither Africa, the land, nor Africans, the people—both fundamental components of the productive forces—have been accessible to Africa for the production and reproduction of real life for Africa and Africans.

Hence Africa has created staggering wealth for imperialism that has benefited the entire European nation—ruling class, middle class, workers and others at our expense. Everything they have was stolen from our labor, resources and knowledge! We have a historical mandate to take back what is ours and fulfill our destiny as a united, independent, self-governing nation in control of our own Continent and future.

This is an immensely profound reality that must be internalized by Africans and all peoples throughout the globe who have an interest in destroying forever this blood-sucking culture of violence stemming from U.S.-European imperialism.

Therefore, historical necessity—the absolute requirement of any people to produce and reproduce life as a condition of existence, survival and a meaningful future—*requires* the consolidation of the African nation. The consolidation of the African nation is a prerequisite for overturning the abject, genocidal conditions of existence of Africans everywhere.

There is no separate solution for the liberation of African people based on colonially-defined borders or identity any place on Earth. Clearly the African Liberation Movement has run into its limitations when fought within the context of these borders. Civil rights and "flag independence" only serve to obscure our oppressive exploitation, not overturn it.

Millions of Africans have been forcibly dispersed from Africa throughout the world. Europeans and others have come to Africa, some as colonizers, some as subjects of colonial powers who were allowed privilege in Africa as intermediary colonial agents functioning as buffers between Africans and our oppressors, a situation contributing to absolute African dependency and the atrophy of African productive forces. Other occupants of Africa are descendants of the Arab conquest in Africa preceding that of Europe.

How do these various forces fit into our definition of the African nation?

First of all, all black people forcibly transported to diverse parts of the world as part of the process giving rise to capitalism and the European nation are Africans. Period.

Secondly, all black people throughout the world are potentially part of the African nation, whether they were part of the forcible dispersal or whether their presence in other places predates the assault on Africa. This includes black people in Australia, India and other places who generally experience a sense of sameness associated with African blackness and the oppression we share because of our blackness. Under imperialist world domination, blackness is universally perceived as justification for our oppression.

For those Africans forcibly dispersed from Africa, we are directly connected to each other by the parasitic capitalist world economy under whose weight we continue to groan in poverty and oppression as the economic foundation of the European nation. All our cultural expressions, found everywhere we are dispersed—music, dance and other art forms and traditions—have their foundation in Africa.

The African nation and Arabs, whites, others in Africa

On the continent of Africa, our national homeland, there are many Europeans who came as colonizers. They have chosen to remain in Africa after nominal independence was declared in some territories, including Zimbabwe, Namibia, Kenya and South Africa as prime examples. In South Africa white people called themselves Africans prior to independence. Are these white people genuinely a part of the African nation by just declaring themselves so? The fact is that all Europeans, including those in Africa, are beneficiaries of the imperialist economy derived from African colonialism and slavery. This means they live at the expense of Africans. This places them concretely and objectively in the category of the European nation, even as they may now be forced to disguise their

European national identity for the purpose of maintaining a parasitic attachment to Africa. This attachment of European colonizers to Africa objectively undermines the consolidation of the African nation whose blackness is an identifying badge of exploitation and oppression.

This does *not* mean that whites from the colonizing nation cannot become a part of the African nation. What it does mean is that whites would have to commit "national suicide," abandoning the interests of the European parasitic oppressor nation and uniting with the historical trajectory of the African nation to achieve "black power."

Whites in Africa must unite with the capture of total economic and political power by African workers in a borderless continent. Power in the hands of African workers is the only way to unleash the productive forces of Africa, allowing Africa and Africans to engage fully in the process of producing life for Africa and Africans the world over. Objectively this would mean white people in Africa would have to voluntarily relinquish to the African nation the vast resources they have accumulated through their past identification with the parasitic European nation.

In the final analysis the struggle against world capitalism, resting as it does on the exploitation of the majority of the peoples of the world, will require the destruction of the "white" or European nation that requires for its existence a parasitic relationship to the majority of humanity.

The national liberation of Africa and African people will be a leading force in that destruction. The role of genuine white or European communists will be to actively engage in the commission of national suicide by becoming one with the national liberation of Africans and others. This is a far cry from the current position of most self-declared white communists who talk instead about the need of the oppressed of the world to unite with their narcissistically-defined European version of history.

A similar situation is that of the Arabs who came into Africa as conquerors, initiating their enslavement of African people that lasted 1,500 years, and paved the way for the European trans-Atlantic slave trade. Similar to Europeans, Arabs must embrace the historically necessary trajectory of Africa toward black power as their own.

We saw the potential for this kind of unity in the 1960s when Gamal Abdel Nasser of Egypt stood as one of the strongest allies of Kwame Nkrumah in his attempt to create a united Africa. Ahmed Ben Bella, revolutionary fighter and first president of liberated Algeria, was another who cast his lot with the African nation. Both men shared with Africa a sense of sameness that showed promise for consolidating all of North Africa into the African nation.

In addition to the practical examples of Nasser and Ben Bella there is the example of black Haiti, which upon achieving independence from France in 1804, created a constitution declaring citizenship and land ownership for blacks only, but which defined whites, including the Poles who fought with Africans in the struggle for independence, as "black" for the purposes of citizenship. This was a historic case of whites committing national suicide and consciously abandoning the pedestal upon which the European nation rests as a parasite on Africa and the world. This is a case of Europeans accepting as their own the struggle for the achievement of revolutionary black power.

We also mentioned the presence in Africa of people from India and other former colonies who were brought to the Continent by the British for the express purpose of acting as a colonial buffer between the imperialists and the often-resisting African masses.

There are literally millions of Indians in Africa today, most of whom live at a much higher standard of living than both the majority of Africans and the majority of people in India. This shows how the pedestal upon which Europeans sit on our backs can be and has been opened up to petty bourgeois sectors of formerly colonized countries who now enjoy the benefits of white power at our expense.

Thus, Arabs, Europeans and residents of Africa from other European colonies can become African if they commit national suicide and abandon their parasitic relationship to African people. They must financially, politically and in every other way unite with the leadership of and become one with the African working class and the aims of a united and liberated Africa.

We are Africans because we say we are!

The African nation, then, is a community of people whose core identity is based on historical ties to the equatorial continent of black Africa, contributing to a common culture, history and physiognomy.

The African nation is also comprised of all those African people who have been forcibly dispersed to various places in the world through colonial slavery. Dispersed Africans were part of the process of the development of capitalism and the European nation, a process that requires our subjugation and national incoherence.

Additionally, the African nation is comprised of many who experience a sense of sameness, a subjective connection to Africa, mainly because of skin color that helps to define their imperialist-inspired impoverished and oppressed state of existence. The Dalit in India, the Indigenous of Australia and other areas where the African presence goes back to earliest times, such as in the Asia-Pacific region, are included in this category.

Finally, the African nation can include people of other nationalities living in Africa who commit national suicide, becoming part of the African working class and abandoning all allegiance to a predatory, colonial relationship to African people.

The truth, stated simply, is: we are Africans, whatever else we may be called, because we say we are Africans and we feel like we are Africans.

Africa is the national homeland of all black people worldwide. It is the land to which the identity of the African nation is firmly and irreversibly affixed. Our historical connection to Africa represents the critical element of the material basis for African nationality. For although we have been forcibly dispersed by colonial slavery and related factors subsequent to the initial European attack on Africa, our current conditions of existence, both in Africa and abroad, are essentially defined by the consequences of our forced dispersal.

Here we remind ourselves that it was Europe that divided Africa with the illegitimate borders that now still function to facilitate the theft of Africa's still vast resources by various imperial forces. The colonial division of Africa continues to separate Africans from each other and from our resources that are being expropriated without cessation.

The 54 delineated territories currently characterized as African nations were created in a conference held in Berlin, Germany in 1884-1885, attended by contending European states that parceled Africa out among themselves, resulting in the map that is known as Africa today.

The result of this European invention has been the evolvement of a false national consciousness that fits the interests of the imperialists who created it at the expense of Africans ourselves. There were no pre-colonial borders separating Africans from each other. Now borders surround

54 colonially-created entities, many of which cut right down the middle of ancient family or kinship territories, dividing and pitting against each other Africans that lived together for time immemorial. Clearly, this physical and psychological separation has facilitated false national consciousness, not to mention a myriad of other traumas.

The practical significance of this clarification concerning the African nation and its relationship to the European imperialist nation was discussed in our book, *One People! One Party! One Destiny!*:

> *The anti-imperialist struggles of the world's peoples for repossession of our sovereignty and resources, both human and material, are the basis of the current, deep crisis of imperialism. They are struggles to remove the pedestal upon which the entire rotten edifice of imperialism rests. They are struggles that enlist the vast majority of humanity, the laboring masses of every nation, in the creation of a new world without exploitation and oppression, without slaves and slave masters and, ultimately, without borders.*
>
> *We recognize that the struggle for the liberation and unification of Africa and African people, the struggle for the consolidation of the African nation is ultimately a struggle that undermines the solidarity of the European nation-state. We understand that under imperialism those who were enslaved, colonized and oppressed as a people will have to win liberation as a people.*
>
> *We are also clear that the successful nation-building struggles of Africans and others under the leadership of the working class is at the same time*

> *the beginning of the process of the withering away of nations.*
>
> *The European nation was born as a bourgeois nation at the expense of whole peoples and their territories. As we have seen in this discussion, it is a nation that requires the oppression and exploitation of whole peoples for its successful existence.*
>
> *Hence, African people have to resist the imperialist bourgeoisie as a people. Our assumption of consolidated nationhood will function to destroy the bourgeois nation. Thus the rise of revolutionary worker nation-states destroys the material basis for the existence of nations and borders that function to distinguish and separate one people from another.*
>
> *This is easier to understand when we finally realize the significance of the fact that capitalism at birth came wrapped in the skin of the racialized European nation-state. It is this reality that made impotent the Marxian assumption of communism resulting from the withering away of the European bourgeois industrialized state.*
>
> *However, the fact that the European bourgeois nation-state achieves life and definition from its relationship to Africa and the oppressed peoples of the world means that our victory over imperialism, with the African working class at the helm will result in the withering away of nations. This will leave bare and make possible the withering away of the bourgeois state, which will have become historically redundant.*

Consolidating the African nation and building the African People's Socialist Party as the tool to achieve that goal must be at the top of the agenda of every African on Earth. Every struggle must lead to this end; every border must be broken down; the crisis of imperialism must be deepened daily. It is on the shoulders of Africans alive today to complete the struggle that our people have waged for more than 500 years: the liberation of Africa and reunification of African people everywhere—the consolidation of the African nation.

Independence, unification and socialism in our lifetime!

Part II

Resolutions from the Seventh Congress of the African People's Socialist Party USA

RESOLUTION 1

Preserve, protect and publish the Party's history

WHEREAS, the African People's Socialist Party has a glorious 46-year history of struggle and leadership of the worldwide African liberation struggle, which has been documented in the pages of *The Burning Spear* newspaper, in photos and on video and audio tape; and

WHEREAS, these materials are not easily accessible or available for use by the Uhuru Movement, students, activists, journalists, filmmakers and historians; and

WHEREAS, the organizing and dissemination of these materials will ensure that the theory, strategy and practical leadership of the African People's Socialist Party (APSP) and Chairman Omali Yeshitela will be forever available to future generations, providing continued guidance and serving as documentation of the role that the APSP has played in keeping the African struggle alive following the military defeat during the counterinsurgency and leading the way to victory against imperialism for all colonized and oppressed peoples;

NOW, THEREFORE, BE IT RESOLVED BY THE SEVENTH CONGRESS OF THE AFRICAN PEOPLE'S SOCIALIST PARTY, HELD IN ST. LOUIS, MISSOURI ON THE DATES OF OCTOBER 6-12, 2018:

SECTION ONE: That the APSP Department of Agitation and Propaganda will embark on a project to digitize and catalog the Party's over 40 years of archives of *The Burning*

Spear newspaper, video, audio and photographic materials; and

SECTION TWO: That the APSP Department of Agitation and Propaganda will establish ongoing processes and protocols for the digital tagging, organizing and storage of all print, video, audio and photo documentation of the work of the Party and all its departments and mass organizations going forward from this point in the Party's history; and

SECTION THREE: That the APSP Department of Agitation and Propaganda will set up redundant digital backup storage systems combining in-office storage with secure cloud storage of all materials; and

SECTION FOUR: That this resolution shall be in full force and effect immediately upon its adoption and approval in the manner provided by the Constitution of the African People's Socialist Party and the Rules of Procedure of this Congress.

RESOLUTION 2

Build an army of propagandists

WHEREAS, the African People's Socialist Party's Department of Agitation and Propaganda has the responsibility to wage the war of ideas and to win the hearts and minds of the African working class masses to revolutionary conclusions; and

WHEREAS, the colonial-capitalist state works daily to control the minds of African people, through TV, radio, newspapers, social media and culture; and

WHEREAS, African people under colonialism are denied access to the skills, training and equipment necessary to be self-determining and carry out our work for the Revolution;

NOW, THEREFORE, BE IT RESOLVED BY THE SEVENTH CONGRESS OF THE AFRICAN PEOPLE'S SOCIALIST PARTY, HELD IN ST. LOUIS, MISSOURI ON THE DATES OF OCTOBER 6-12, 2018:

SECTION ONE: That the APSP Department of Agitation and Propaganda will recruit into the offices of its primary propaganda tools: *The Burning Spear* newspaper, especially in the area of distribution, and Black Power 96.3 FM radio station; and

SECTION TWO: That the APSP Department of Agitation and Propaganda will train its department members as well as the general membership of the Party on writing for *The Spear*, selling *The Spear*, radio engineering, audio/visual services, graphic design and website development.

SECTION THREE: That this resolution shall be in full force and effect immediately upon its adoption and approval in the manner provided by the Constitution of the African People's Socialist Party and the Rules of Procedure of this Congress.

RESOLUTION 3

Build the economic self-sufficiency of the Department of Agitation and Propaganda

WHEREAS, the Department of Agitation and Propaganda has been performing its daily operations in a state of economic crisis; and

WHEREAS, the Party and its Chairman has mandated that the Party's Department of Agitation and Propaganda must be able to pay staff and fund production of all types of media materials to win the war of ideas; and

WHEREAS, the Department of Agitation and Propaganda has the capacity to bring in the most resources after the Office of the Deputy Chair, through our ability to sell the Party line; and

WHEREAS, the Department of Agitation and Propaganda has been without a person formally identified as the Economic Development Coordinator for the overall department or any of its institutions;

NOW, THEREFORE, BE IT RESOLVED BY THE SEVENTH CONGRESS OF THE AFRICAN PEOPLE'S SOCIALIST PARTY, HELD IN ST. LOUIS, MISSOURI ON THE DATES OF OCTOBER 6-12, 2018:

SECTION ONE: That the Department of Agitation and Propaganda will expand its products and services, as well as reinitiate programs that have existed in the past, to identify consistent revenue streams; and

SECTION TWO: That the Department of Agitation and Propaganda will resolve to build Burning Spear A/V, with the tagline "Vanguard Audio/Visual Services," as a professional events production service, providing audio, video and live broadcasting services as a fundraising business; and

SECTION THREE: That the Department of Agitation and Propaganda will build Burning Spear Publications by creating a large catalog of Party books and posters, along with a product line containing African Internationalist merchandise and gear; and

SECTION FOUR: That the Department of Agitation and Propaganda resolves to identify an Economic Development Coordinator on the leading committee for Agitation and Propaganda to oversee all economic development work for the department, and that the department will recruit into the managerial positions of Burning Spear Publications, Burning Spear A/V and department treasurer to ensure the development of these new programs and institutions; and

SECTION FIVE: That this resolution shall be in full force and effect immediately upon its adoption and approval in the manner provided by the Constitution of the African People's Socialist Party and the Rules of Procedure of this Congress.

RESOLUTION 4

Utilize the Party's regional structure to expand distribution of *The Burning Spear* newspaper

WHEREAS, *The Burning Spear* newspaper is the official organ of the African People's Socialist Party, and constitutionally mandated to be distributed by the Party's call for members to distribute its press; and

WHEREAS, selling *The Burning Spear* newspaper in the African community is the primary means by which members of the African People's Socialist Party can organize and influence African workers on a daily basis, and recruit members into the Party or our other organizations; and

WHEREAS, the African People's Socialist Party has engaged in a regional strategy to build dual and contending power in the colonies throughout the U.S. through the consolidation of regional hubs;

NOW, THEREFORE, BE IT RESOLVED BY THE SEVENTH CONGRESS OF THE AFRICAN PEOPLE'S SOCIALIST PARTY, HELD IN ST. LOUIS, MISSOURI ON THE DATES OF OCTOBER 6-12, 2018:

SECTION ONE: That regional representatives or identified Regional Spear Agents of the African People's Socialist Party will develop and lead strategies to centralize and collectivize the sale of *The Burning Spear* newspaper throughout their respective regions; and

SECTION TWO: That regional representatives or identified Regional Spear Agents of the African People's Socialist Party will do everything possible to get *The Burning Spear* newspaper carried by African bookstores, African businesses and colleges within their respective regions; and

SECTION THREE: That regional representatives or identified Regional Spear Agents of the African People's Socialist Party will ensure that local Party organizers within their respective regions establish regular *Burning Spear* study groups to include Party members as well as Party followers and members of the Party's mass organizations; and

SECTION FOUR: That this resolution shall be in full force and effect immediately upon its adoption and approval in the manner provided by the Constitution of the African People's Socialist Party and the Rules of Procedure of this Congress.

RESOLUTION 5

Protect the Party from social media security breaches and ensure responsible social media use

WHEREAS, social media tools like Facebook, Twitter and Instagram are owned, designed and controlled by the colonial-capitalist enemies of African liberation; and

WHEREAS, data-gathering companies like Facebook, Google and others are known to share their information on users with counterinsurgency wings of the imperialist state like the NSA, FBI and others; and

WHEREAS, information voluntarily posted by political activists to social media and Google searches has been used to imprison and attack these activists and to compile profiles on the personal, family, job and daily whereabouts of such activists for the purposes of surveillance and manipulation;

NOW, THEREFORE, BE IT RESOLVED BY THE SEVENTH CONGRESS OF THE AFRICAN PEOPLE'S SOCIALIST PARTY, HELD IN ST. LOUIS, MISSOURI ON THE DATES OF OCTOBER 6-12, 2018:

SECTION ONE: That the APSP Department of Agitation and Propaganda will produce for the entire Party a manual dealing with social media and cybersecurity, presenting a process and protocols to centralize the organization of our Party online and prevent harmful social media use; and

SECTION TWO: That the APSP Department of Agitation and Propaganda has provided social media protocols and will consolidate a team to make sure they are adhered to. Those protocols are as follows:

What types of posts aren't permitted?

1) Sexually explicit posts. 2) Posts about weapons. 3) Posts about killing someone, even if it's concerning inevitable revolutionary violence. A call to kill/inflict major bodily harm on someone is not permitted as it can lead to state targeting and even result in a "criminal" offense. 4) Gossip posts. Gossip is in direct violation of our Rules of Party Discipline. Criticisms of our comrades, the work or any Party-related information discussed in a meeting that has not gained approval for discussion among the public is prohibited. Internal struggles that we have must be just that—internal to our Party. 5) Posts that slander/undermine the African working class. This goes for sharing posts that appear to be comedic but are at our people's expense. The Party's responsibility is to uplift the African working class! 6) Public criticisms of Party members or Party work/decisions. Similar to the reasoning of Point 4, we must not make our struggles public unless otherwise advised. Violation of this point will be viewed as an attack on the Party; and

SECTION THREE: That the APSP Department of Agitation and Propaganda will enforce disciplinary actions when Party members are in violation of these social media protocols; and

SECTION FOUR: That this resolution shall be in full force and effect immediately upon its adoption and approval in the manner provided by the Constitution of the African People's Socialist Party and the Rules of Procedure of this Congress.

RESOLUTION 6

Build the African People's Solidarity Committee in South Africa

WHEREAS, white people live in South Africa as an occupying, colonizer population, living off the land stolen from African people; and

WHEREAS, South Africa is a country run by the white bourgeoisie and despite the transfer of the administration to the African petty bourgeoisie, the vast resources produced by the African working class are still in the hands of white settlers from England, the U.S., Holland and elsewhere; and

WHEREAS, the formal end of apartheid has allowed the white bourgeoisie to expand in other African countries, increasing the general wealth of the white settler bourgeoisie; and

WHEREAS, white people in South Africa have never been challenged by revolutionary politics;

NOW, THEREFORE, BE IT RESOLVED BY THE SEVENTH CONGRESS OF THE AFRICAN PEOPLE'S SOCIALIST PARTY, HELD IN ST. LOUIS, MISSOURI ON THE DATES OF OCTOBER 6-12, 2018:

SECTION ONE: That an African People's Solidarity Committee (APSC) be created, working under the leadership of the Party to take African Internationalism into the white community, winning material solidarity for black power and self-determination; and

SECTION TWO: That an African Day of Solidarity be organized that will allow our Party to win white and other non-African people to provide solidarity to African liberation under the leadership of the African People's Socialist Party; and

SECTION THREE: That this resolution shall be in full force and effect immediately upon its adoption and approval in the manner provided by the Constitution of the African People's Socialist Party and the Rules of Procedure of this Congress.

RESOLUTION 7

Produce *The Burning Spear* in South Africa

WHEREAS, the war of ideas is the struggle to defeat all the wrong ideas of imperialism that bombard the oppressed African nation and make us incapable of thinking of our own interests and how to transform our reality; and

WHEREAS, the spread of African Internationalism, for the education of the African nation under the leadership of its Advanced Detachment, the African People's Socialist Party, requires an organized process in South Africa to include writers, proofreaders, illustrators and graphic designers; and

WHEREAS, the creation of a *Burning Spear* Bureau in South Africa is necessary to ensure the continuity of the production and distribution of *The Burning Spear* newspaper;

NOW, THEREFORE, BE IT RESOLVED BY THE SEVENTH CONGRESS OF THE AFRICAN PEOPLE'S SOCIALIST PARTY, HELD IN ST. LOUIS, MISSOURI ON THE DATES OF OCTOBER 6-12, 2018:

SECTION ONE: That *The Burning Spear* newspaper will be produced in South Africa to facilitate a more efficient and scientific approach to the spread of African Internationalism throughout the Southern Africa region; and

SECTION TWO: That printing *The Spear* in South Africa will ensure reliability and consistency in the training and consolidation of all Party units throughout the region of Southern Africa; and

SECTION THREE: That this resolution shall be in full force and effect immediately upon its adoption and approval in the manner provided by the Constitution of the African People's Socialist Party and the Rules of Procedure of this Congress.

RESOLUTION 8

Hold an annual African Liberation Day in South Africa

WHEREAS, there are many African people from throughout the Continent and from outside the Continent who live in South Africa (there are at least 1 million people from Zimbabwe living in South Africa); and

WHEREAS, the question of African unity can find a new expression with a revolutionary call for a united socialist state of Africa; and

WHEREAS, the white bourgeoisie and the African petty bourgeoisie regularly incite ethnic hatred and clashes to break the solidarity between African workers who are native to South Africa and those who are originally from elsewhere but now live in South Africa; and

WHEREAS, the question of nationality and immigration can only be solved by the revolutionary African working class under its Advanced Detachment, the African People's Socialist Party, carrying out intense and constant political education and propaganda work; and

WHEREAS, the borders imposed on us by the imperialists only benefit those who have an agenda of oppressing and looting Africa, and separate Africans from each other while protecting the African petty bourgeoisie from the anger and wrath of the people;

NOW, THEREFORE, BE IT RESOLVED BY THE SEVENTH CONGRESS OF THE AFRICAN PEOPLE'S

SOCIALIST PARTY, HELD IN ST. LOUIS, MISSOURI ON THE DATES OF OCTOBER 6-12, 2018:

SECTION ONE: That an international African Liberation Day will be held each year in South Africa to unite all African people on the Continent and around the world; and

SECTION TWO: That the African People's Socialist Party will organize all African people who are living in South Africa, including those who are not originally from South Africa, to be an essential part of this African Liberation Day; and

SECTION THREE: That this resolution shall be in full force and effect immediately upon its adoption and approval in the manner provided by the Constitution of the African People's Socialist Party and the Rules of Procedure of this Congress.

RESOLUTION 9

Engage in reparations enforcement

This resolution was initiated by Kamm Howard, Chair of the Reparations Working Group for the Black is Back Coalition for Reparations, Peace and Social Justice. It was put forward at the APSP Seventh Congress by the Constitution and Resolutions Committee of the Congress on his behalf.

WHEREAS, the United Nations Human Rights Commission sponsored the World Conference against Racism, Racial Discrimination, Xenophobia and Related Intolerance in 2001 in Durban, South Africa, also known as the World Conference Against Racism (WCAR); and

WHEREAS, the World Conference Against Racism produced an outcome document—the Durban Declaration and Program of Action (DDPA); and

WHEREAS, the Durban Declaration and Program of Action declared that the trans-Atlantic slave trade, slavery and colonialism were crimes against humanity; and

WHEREAS, crimes against humanity are recognized as the most egregious crimes a state can commit or allow to be committed against a civilian population; and

WHEREAS, crimes against humanity have no statute of limitations; and

WHEREAS, reparations are the internationally adopted means of redress for crimes against humanity, i.e., "reparations are a human right;" and

WHEREAS, reparations under international law means "full repair," and full repair means that "all consequences" of the crime must be wiped out; and

WHEREAS, all citizens within a state are obligated to affect redress for crimes against humanity regardless of when they became citizens of the state; and

WHEREAS, the United States of America engaged in the crimes of the trans-Atlantic slave trade, slavery and colonialism; and

WHEREAS, the United States of America allowed and assisted corporations, institutions and private citizens to engage in the crimes of the trans-Atlantic slave trade, slavery and colonialism; and

WHEREAS, the United States of America, many corporations, institutions and private families that engaged in crimes against humanity via the trans-Atlantic slave trade, slavery and colonialism, still exist; and

WHEREAS, the United Nations Human Rights Commission stated in September of 2017 that the United States must address reparations for people of African descent in America; and

WHEREAS, there has been no action on the part of the United Sates of America, its corporations, institutions or private families that are guilty of crimes against African humanity, to engage the Africans in this country for redress, i.e., reparations; and

WHEREAS, African people have the human right to enforce their right to be repaired, i.e., make a demand for reparations from any of the above criminal entities;

NOW, THEREFORE, BE IT RESOLVED BY THE SEVENTH CONGRESS OF THE AFRICAN PEOPLE'S SOCIALIST PARTY, HELD IN ST. LOUIS, MISSOURI ON THE DATES OF OCTOBER 6-12, 2018:

SECTION ONE: That in cities where the African People's Socialist Party exists, we will expose entities that are guilty of crimes against humanity; and

SECTION TWO: That the African People's Socialist Party will use its forces and resources to engage any such entity in a demand for reparations utilizing the DDPA as a basis for its reparations enforcement action; and

SECTION THREE: That this resolution shall be in full force and effect immediately upon its adoption and approval in the manner provided by the Constitution of the African People's Socialist Party and the Rules of Procedure of this Congress.

Part III

Solidarity Statements to the Seventh Congress of the African People's Socialist Party USA

Benjamín Prado

Under-Secretary General, Unión del Barrio

Uhuru Comrades of the Central Committee of the African People's Socialist Party, Comrade Chairman Omali Yeshitela, Comrades of the African People's Socialist Party.

On behalf of the Central Committee of Unión del Barrio and its general membership, I would like to salute the APSP and the convening of its membership to this historic Seventh Congress.

It constitutes a profound honor for the delegation of Unión del Barrio to participate in this gathering, for the significance that the Congress represents and the consolidation of a political Vanguard for the African working class, in our shared struggle to defeat our common enemy: U.S. settler colonialism, parasitic capitalism and U.S. imperialism.

We attend this Congress in a moment of deep sorrow for the loss of our Comrade Pablo Aceves. And we say that Comrade Paul, Pablo Aceves, would want us to be here more than in any other place in this historic moment. We say not one moment of silence, but a lifetime of struggle, a lifetime of organization and a lifetime of unity!

Comrades, it is 35 years that Unión del Barrio has been in unity with the African People's Socialist Party. Thirty-five years! It is 35 years of principled struggle, of principled unity, of standing together in our common fight against our common enemy of humanity. We are inspired by the trajectory of our two peoples' struggle.

Unión del Barrio stands in unity with the Seventh Congress. This nearly 35 years of principled relationship among the African people and Mexican people cannot be underestimated. Because it is our peoples who have been suffering the terrible colonial oppression that European colonialism has imposed, not only on the Americas and our peoples, but on humanity as a whole.

We are inspired by the diversity and significance of the Black Power Blueprint and every single project that the African People's Socialist Party has taken on.

It is an inspiration for Unión del Barrio to continue to unite and continue to build. The physical, real representation of self-determination, embodied by Black Star Industries, by Uhuru Foods & Pies, by the history of building and consolidating the working class as expressed by *The Burning Spear,* has inspired our organization, educated our membership and provided profound ideological vision for what Unión del Barrio is today.

The influence of the African People's Socialist Party on Unión del Barrio is profoundly significant. It has been that important unity that we have seen grow.

We stand here on the shoulders of giants. We cannot speak of being here without remembering our Comrade, Ernesto Bustillos.

Ernesto Bustillos ¡Presente! Uhuru! Long Live Ernesto Bustillos! Long Live Pablo Aceves!

Since 1981 we have worked consistently and tirelessly to build the necessary organization that will inform and lead the Mexican and Latin American working class to liberate our lands from the U.S. colonial laws and their settler institutions. We recognize that our struggle as an Indigenous people for self-determination against colonialism, capitalism and imperialism must be in unity with the African people in their struggle for a united Africa and a united socialist Nuestra América.

That is why today we unite with this struggle, to motivate us in that long history of anti-colonial struggle that we ourselves assume as a necessary component to build our own liberation struggle and build a political vanguard that can advance our people's struggle for self-determination and national liberation.

We do not recognize the colonial borders or those colonial laws that attempt to subject our people as foreigners on our own land. The basis of our unity with all people is a unity to reclaim our labor, to reclaim our land, to reclaim our natural resources, so that we can build a future for all of us in a sustainable fashion that does not destroy our Mother Earth.

We know that there is a methodical war being waged against our communities, the working class people, here and around the world. This capitalist offensive is bent on sustaining itself on permanent war. We recognize that the only way that we're going to be able to liberate ourselves is to organize principled political struggle. And that is why we recognize the significance of this Congress to bring unity to our peoples, to bring unity to the African people, to bring unity to the Mexican people and to bring unity for all anti-colonial struggle, to do away with false political borders that continue to divide our peoples and nation.

We unite with the Political Report, with the political document for the Congress because we see that parasitic capitalism as it exists today is unsustainable. It has been unsustainable since the day they kidnapped the first African out of Africa and brought them to what we know as the Americas.

We know the assault that happened more than 500 years ago continues to this day and that we have never been at peace. We have lost a way of life as a consequence of this European invasion, war and occupation of our lands and the continued imposition of a political economic system that exploits our land and our labor, that keeps us captured in these concentration camps known as prisons.

We know that the only way we're going to get out of this is by fighting back, by uniting with the African People's Socialist Party, by uniting with all the other peoples around the world who are also waging a fierce struggle for liberation of their lands, their resources and to build a socialist future.

Unión del Barrio salutes this gathering and we offer our unity with the objectives to bring our peoples closer and to build a united and coordinated political, organic struggle—organic unity and unity of action.

We feel in this moment, the political conditions have only sharpened. We recognize that at no point in U.S. history have the colonial representatives that occupy the White House, ever represented the interest of our peoples.

So it is profoundly important and inspiring to be here with you today, to share this Congress with you and to take back the message of organization and unity. Take back the message of building the Black Power Blueprint in every community, in every school where we find ourselves, in every barrio that we find ourselves, even in the prisons where the majority of our people continue to be locked up and oppressed.

Wherever our people may be, we must expose them to the thoughts and ideas of this Congress, of these documents that have been produced by Comrade Omali Yeshitela. We recognize the profound leadership of Omali Yeshitela.

We don't take this responsibility lightly. It is one of historical significance, not only for our organization Unión del Barrio, but for our people in order to advance the necessary theory that can take us into a liberated, free world, beyond U.S. imperialism.

We thank you comrades for this invitation. We are profoundly honored. And we will continue to work side by side, so that we can bring about that world that we all aspire to build.

United we shall win, Uhuru!

Ramiro Sebastián Fúnez

Chairman, Anticonquista

My name is Ramiro Sebastián Fúnez. I live in Los Angeles, California and I'm a proud member and Chairman of ANTICONQUISTA, the Communist Party of the Latin American and Caribbean Diaspora.

On behalf of ANTICONQUISTA, the Central Committee and all of our members, I want to congratulate all of you, the African People's Socialist Party on your Seventh Party Congress in St Louis, Missouri. It's truly an honor to be able to share this moment with you all and to send you a solidarity message from the bottom of our hearts.

ANTICONQUISTA, which was founded just a year ago, offers its full support to the African People's Socialist Party. We support your effort to liberate Africa and the African people from the constraints of the global capitalist, imperialist, racist system headed by the United States, the European Union and all other first world nations. We support the unification of Africa and all of its people under one strong united and powerful motherland.

We support the revolutionary theory and practical application of African Internationalism. We know that the liberation of Latin America and the Caribbean from capitalism and imperialism is impossible without the liberation of Africa from the very same racist systems. Like Comandante Hugo Chávez from Venezuela once said, we reject the idea that Spain is our motherland, we know that Latin America and the Caribbean is our motherland, that Africa is our great motherland. After all, over 10 million enslaved Africans were kidnapped by white colonizers and taken to the Americas against their will.

We owe a lot to Africa. Our food has roots in Africa, our music has roots in Africa, our people have roots in Africa. Even revolutionary figures Juan Almeida from Cuba and Maurice Bishop from Grenada are African people.

One can't speak of the contributions of Latin America and the Caribbean, all of the amazing things we've done in music, science, culture and politics, without mentioning Africa and the African people. That's why ANTICONQUISTA, the Communist Party of the Latin American and Caribbean Diaspora, stands shoulder-to-shoulder with the African People's Socialist Party in the fight, in the struggle, to liberate Africa from colonialism and imperialism.

So on behalf of my Party and my Compañeras and Compañeros, I want to thank you all for the work that you're doing. We support you, we love you, we are here to help any way we can and we hope that someday Latin America and the Caribbean can come together under a united socialist movement and that Africa can come together under a united socialist movement and build a better world, free from capitalism, free from colonialism and free from imperialism.

Lisa Davis

Vice Chair, Black is Back Coalition for Social Justice, Peace and Reparations; Member of the People's Organization for Progress

Uhuru Comrades!

First of all, let me start by stating that I wish you an extraordinary and powerful Congress, as I know that it will be. Regrettably, I cannot be there in person, as the politics of the plantation does not make that possible; hence my desire grows stronger every day to not just liberate myself and my people from these damned plantations, but to completely turn them inside out, upside down, shred them to pieces, overthrow them and to obliterate every trace of their existence from every fiber of our beings. I stand in complete solidarity with the mission of the African People's Socialist Party's call for the complete liberation of African people. And although I am not able to be there with you physically, I am there with you in power, vision and determination.

I will never forget the first time I'd ever heard of Chairman Omali Yeshitela, *The Burning Spear* newspaper and the

African People's Socialist Party (APSP). It was at a meeting of the People's Organization for Progress in Newark, which was over 15 years ago. He was introduced to us that night as a very profound and exciting speaker who was going to deliver a message to us in a way that we would not forget.

Needless to say, that was an understatement. His in-depth analysis of the development of early European society had a profound impact on me. It caused a major shift in my perspective and supplied me with much needed language to further destroy the lie of European supremacy. And today I'll defiantly tell anybody that it is Europe that needs Africa for its survival, and not the other way around. I knew from that night onward that I wanted to find out more about the work of Omali Yeshitela and I hoped that I would get the chance to work with him at some point.

And sure enough, some years later when the chance presented itself to me, I was ready for the opportunity. When Glen Ford announced the formation of the Black is Back Coalition for Social Justice, Peace and Reparations in the *Black Agenda Report*, I was determined to become an active member of that Coalition. Today, I am its Vice Chair.

I am so proud of the work of the Black is Back Coalition and of the comrades that I have met in the International People's Democratic Uhuru Movement and the APSP. From its inception, we hit the ground running and the APSP's contributions to the success of the Black is Back Coalition are immeasurable. Many are the times that I have called the Chairman from New Jersey, with concerns about something going on in another part of the country, to have him put me in touch with APSP comrades on the ground in that area. I've worked on actions with people from Oakland, Philadelphia, North Carolina, etc. There has never been a time when I have reached out to the Chairman with a concern and he did not respond with an action plan.

And while there is so much to be said about all of the institutions that the APSP is building, such as its Black Power Blueprint, the All African People's Development and Empowerment Project, etc., one of the most significant contributions it has made is in the shaping of the political discourse for African liberation.

Terms such as "Uhuru," "African Internationalism," and "parasitic capitalism" are fast becoming part of our Movement's vernacular. Its publications of *The Burning Spear* newspaper, and numerous books, along with its production of Black Power 96 radio and the "Omali Taught Me" study series, encourage studying, while providing powerful opportunities for us to challenge mainstream assumptions, and to develop analytical thinking prowess. These skills are necessary for becoming strong African-minded people as we navigate these white racist systems of oppression. The fruits of the APSP precede you, as I am constantly hearing people in our community commend the political analysis that the Uhuru Movement brings to any situation.

Again, I salute the work of the African People's Socialist Party and I look forward to seeing you at the Black is Back Coalition's annual march on the white people's house in November.

Asa Anpu

Secretary General, African People's Socialist Party South Africa

Uhuru, Mafrika!

On behalf of the Chairman of the African People's Socialist Party Occupied Azania, as well as the Uhuru Movement, one thing we know for sure is that we are excited about being able to see the Seventh Congress happen.

Even though we won't be there physically due to certain colonial circumstances, we unite with the mandate of the Party to organize our people, as well as the allies who are working in conjunction with African liberation.

We want to say, "Forward to the Seventh Congress!" Let's get it in. Africa is getting free, the whole world is changing. It's the tipping point, that's what it is.

I want to salute the delegation. I want to salute the brothers and sisters, Chairman Omali Yeshitela, sister Deputy Chair Ona Zené Yeshitela, Comrade Secretary General Luwezi, all my elders, Kefing. All the comrades, we just want to say shouts to you and we love you for what you're doing. Africa is getting free, history is in motion. Uhuru!

M. Kask

African People's Socialist Party Kenya

Uhuru! This is Comrade M. Kask from Nairobi, Kenya and I'd like to send out my revolutionary greetings to the entire African People's Socialist Party watching from all over the world.

I am saddened that I could not join my comrades in St. Louis for this historic Congress and it's also sad that I didn't make it to the Regional Congress in Azania because of these stupid borders, but anyway, tuko pamoja[1] comrades!

My special shout outs to Chairman Omali Yeshitela, Deputy Chair Ona Zené Yeshitela, Luwezi Kinshasa and the entire National Central Committee. And my special greetings to all members of the African People's Socialist Party.

Comrades, I will be there with you in spirit and I unite with the Seventh Congress. Onward! Tuko pamoja! Uhuru! Thank you!

---

1 Swahili for "we are together"

Part IV

Photos from the Seventh Congress of the African People's Socialist Party USA

1. Ngoma in Motion drummers. **2.** ASI Secretary General Luwezi Kinshasa convenes the APSP Seventh Congress. **3.** Chairman Omali Yeshitela with Unión del Barrio Under-Secretary Benjamín Prado. **4.** Members of the National Central Committee (NCC) Aisha Fields, Yejide Orunmila and Akilé Anai **5.** NCC members Luwezi Kinshasa, Ona Zené Yeshitela, Kalambayi Andenet, Nana Yaw Grant and Kobina Bantushango. **6.** Chairman Omali Yeshitela reads from the Political Report. **7-10.** APSP veterans Omowale Kefing, Chimurenga Selembao, Vince Lawrence and Gaida Kambon were saluted for their unending devotion to African liberation.

1. Chief of Staff Ekenge Mayele holds a copy of the Political Report. **2.** Nana Yaw Grant holds appreciation gifts given to Party supporters. **3.** New York state assemblyman Charles Barron with APSP Deputy Chair Ona Zené Yeshitela. **4.** Office of Deputy Chair members discuss the Party's successful and long-standing institutions and upcoming projects in workshop "The Political and Economic are One: Dual and Contending State Power." **5-6.** Many answer the Party's call to join. **7.** Chairman Omali Yeshitela in the dressing room before the reading of the Political Report **8.** Deputy Chair Ona Zené Yeshitela with comrades from her department.

1-3. Attendees dress to impress at the Black Power Masquerade and Awards Ball. **4.** African stilt walkers. **5.** Charles Oliver and Tommy Washington, from the Office of the Deputy Chair. **6.** Brandi Arrington (center) and Ticharwa Masimba (right), from the Office of the Deputy Chair, surrounded by family members. **7.** Chairman Omali Yeshitela and Deputy Chair Ona Zené Yeshitela. **8.** The Chairman with members of the delegation from Unión del Barrio. **9.** Aisha Fields, Tommy Washington and Kobina Bantushango strike a pose.

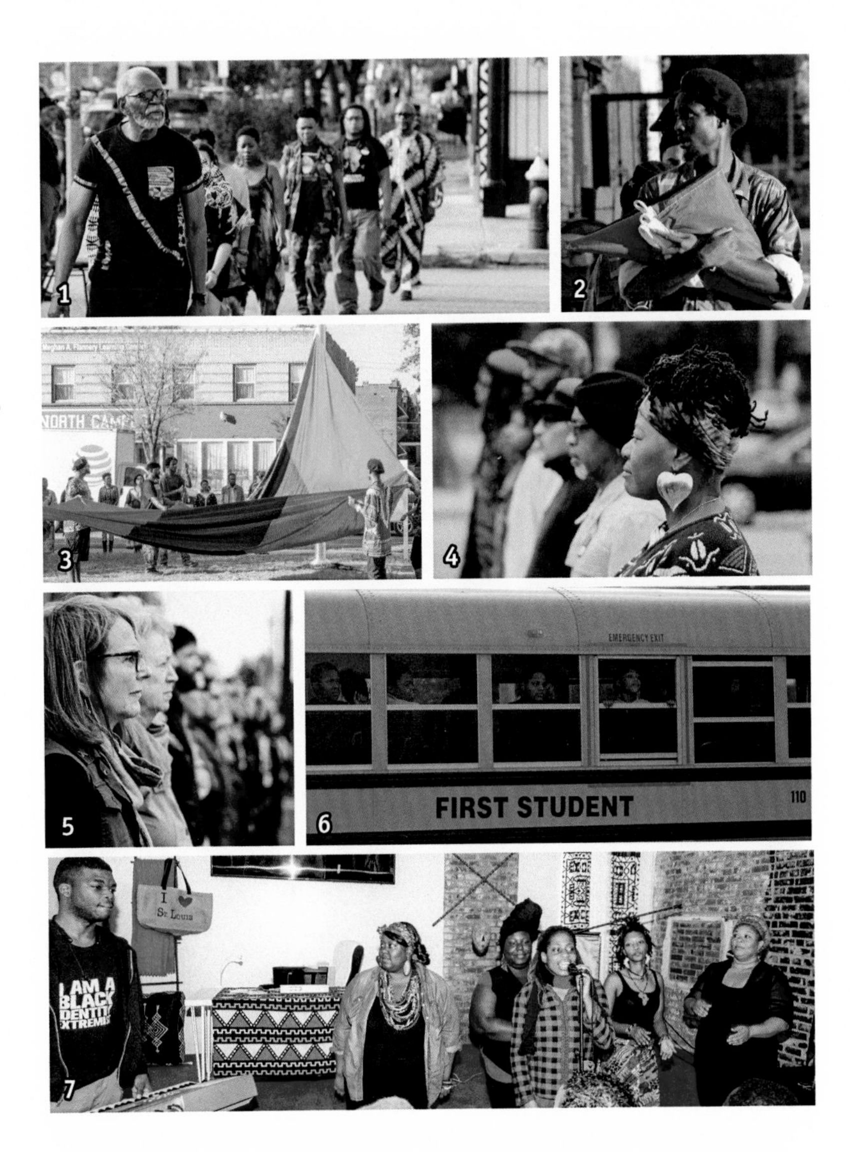

1. Chairman Omali Yeshitela leads the Party's NCC to the flag raising. **2-3.** The honor guard carries and raises the Red, Black and Green flag of the African nation. **4.** Party members watch the flag raising. **5.** African People's Solidarity Committee leaders and members watch from across the street. **6.** African children on their way to school watch the flag raising ceremony. **7.** The Freedom Mass Choir and Band.

1. Elikya Ngoma, director of the Freedom Mass Choir and Band. **2.** ANWO President Yejide Orunmila. **3.** AAPDEP Director Dr. Aisha Fields. **4.** Members of the Office of the Chairman: David Lance, Elikya Ngoma and Ekenge Mayele. **5.** Agit-Prop Director Akilé Anai recognizes Themba Tshibanda as top *Spear* seller. **6.** Southern Regional Representative Kobina Bantushango. **7.** Northern Regional Representative Nana Yaw Grant. **8.** InPDUM International President Kalambayi Andenet. **9.** The Party exercises the power to govern during the voting process. **10.** Renaming ceremony for Comrade Kundai Alongi Bajikikayi. **See more Congress photos at apspuhuru.org.**

Bibliography

"African Socialist International Manifesto," 2000, *asiuhuru.org*.

Brzezinski, Zbigniew. *Second Chance: Three Presidents and the Crisis of American Superpower*, Basic Books, 2007.

Buchanan, Patrick J. *Day of Reckoning: How Hubris, Ideology, and Greed Are Tearing America Apart*, Thomas Dunne Books/St. Martin's Press, 2007.

Buchanan, Patrick J. *Suicide of a Superpower: Will America Survive to 2025?*, Thomas Dunne Books, 2011.

Cabral, Amilcar, *Revolution in Guinea*, Stage 1, 1974.

Cannadine, David. *The Undivided Past: Humanity Beyond Our Differences*, Alfred A. Knopf, 2013.

Césaire, Aimé. *Discourse on Colonialism*, Présence Africaine, 1955.

Churchill, Ward, and Jim Vander Wall. *The COINTELPRO Papers: Documents from the FBI's Secret Wars Against Domestic Dissent*, South End Press, 1990.

Diop, Cheikh Anta. *The Cultural Unity of Black Africa: The Domains of Patriarchy and of Matriarchy in Classical Antiquity*, Third World Press, 1978.

Fukuyama, Francis. "The Future of History: Can Liberal Democracy Survive the Decline of the Middle Class?" *Foreign Affairs*, January/February 2012.

"Geneva Conventions," *Wikipedia.org*.

Hill, Robert, Editor. *The Marcus Garvey and Universal Negro Improvement Association Papers, Volume II*, University of California Press, Berkeley, 1983.

Huntington, Samuel P. *Who Are We? The Challenges to America's National Identity*, Simon and Schuster, 2004.

Jaffe, Hosea. *A History of Africa*, Zed Books, 1986.

Johnson, Walter. "King Cotton's Long Shadow," *The New York Times*, March 30, 2013.

Kadalie, Modibo M. *Internationalism, Pan-Africanism and the Struggle of Social Classes: Raw Writings from the Notebook of an Early Nineteen Seventies African-American Radical Activist,* One Quest Press, 2000.

Ki-Zerbo, Joseph. "African Personality and the New African Society," *Readings in African Political Thought*, Heinemann, 1975.

Lenin, V.I. *Collected Works, Vol. 5*, Foreign Language Publishing House, Moscow, 1961.

Lenin, V.I. *Collected Works, Vol. 7*, Foreign Language Publishing House, Moscow, 1961.

Lenin, V.I. *Imperialism and the Split in Socialism,* Foreign Language Publishing House, Moscow, 1954.

Lenin, V.I. *Imperialism, the Highest Stage of Capitalism,* Foreign Language Publishing House, Moscow, 1952.

Martin, Tony. *Race First: The Ideological and Organizational Struggles of Marcus Garvey and the Universal Negro Improvement Association*, The Majority Press, 1986.

Marx, Karl. *A Contribution to the Critique of Political Economy,* Progress Publishers, 1859.

Marx, Karl. *Capital: A Critique of Political Economy, Volume 1,* International Publishers, New York, 1967.

Marx, Karl. *The Poverty of Philosophy.* Charles H. Kerr & Company, 1920.

Marx, Karl, and Friedrich Engels. *Selected Works*, International Publishers, 1986.

McCoy, Alfred W. *The Politics of Heroin: CIA Complicity in the Global Drug Trade,* Lawrence Hill Books, 1972.

Newton, Huey P. "The Last Speeches of Huey P. Newton," Burning Spear Publications, 1990.

Nkrumah, Kwame. *Neo-colonialism, The Last Stage of Imperialism*, International Publishers, 1966.

Padmore, George. *The Life and Struggles of Negro Toilers*, Sun Dance Press, 1971.

The Burning Spear newspaper, June 15-29, 1970.

The Burning Spear newspaper, November 2017.

The Sentencing Project, sentencingproject.org.

"The Communist Party USA and African Americans," *Wikipedia.org*.

Turse, Nick. "The war you've never heard of," *Vice.com*, May 18, 2017.

Webb, Gary. *Dark Alliance: The CIA, the Contras, and the Crack Cocaine Explosion*, Seven Stories Press, 1998.

"Who Gave the 'Messenger' the Message?" *Race for the Times*, raceforthetimes.com/who-gave-messenger-message.

"Woman honored as foster mother guilty of abuse," *Los Angeles Times*, June 6, 1996.

Yeshitela, Omali. *A New Beginning: The Road to Black Freedom and Socialism*, Burning Spear Publications, 1982.

Yeshitela, Omali. *An Uneasy Equilibrium: The African Revolution versus Parasitic Capitalism. The Political Report to the Sixth Congress of the African People's Socialist Party*, Burning Spear Publications, 2014.

Yeshitela, Omali. *Black Power Since the '60s: The struggle against opportunism within the U.S. front of the Black Liberation Movement*, Burning Spear Publications, 1991.

Yeshitela, Omali. "Build and Consolidate the African People's Socialist Party," Marcus Garvey Club, 1986.

Yeshitela, Omali. *Izwe Lethu i Afrika (Africa is Our Land): Political Report to the 3rd Party Congress of the African People's Socialist Party*, Burning Spear Publications, 1991.

Yeshitela, Omali. *Omali Yeshitela Speaks*, Burning Spear Uhuru Publications, 2005.

Yeshitela, Omali. *One People! One Party! One Destiny! The Political Report to the Fifth Congress of the African People's Socialist Party-USA*, Burning Spear Uhuru Publications, 2010.

Yeshitela, Omali. *Organize to Win! Organize to Govern! Political Report to the 2016 Plenary of the African People's Socialist Party*, apspuhuru.org/2016-plenary-political-report/

Yeshitela, Omali. *Putting Revolution Back on the Agenda: Political Report to the 2017 Plenary of the African People's Socialist Party,* apspuhuru.org/2017-plenary-political-report/

Yeshitela, Omali. *Report by Omali Yeshitela to the National People's Democratic Uhuru Movement Founding Convention,* April 6, 1991, archive.org/details/NationalPeoplesDemocraticUhuruMovement

Yeshitela, Omali. "Social Justice and Economic Development for the African Community: Why I Became a Revolutionary," Burning Spear Uhuru Publications, 1997.

Yeshitela, Omali. "Tactics and Strategy for Black Liberation," Burning Spear Publications, 1982.

Yeshitela, Omali. "The Dialectics of Black Revolution: The Struggle to Defeat the Counterinsurgency in the U.S.," Burning Spear Uhuru Publications, Second Edition, 1997.

Yeshitela, Omali. *The Road to Socialism is Painted Black,* Burning Spear Publications, 1987.

Yeshitela, Omali. *The Struggle for Bread, Peace and Black Power: Political Report to the First Congress of the African People's Socialist Party,* Burning Spear Publications, 1981.